Community Recycling
System Design to Management

Nyles V. Reinfeld

With contributions by
Carl M. Layman III, Nick E. Reinfeld, A.C. Rosander,
Albert C. Schulz, *and* Mary L. Wiard

PRENTICE HALL
Englewood Cliffs, New Jersey 07632

Library of Congress Cataloging-in-Publication Data

Reinfeld, Nyles V.
    Community recycling : from system design to management / by Nyles
  V. Reinfeld with Nick E. Reinfeld ... [et al.].
      p.   cm.
    Includes bibliographical references and index.
    ISBN 0-13-155789-0
    1. Recycling (Waste, etc.) 2. Community development.
  I. Reinfeld, Nick E. II. Title.
  TD794.5.R444 1992
  363.72'82--dc20   91-33118
                                                            CIP

Editorial/production supervision: *Brendan M. Stewart*
Prepress buyer: *Mary McCartney*
Manufacturing buyer: *Susan Brunke*
Acquisitions editor: *George Z. Kuredjian*

© 1992 by Prentice-Hall, Inc.
A Simon & Schuster Company
Englewood Cliffs, New Jersey 07632

Chapter 5 written by Albert C. Schulz; Chapters 7 and 8
by Nick E. Reinfeld; Chapter 9 by Carl M. Layman, III;
Chapter 10 by Mary L. Wiard; and Chapter 15 by A.C. Rosander

The publisher offers discounts on this book when ordered in bulk quantities. For more information, write: Special Sales/Professional Marketing, Prentice Hall, Professional & Technical Reference Division, Englewood Cliffs, NJ 07632.

Printed in the United States of America
10 9 8 7 6 5 4 3 2 1

ISBN 0-13-155789-0

Prentice-Hall International (UK) Limited, *London*
Prentice-Hall of Australia Pty. Limited, *Sydney*
Prentice-Hall Canada Inc., *Toronto*
Prentice-Hall Hispanoamericana, S.A., *Mexico*
Prentice-Hall of India Private Limited, *New Delhi*
Prentice-Hall of Japan, Inc., *Tokyo*
Simon & Schuster Asia Pte. Ltd., *Singapore*
Editora Prentice-Hall do Brasil, Ltda., *Rio de Janeiro*

The future isn't what it used to be-

Contents

v

     RECYCLING AND SCRAP-PROCESSING CENTER   47

     Paper Handling, 48
     Plastics Handling, 49
     Handling Aluminum and Steel Cans, 51

6   MARKETING   55

     Source Reduction: Reducing the Amount of Waste, 59
     Creating a Market, 60
     Shifts in the Market, 60
     Is Economics the Only Answer? 62
     Establishing a Market Economy in Recycling, 64
     The Market System: Price Negotiation, 71
     A Case Study: The Market Potential of Recycling, 72
     Spreading the Word on New Breakthroughs, 76

7   PRIVATE VERSUS PUBLIC OPERATION   87

     Competition, 89
     Refuse Service Recycling, 90
     Deposit Programs, 90
     The Need to Cooperate! 91

8   PLANNING FOR CONVENIENCE   93

     Convenience in the Home, 93
     Convenience for Businesses and Government Offices, 94
     Drop-off Recyclers, 95
     Convenience in Operating the System, 95
     Convenience for the Recycler, 96

9   LEGAL AND PRACTICAL ASPECTS OF RECYCLING
     FOR THE SMALLER COMMUNITY   98

10   BUILDING SUPPORT FOR A COMMUNITY
     RECYCLING PROGRAM   104

     Know the Ground Rules: State and Federal Policies and
     Regulations, 105
     Look for Help: Sources of Information, Technical
     Assistance, and Financial Aid, 106
     Begin the Planning Process: Include Affected and
     Interested Parties, 107
     Understand the Waste Management System, 108

Human Error, 205
The Cost of Quality, 207
Developing a Quality Program, 208

Preface

There is so much to be learned with enormous opportunities in the area of recycling! To grasp the potential we need only visualize the more than 64,000 communities in America, each one providing numerous opportunities in recycling, creating an especially exciting future for the energetic, the bold, and the creative.[1]

What has been accomplished to date has not even scratched the surface of the many possibilities in the reuse of waste. Our minds are overwhelmed by the enormity of the problem and by society's apparent inability to come to grips with the sheer magnitude of its waste generation. Thus, for us today, we have been creating one massive landfill out of America.

Our immediate reaction is to move with haste. Hence, we pass laws mandating recycling. We spend enormous sums to achieve questionable results. We grasp at straws and fail to see the potential.

But the future uses for waste materials have only begun to emerge. Our massive landfills may well be the valuable reserves of the twenty-first century. Fast becoming our biggest industry, recycling in the next few years offers employment and technological challenges unmatched by any other foreseeable field. Recycling is the growth industry of the future.

It is the purpose of this book to look beyond today and consider not only the problems of recycling and mass waste removal and reuse, but to stress the need for management and professional achievement. Waste management is in need of creative contributors as great as the giants who ushered in the Industrial Revolution.

Waste management, or recycling, is a business and must be treated like any other business. This means that it must be logically planned and structured. Like any other business, we need to establish goals and objectives, to state what we want to accomplish, and then lay out plans to do it. We must learn how to operate effectively and efficiently. And, just as with any other business, we must learn our business thoroughly. We must learn to produce quality products that command

---

[1]The Statistical Abstract of the U.S. lists almost 65,000 local governments with taxing power, including counties, municipalities, and townships. It also lists another 26,000 special districts.

good prices in the marketplace. We need to develop these markets and build demand. We need to apply all the standards, controls, and incentives that help build and accomplish efficiency and creativity, just as the best-run businesses do. After all, this is a new, fledgling industry with enormous potential. Unlike many other businesses, it is here to stay. The future is guaranteed.

Please note, that in a book of this type, with several authors, certain important ideas are expressed more than once. What is particularly interesting is that the contributors range from different backgrounds, experiences, and perspectives. Ms. Wiard, for example, gained her experience by working for the state, (she is now a lobbyist and consultant) and she sees the problem from the public servant point of view. She approaches recycling as a public service and responsibility. Al Schulz and Nick Reinfeld work in the private sector, on the other hand, and they see the problems from a business and technical perspective. At the same time, Carl Layman fits somewhere in the middle, working both as a public servant and a private operator. Hence, all these views are brought together and presented in one book, sometimes not quite in conflict, but certainly each with his/her own beliefs and integrity. This diversity of background and experience thus gives the reader a much broader and more practical overview of recycling than might otherwise be the case. The result, I believe, makes a better book. Since this is the first book of its type written to date, it is hoped that it will provide the standard and guidelines for future approaches to the subject.

Waste is not only "our fastest growing resource," you see, but also *our fastest growing opportunity!*

—*Nyles V. Reinfeld*

List of
Contributors

Nyles V. Reinfeld, the Director of the National Institute of Management, and Chairman of Comprehensive Environmental Recycling Systems, Inc. (CERS), is a member of the boards of several firms, and has been active in recycling for more than eight years. One division of CERS builds and designs special machinery. These machines are located from coast to coast and are sold to communities and private businesses. The consulting division sets up turnkey recycling operations for scrap yards and communities, as well as offering special training to communities and officials.

Mr. Reinfeld has also served as a visiting professor of management in Kansas and was chairman of the Governor's Conference on Waste Management. He also served as the first executive director of the Kansas Business Hall of Fame.

Mr. Reinfeld has written seven other books on management published by Prentice Hall and Reston Press.

For the past three years, Mr. Reinfeld has been the Conference Chairman for three national conferences on "Guiding Society Into The Future," held in cooperation with the World Future Society and the Institute for Global Action (of which he is Chairman). The latest of these in Chicago featured a number of world-renowned speakers, with a section devoted to recycling and ecology.

Mr. Reinfeld is an Honorary Life Member of the American Production and Inventory Control Society and was awarded the annual H.B. Maynard Award for outstanding work in consulting. With an M.A. from the University of Michigan and a B.A. from the University of Akron, Mr. Reinfeld has served as a consultant to state and federal agencies, including the Pentagon, ordnance supply agencies, several foreign nations, plus a number of major firms and hospitals. He has written almost 200 articles and has lectured widely both in America and overseas.

Carl M. Layman, III is founder and President of Universal Recycling Corporation. He is an attorney licensed in Ohio since 1973, and currently Law Director of the village of Silver Lake, Ohio, as well as in private practice in Stow, Ohio. Mr. Layman has over ten years' experience advising small communities with regard to their legal needs. He is a member of the Ohio Alliance for the Environment and an active recycler since 1976.

Nick E. Reinfeld, former President of Reinfeld Recycling Equipment, Inc. (R^2E), and Vice-President and Operations Manager of Comprehensive Environmental Recycling Systems, Inc. (CERS), has been involved in manufacturing and designing special machinery for recycling for eight years. Because he ships machinery all over the country to various recycling centers, he has visited and worked in numerous operations. He often spends time working as a laborer at these operations, observing how his equipment works in the field, to study other ways to do the job. Mr. Reinfeld can speak knowledgeably about the ways recyclables are handled in Arizona, for example, versus those same items in New Jersey. As a result, he has been able to synthesize and bring together an amalgam of those operations and procedures that seem to work best.

Prior to becoming a part of CERS, Mr. Reinfeld was active in formalizing the operations of CanQuest, a multi-county recycling operation.

A. C. Rosander has been one of the pioneers in the introduction of quality control methods into the service sector of the economy. Mr. Rosander described the application of statistical quality control methods to tax operations by the Internal Revenue Service as early as 1958. In his book, *Applications of Quality Control in the Service Industries* (New York; Marcel Dekker, Inc., 1985), he describes the application to banking, insurance, government, health services, transportation, retail trade, personal services, and public utilities. In this book, Mr. Rosander now shows how to apply these ideas to recycling services as well as any similar activity.

Albert C. Schulz is President of Counselor Engineering, Inc., and has been actively associated with the scrap-processing industry in all facets of operation for 30 years. He has acted as a consultant, engineer, and provider of equipment to the scrap-processing industry. Mr. Schulz has worked with and for a number of equipment providers, including balers, shears, shredders, and glass crushers.

Counselor Engineering, Inc. is actively engaged in providing both new and used equipment to the recycling industry. As a member of the American Society of Appraisers for machinery and equipment, Counselor Engineering, Inc. also appraises scrap-processing and recycling equipment.

Mary L. Wiard is President of Waste Reduction Strategies. After beginning a career as a teacher, Ms. Wiard went into the building construction industry for seven years, handling scheduling and management for a small apartment construction firm.

After serving on the gubernatorial campaign of 1982, she was asked to organize the Litter Prevention and Recycling Division of the Ohio Department of Natural Resources. Ms. Wiard served as chief of the division for seven years.

In 1985, Ohio hosted the National Recycling Congress (NRC) in Columbus for more than 450 people. As one of the key organizers, Ms. Wiard became active in its growth and increased prestige. In 1990, she became the sixth president of the association which now maintains a full-time staff with offices in Washington, DC (see appendix for address).

One of Ms. Wiard's projects at NRC is to establish guidelines for measuring standards and quality. She is the first woman and first state official to serve as president of NRC.

1

Recycling as a Learning Process

THE CURRENT STATUS OF RECYCLING

Recycling is not new. Until the mid-1930s, scrap dealers rode through the neighborhoods with horse and buggy, shouting: "Any rags or metal today?" And the kids on the block ran out from their houses with batteries, scrap metal, rags, and anything he would buy to make a few pennies. People saved their "valuables," awaiting the next trip through by the scrap dealer. Until at least 1967, machine shops in northern Ohio sold their steel shavings to scrap dealers and donated the money to the employees' fund. After that, the value of steel chips produced on lathes and mills dropped so low that the only way a shop could dispose of its waste was to pay to have it hauled away.

Even today, machine shops separate their shavings into containers for steel, brass, and aluminum. While they are paid for brass and aluminum, they must pay to rid themselves of scrap steel.

In fact, as long as waste products have had sufficient value, they have always been recycled. Gold and silver, for example, have been recycled since the time of the Pharoahs and, perhaps, since the days of the cavemen. The gold which fills your teeth or the silver plate on your dinnerware is too costly to recycle, so it ends up in its own special landfill when you pass on. Even then it may be removed and recycled in the wee hours of the night, if the incentive is high enough.

What has been recycled in the past, therefore, has been whatever generated income. Unfortunately for modern society, we have become so efficient and diverse that it is cheaper for industrial societies such as the United States to produce materials from scratch rather than rework the scrap. Furthermore, at least with respect to steel (and also other products such as paper and plastics), there are over 30,000 grades of steel which are not interchangeable. Truly high-grade specialized steels must be produced from virgin sources in order to ensure the chemical content and qualities needed. When steel is produced from scrap metal, the result is an amalgam of unknowns, and the product's specifications are uncertain. Steel from car axles and auto bodies, for example, mixed together cannot be reused for either purpose because both have special properties incompatible with the other. This doesn't mean that steel cannot be recycled, but it does explain why it has so little scrap value. Since, it would be prohibitively expensive to analyze and sort out every grade of scrap steel before reusing it, the recycled steel is often of little value to the user. Even when scrap steel is used to produce the cheapest grades of steel, it often contains hard and soft spots that tear up the tooling and increase production expenses beyond any savings. The same problems occur in the reuse of papers and plastics. This explains why so much time is spent in separating the materials prior to actual recycling.

One method used for recycling of waste is to mix a small percentage of the old material in with the virgin material. For example, finely ground tires can be mixed with virgin tire stock to produce new tires, but the amount of waste used can only be a small percentage. Obviously, most of us want our tires to be dependable without any lowering of safety standards. Similarly, recycled plastic containers often split or crack in use. Hence, safety and dependability are important factors to be considered and lead to resistance toward recycling. It is not just cost alone, therefore, but many other factors which must be overcome to achieve a sound program of recycling.

There are many such nagging problems facing those who attempt to recycle. As a result, a nationally mandated program of recycling to solve the country's landfill problem may actually create a whole new problem with no immediate solution. Instead of *in* the earth, we could be parking waste on *top* of the earth, or even in outer space, as we shall see. Remember, for example, when New York hailed the automobile as the solution to horse manure in the streets at the start of the century? Did we not merely trade dirty streets for dirty air?

We may not even have a clearly defined understanding of what constitutes desirable and undesirable waste. Typically, society has always been a great producer of useless trash—the great defiler of nature. (The contamination of nature did not just begin in our time.) When the caveman cooked over a fire, he left shards and residues that are still being analyzed today for clues to the past. Pottery shards, in fact, are the first nonbiodegradables of humankind. These sources of important insights into the past have revealed arts, crafts, and religious beliefs that would be unknown to us today (if they had degraded). These are often the great treasures of society because a civilization's residue often reveals the glory of its past. Unfortunately, all things eventually do degrade over time because nature is the great leveler. Thus, marble structures, monuments, medieval cathedrals, paintings, and stained glass are all sadly degrading, speeded along by our own contributions to polluted air and stream. Indeed, to reverse or retard this process of "natural recycling," a whole new field has sprung up to attempt to stop or delay the decay and save the past.

The study of the wastes of the most recent past is new to our generation, dating only since World War II. We are now learning much about our own pre-colonial period by digging up rubble left by the early American pioneers. We are finding out how they made things and what implements and foods they had, which are not often revealed in books. History books, as the blacks point out, tell us about the elite of society, not the common man.

Since the 1970s, the University of Arizona's Garbage Project has begun looking into landfills and garbage just recently buried. Headed by Dr. William L. Rathje, the study has produced unexpected results. Dr. Rathje points out in *The Atlantic* (December 1989) that Americans once produced as much as 1,200 pounds of ashes annually per person at the turn of the century. Orange peels which used to be dumped in the garbage, when each household made its own juice, are now converted into feed by the large producers. "In reality, Americans, as individuals, are not suddenly producing more garbage. Per capita our record seems to be one of relative stability," he tells us. In fact, as he points out, modern systems of packaging and refrigeration have greatly reduced the amount of waste in this category.

> Over the past two years, he tells us, "the Garbage Project team has dug into seven landfills; two outside Chicago, two in the San Francisco Bay area, two in Tucson and one in Phoenix. In eight tons of garbage and dirt cover, there were fewer than 16 pounds of fast-food packaging—about a tenth of 1 percent of the landfills content by weight . . . The real "culprit" in every landfill is plain old paper—non-fast-food paper—which accounts for 40 to 50 percent by weight . . . Conspicuous are newspapers, which make up 10 to 18 percent of a typical municipal landfill by volume. During a recent dig in Phoenix, I found newspapers dating back to 1952, that looked so fresh you might read one over breakfast.[1]

He also adds that plastic, which is hardly biodegradable, "may actually be a great virtue. Being inert, it doesn't introduce toxic chemicals into the environment." His observations are confirmed by Jan Beyea, Senior Scientist for the National Audubon Society, who states that "plastics in landfills are no problem."[2]

Dr. Rathje concludes that "perhaps the biggest challenge we face is to recognize that the conventional wisdom about garbage is often wrong."

---

[1] From the article "Rubbish!" by William J. Rathje, *The Atlantic*, Dec. 1989, pp. 62–63.

[2] Ibid., p. 63. (Quoted by Dr. Rathje). Note this comment also: "The polystyrene hamburger clamshell uses 30 percent less energy than paperboard. Its manufacturing results in 46% less air pollution and 42 percent less water pollution." (Lynn Scarlett, V.P. Research, Reason Fdtn., quoted in *Wall Street Journal*, editorial page, Jan. 14, 1991.)

Dr. Rathje's findings need to be considered carefully by society in developing an approach to recycling. They have the weight of being supported by careful study and analysis. Dr. Rathje has avoided drawing hasty conclusions based on insufficient knowledge, which has sometimes guided public reaction and demand. In a sense, what Dr. Rathje is saying is that landfill problems involving traditional wastes are most effectively solved when left up to those who work in the field.

This is also often true of toxic wastes. While public interest and concern are vital, the means for controlling and neutralizing these threats to society are most wisely left to the professionals. They may need to be nudged, but the means for responding is most clearly their task. We discuss these ideas in more detail later.

One area in which the public can make an immediate contribution is in enforcing cleanups and restrictions on eyesore dumping, such as junk autos and appliances left in fields and neighborhoods.

There is no doubt that a major contributing factor to the rising public demand for recycling is an urgent awareness of the sheer volume of waste produced by modern society. Even if the per capita volume has not changed over the years, as suggested by Rathje, the fact that the world is beginning to overflow with people means that the problem of waste disposal is now upon us in full force. Action is often taken without careful thought with the result that instead of solving problems, we sometimes create new ones or exacerbate old ones. We find ourselves killing cockroaches in the dining room, instead of searching out and destroying the breeder. Consider, for example, the case of newsprint. Where we once got as much as $50 a ton for it, we now pay as much as $25 to have it hauled away, or we store it for use at some point in the unforeseeable future. Hence, instead of curing the problem at its source, we are hiding the problem from public view by implying that we are recycling, when in fact we are not!

It is not quite fair to suggest that no one saw the situation developing. Conservationists and waste management specialists realized several years ago that our approach to the problems of recycling and waste management needed more planning and thought. It became apparent that there were too many cooks in the kitchen—too many "experts" with special programs. In some ways, this was good in that it made people aware of the need for action. But it too frequently committed the sin of ignoring the practical aspects such as economics to achieve special goals, or resulted in paradoxical contradictions of purpose. It produced young idealists, for example, who threw paint on fur coats, but carried leather purses and wore imported Italian boots, as *The Wall Street Journal* reported.

My book, *Perspectives on the Future* (published in 1992 by the Institute for Global Action), contains material on the environment contributed by Joseph F. Harkins and Margaret A. Baggs. Mr. Harkins was Director of the Environmental Agency for Kansas. Ms. Baggs was his assistant. Mr. Harkins was also at the Health Department for a number of years. These authors' main concern is with the lack of coordination within environmental planning being discussed here. Although the authors are most directly experienced with health and water safety problems, they are concerned with all areas of the environment, including recycling. Here's what they say:

> For decades, federal and state governments have enacted environmental programs on the "squeaking wheel" basis—whichever problem made the most noise, got the oil. Many of these programs were developed as responses to specific environmental incidents. As a result, there is a vast array of laws and programs at the federal level which includes the Clean Water Act; Safe Drinking Water Act; Toxic Substance Control Act; Federal Insecticide, Fungicide, and Rodenticide Act; Resource, Conservation and Recovery Act; Comprehensive Environmental Response, Compensation, and Liability Act; Leaking Underground Storage Tanks; and National Environmental Policy Act. Each program concentrates only on its narrowly defined mission, often ignoring critical interrelationships. In the area of federal water programs alone, responsibility rests with 18 federal agencies. At least 25 separate water programs and some 70 separate Congressional appropriations accounts have been identified. These programs are governed by more than 200 federal rules, regulations and laws. This categorical approach to environmental protection has led to a fragmented, piecemeal, and incomplete set of programs with no conceptual framework. This unplanned, evolutionary development of environmental protection programs has caused a variety of obstacles which can severely retard, if not ultimately prevent, the implementation of an environmental protection program which can effectively respond to an ever-increasing number of pollution problems.

> At the state level, the public health model was the original framework within which environmental programs evolved. The model was developed with a clear focus and based on a sound concept. For over 70 years after the turn of the century, this model was successful in addressing public health issues and remained essentially intact.

> The environmental movement of the 1970s resulted in the detachment and dispersion of many public health based environment components. In some cases, programs remained in public health agencies while in others, programs were spun off and formed the basis of new environmental agencies. In still other cases, environmental programs were folded into new or existing natural resources agencies. The missing ingredient of the "environmental movement" was a clear conceptual model to provide structure for the organization and management of environmental programs. This has resulted in a potpourri of programs in a variety of configurations that function with relative independence and little coordination. There remains a need to adopt a comprehensive environmental protection strategy that will provide a framework in which programs can be managed effectively.

> The very nature of comprehensive natural resources management precludes the option to isolate interrelated issues so that they might be planned and operated independent of each other. For example, water quality is interrelated to water supply. Frequently, the issue of water supply is directly linked with flood management interventions, i.e., multipurpose impoundments. And, clearly, the issue of fish, wildlife and recreation is inextricably linked to water supply and water quality issues. This is not to say plans cannot be classified into subparts dealing with major issues such as water supply, water quality and flood control but these subplans must be complimentary to each other.

Incrementalism, or intermittent policy development based upon highly visible issues, is a legacy for our nation's environmental protection effort. Leaders proposing to abandon this approach will encounter considerable opposition. There is an entrenched federal/state bureaucracy in place which is threatened by the specter of such a change. When the concept was presented to a group of state representatives attending a National Governor's Association meeting on environmental issues, there were two reactions. First, there was a general consensus the concept was the right thing to do. Second, many expressed opposition for fear of disrupting the flow of federal funds to state agencies which are administering federally delegated categorical programs. Then there are the thousands of bureaucrats ensconced in narrow categorically oriented programs who dread the thought of change. They are comfortable with a well-defined and familiar area of responsibility. Many can be counted on to lead the opposition through time-tested techniques such as sabotage, passive aggressiveness, and convincing arguments based upon the familiar theme, "it's a good idea but here's why it won't work."

Reorganization at the state and local levels clearly is an option worthy of consideration. Many states have, over the years, moved to consolidating their natural resource agencies. Some have moved much further than others. Reorganization at the local level has also occurred in some states, such as the consolidation of conservation districts and watershed districts into watershed based natural resource districts in Nebraska. But, in no state is there a single agency at the state level and a consolidated unit at the local level that collectively embraces all the authorities and programs that would conceivably be elements of a truly comprehensive effort. An alternative to massive reorganization is the development of an integrated management process that mandates participation by appropriate agencies. Although consolidation of agencies is not essential, modifications within each agency would probably be necessary to establish the ability to interact effectively.

Conversion of long-term strategies into short-term implementation plans, preferably annually, would provide a mechanism to focus on specific issues that cut across traditional areas of agency responsibility. Frequently, the resolution of complex problems is dependent upon the coordinated efforts of several entities at the local, state, and federal levels. A process to cooperatively select priority issues and allocate resources to deal with them would facilitate more effective interventions than possible without a coordinated management effort.

Clearly, policy consistent with a comprehensive natural resources program for this country is emerging at the national level and in some states. The emergence of leaders in widely dispersed loci including private citizens, local governments, state governments, and federal agencies is not so clear. "We are faced with immensely threatening problems—terrorism, AIDS, drugs, depletion of the ozone layer, the threat of nuclear conflict, toxic waste, the real possibility of economic disaster. Even moderately informed citizens could extend the list. Yet, on none of the items listed does our response acknowledge the manifest urgency of the problem. We give every appearance of sleepwalking through a dangerous passage of history. We see life-threatening problems, but we do not react. We are anxious but immobilized."[3] There are no technical or scientific barriers to adopting a comprehensive natural resources

---

[3] John W. Gardner, *On Leadership* (New York: The Free Press, 1990), p. xii.

program in this country. There are, in fact, no truly insurmountable management obstacles. We are awaiting leaders in key management positions at all levels of government to emerge who have the vision to recognize the need for change.[4]

These comments bring home quite clearly the need for careful planning and the gathering of facts before formulating an environmental package.

Another problem involved in our present-day approach to recycling which must be overcome is that those who assume the responsibility for making recycling work often have no experience in the field. By fate, or by law, they are "thrown" into the project and learn to make it work by their own initiative and skills. Most community leaders come from a wide range of fields of interest. Often, their political job is part time or voluntary. Their skills and income come from outside sources. For instance, an assistant store manager, furniture salesperson, college professor, and homemaker are typically the kinds of people who head up our recycling projects. Most are dedicated, but some do not want the job. Often the job evolves because the state has passed mandatory recycling or landfill reduction. Someone at the community level is designated to sort out the program. But virtually no one in the whole community has had experience in waste management/recycling. Even when the program originates locally, it may be more idealistic in its source than arising out of practical experience. In one community, for example, an insurance salesman who had no direct political ties sought out the mayor to advocate that the town get into recycling. The mayor appointed him chairman of an ad-hoc committee to study the idea and submit a plan. Even when the idea originates in council chambers or with the city manager or mayor, the chance that any of these officials has in-depth knowledge in the field is most unlikely. In fact, how could they, when the idea is so new and untried, and the sense of urgency so great?

Virtually everyone today is involved in recycling, getting into it, or thinking about it, and yet there is almost no place to turn because even the experts are feeling their way—and there aren't many experts.

THE NEED FOR PLANNING

One thing we can say for sure based on the preceding discussions and the experience of those who are involved is that the more knowledge, experience, and planning that are applied to the problem, the more successful will be the results.

Planning must be the prelude to all action!

At no time has this been more clearly seen than in the Iraqi War. With no doubt, this was the most successful war ever conducted by a nation. Carried out against an army which was rated by some as the fourth strongest in the world, this war was completed with total defeat of the enemy in 100 hours! Certainly, a

---

[4] Joseph F. Harkins and Margaret A. Baggs, "Our Environment—a Comprehensive Approach," from the text, *Guiding Society into the Future,* edited by Nyles V. Reinfeld, Institute for Global Action, Publisher, to be released in spring 1992.

major contributing factor in this success was the delay imposed by the United Nations, which required the United States and its allies to sit on their hands until a given date on the calendar. During those weeks of waiting and political maneuvering, our army command worked out its strategies for war.

Strategic planning, applied to any activity, will produce greater efficiencies and faster results than moving hastily into a program. Six to eight weeks of careful planning at the community level and training key officials and politicians in the problems, costs, methods, and concepts will pay for itself in the time saved—and every year thereafter in dollars saved. The costs to the community will be reduced significantly, and the results will be better than can otherwise be achieved.

A carefully developed plan actually takes place at several levels. First, both state and local legislation must be integrated into the whole recycling program. Each phase needs to be worked out, evaluated, and then integrated into the total program. This is what Harkins and Baggs are saying. Every attempt to move in a piecemeal fashion, producing hasty, knee-jerk responses to public pressure, can only increase costs, cause discouragement, and worse yet, create hazards and problems of unknown dimensions.

At every level and every stage, there is a need for expert, experienced personnel who are trained in recycling and waste management. This is not a job for amateurs, but it is a job that can be taught to amateurs so they can understand it.

Once the program is in operation, the final system can be either privately or publicly operated. This is often immaterial. (This matter is discussed later in another chapter.) But the design, planning, and initial implementation must be done expertly and with complete understanding of the benefits and problems involved. There must be a clear, concise uniformity of understanding within the community of the goals being sought, so that everyone moves in the same direction. This can only be achieved by training and organized planning.

Our own experience in designing and operating systems makes me believe that a long-term recycling approach in America can make recycling—if planned in advance—a self-supporting operation. *Recyclable waste will be an asset!* Waste is thus our *fastest growing resource!*

2

Overview of the Objectives and Methods of Recycling

The recycling operation with all its facilities and equipment must be laid out for efficiency. It should be easy to clean and should be kept neat and spotless. There is a certain management maxim which was taught to me by a steel mill superintendent, whom I greatly respected. Walking with him through a shop we were visiting one day, he kicked at a piece of steel that partially blocked the aisle. "That's not good!" he scolded. "A clean shop is a well-run shop." We went on walking, and within a few minutes he had made a fairly accurate assessment of the men running the shop.

He was right, of course. Just as a cluttered desk indicates a cluttered mind, so a clean shop indicates a well-run, clean operation. The loose ends are tucked away. Everything has its place and everything gets done on schedule. Emergencies are handled routinely. And there are no surprises. "I hate surprises," was another expression he used with a vengeance. When you worked for him, you kept him informed of potential trouble. You never waited until the problem erupted, hoping it would go away. You told him when you sensed it coming. These are management principles not taught in the books because our schools teach theory, and we are discussing reality. (I taught management at a university for three years, after forty years' experience in the field.)

A scrap yard, a dump, or a waste recycling operation can and should be as neat and clean as a food-processing plant or a laboratory. The well-run ones are that way. Japan, which recycles up to 80 percent of its recyclables, puts so much emphasis on cleanliness that school children visiting the sites are required to wear slippers to maintain neatness.

What difference does cleanliness make? Besides providing a direct clue to the people in charge, it also means that the people who work there are proud to be there. It's a place they can show their friends. How many scrap yards would you like to take your friends to on a tour? And yet, I have seen a few recycling plants, doing all types of recyclables, that I wouldn't hesitate to take my grandchildren to. Besides pride, cleanliness and neatness build morale and inspire creativity. This creative spirit is something you want to develop in your employees because that's where the basic breakthroughs come from. It's your people on the floor who see things that need improving and have ideas that you can use to make the operation better. If they know you care—and cleanliness shows them you care—then they will be proud to come to you when the inspiration hits. What I'm saying is that most good ideas and operational improvements will be generated from the floor, and it's up to you to nurture and use these ideas, so as to encourage more of them.

THE CONCEPT OF RECYCLING

In general, community curb-side recycling programs involve plastics, glass, paper, cans, random discards of batteries, paints, and chemicals from the home,

---

PANEL 2-1: IGA SEMINAR ON RECYCLING*

Recycling

Recycling of materials should be based on two goals:

First, and primary, is the goal to reduce landfill needs; secondly, however, and also important, is the need to create a second value for it—i.e., to make it a sought after asset, after it has lost its original value.

Recycling does not necessarily mean *re-use* as a similar item! A tire used to fuel a generating plant for electricity is giving that tire a second value, reducing landfill and—today—reducing pollution over other fossil fuels, such as coal. (Used tires contain $2\frac{1}{2}$ gallons of oil, and produce more energy per pound than coal.)

The purpose of this one-day seminar is to provide an understanding of the overall problems and procedures used in recycling. It is a collection of over nine years of operating experiences in the field. One advantage of the program is that it brings a widely diversified group of leaders together, with different understandings and interest, and helps them work toward a common goal. The most important benefit, however, for those attending, is the ability to avoid the mistakes of the past and to achieve more rapid, effective progress, at lower cost. One day spent in discussion and observing a step-by-step outline of the way to proceed can save thousands of dollars and much frustration.

---

*One of the handouts at the Institute for Global Action Recycling Seminar given to community leaders. Used by permission.

and, more recently, composts. (Garbage is not included because it is not presently considered a recyclable.)

Our discussion, thus, concentrates on this aspect of recycling. Waste disposal, including hazardous products, represents special problems of disposal and safety, and need to be handled by highly sophisticated and trained personnel. A delineation of this sort thus helps establish the parameters which limit and clarify what constitutes community pick-up (recycling), and what must be treated as outside or beyond the community system. (See Panel 2–1 for a definition of recycling.) Thus, waste from a paint factory or chemical operation within the community must be excluded from curb-side pick-up, even though the paper from the offices of these same operations can and will be included.

Discards from the home or typical business office will from time to time include flashlight batteries, broken toys, oils and greases, car batteries, tires, and a wide range of chemicals such as insecticides and weed killers or office cleaning supplies. Obviously, a means must be established which provides for the disposal of these items as well in a safe way in the normal course of cleaning up the neighborhood. The details of specific laws and regulations to accomplish this are discussed later. Here we concentrate on the home-office, nongarbage aspect of recycling. This is what normally constitutes a community recycling program.

THE RECYCLING SYSTEM: THE EXAMPLE OF ALUMINUM

When we tackle the problem of recycling of plastics, cans, bottles, glass, and papers, we are dealing with a major portion of the landfill problem. We have already seen in the Rathje study that paper represents as much as 50 percent of a landfill by weight. Aluminum beverage cans are in this sense a minor culprit, but aluminum is less biodegradable than paper. And there isn't much excuse for it being in landfills because aluminum is actually the perfect recyclable material for beverage cans. Not only is 99 percent of the can recyclable, but it can in theory be back on the street as a new can in a few days. Recycling saves as much as 95 percent of the energy used in converting bauxite. Consider that the nearly 2.2 million tons of aluminum recycled since 1986 saved about 8 million tons of bauxite, 4 million tons of chemicals, and 30 billion kilowatt hours of electricity. That's enough power to provide all the homeowners in Ohio with electricity for about one year! And yet today in America we still throw away—and pay good money to bury—about 40 percent of our aluminum cans.

The extent of this negligence is seen in the following statistics. First, the per capita consumption of beverages in America produces about one pound of cans per month. This figure is provided by the Can Manufacturers Institute in Washington, DC. According to their statistical department, the total number of aluminum cans *produced* in 1988 was: beverage cans 77.9 billion; food 2.2 billion; miscellaneous 12 million, for a total aluminum production of 80.156 billion cans. The national recycling rate for 1988 was 54.6 percent. It is increasing every year, and now exceeds 60 percent! But in some areas of the rust belt, and specifically in northern Ohio, the recycling rate is only about 30 percent to 35 percent. The remainder end up in a landfill at best, or littering parks and roads at worst.

It takes less than 3,000 cans to fill a cubic yard of landfill. At about 30 cans to the pound, this represents about 100 pounds of cans.[1] At our average consumption rate of one pound per capita per month, this means that two typical American families which fail to recycle are actually filling a yard of landfill every year—with aluminum cans only!

One approach to force these cans back into the stream is to enact can-return laws. There are at present ten states with can-return laws, requiring a deposit of money on a can. The number of such states has been constant for several years. The reason is that it costs a supermarket as much as $30,000 a year to recycle such containers. Costs such as these plus the threat of can-return laws, comparable to bottle deposits, are an urgent concern of all businesses engaged in selling and distributing beverages. They thus become active supporters of voluntary recycling programs, many of which have evolved through entrepreneurs anxious to set up a profitable business.

To avoid or limit "bootlegging" from border states, these deposit states have gone to coding the cans. However, if the cans are damaged, the codes may become illegible. Hence, each can returned to the store must pass through a reading device to verify that it is qualified for a refund. Even so, Michigan, which has a 10¢ deposit requirement on every can and is the highest in the United States, only achieves a rate of recycling in excess of 90 percent. By contrast, voluntary recycling in nondeposit states is now approaching this figure and is expected to be nearly equal to that of the can-deposit states within this decade. Recycling of aluminum cans is growing about 16 percent a year according to the Can Manufacturers Institute. (See Figures 2–1 and 2–2.)

There is in fact a ground swell of support for recycling by businesses, distributors, clubs, and nonprofit groups plus the general public. But a problem has been the lack of convenience, opportunity, and consistency.

Another deterrent to a can-return law is that groups throughout the United States are organizing fund-raising campaigns, in which the major source of their income comes from aluminum cans. These drives are not possible in a can-return law state. These charity groups include P.T.A.s, burn centers (supported by fire departments), churches, scouts, schools, and other groups.

Hence, recycling is more than a business. It's becoming a *cause* for many! As CanQuest's operating Vice President Nick Reinfeld remarked after meeting with several schools to develop a local campaign to raise funds for children, "This is not just a business. We are helping raise money for burned children, to buy them toys, and to help other people who need money. It's a business with a heart and soul." Not only do those involved in recycling care about the environment, but they also care about people.

---

[1] Some cans use a thinner aluminum than others and the can's weight varies by type of beverage and geographic area, so that it takes from 22 to 30 cans to make a pound. The number of cans per pound has increased over the years, as we learn to roll thinner sheet aluminum.

**Can
Manufacturers
Institute**

1625 Massachusetts Avenue, N.W.
Washington, D.C. 20036
Telephone: 202/232-4677

news release

AMERICA RECYCLED 42.5 BILLION
ALUMINUM CANS IN 1988, FOR A 54.6%
NATIONAL RECYCLING RATE

Washington, D.C. -- Americans recycled a record 42.5 billion aluminum soft drink and beer cans in 1988 and raised the national aluminum can recycling rate to 54.6 percent -- a significant increase over the 50.5 percent rate posted in 1987.

In exchange for its efforts, the recycling public earned an estimated $700 million in 1988. Since 1981, recyclers have earned nearly $3 billion, according to industry estimates.

Last year's record volume, which amounts to some 1.5 billion pounds of aluminum, topped the 1987 mark by almost six billion cans, a 16 percent increase over the previous year. Six billion cans, put end to end, would circle the earth 17 times.

Figure 2–1   A periodic news release prepared for public information about recycling.

Beverage can recycling (alumimum only)

Year	Cans shipped[1]	Cans collected[1]	Recycling rate (%)
1972	7.8	1.2	15.4
1973	9.9	1.5	15.2
1974	13.1	2.3	17.5
1975	15.2	4.1	26.9
1976	19.7	4.9	24.9
1977	25.0	6.6	26.4
1978	29.2	8.0	25.7
1979	33.1	8.5	25.7
1980	39.7	14.8	37.3
1981	46.8	24.9	53.2
1982	51.0	28.3	55.5
1983	55.6	29.4	52.9
1984	60.4	31.9	52.8
1985	64.9	33.1	51.0
1986	68.0	33.3	49.0
1987	72.5	36.6	50.5
1988	77.8	42.5	54.6
1989	42.6	24.7	58.0

[1]Figures in billions.

Beverage can production

Year	Aluminum cans[1]	Bi-metal cans[1]	Total cans[1]	Percent aluminum
1964	N.A.	N.A.	N.A.	2.0
1970	N.A.	N.A.	N.A.	14.0
1973	N.A.	N.A.	N.A.	25.0
1975	16.321	26.304	42.625	38.3
1976	20.928	25.509	46.437	45.0
1977	25.806	25.400	51.206	50.4
1978	30.064	24.309	54.373	55.3
1979	33.674	20.768	54.442	61.9
1980	41.577	13.662	55.239	75.3
1981	47.684	8.642	56.326	84.7
1982	51.700	6.234	57.934	89.2
1983	56.658	4.798	61.456	92.2
1984	61.501	4.143	65.644	93.7
1985	65.726	4.451	70.177	93.7
1986	68.965	3.937	72.902	94.6
1987	73.747	3.026	76.773	96.0
1988	77.941	3.239	81.180	96.0
1989[2]	42.616	1.566	44.182	96.4

N.A. Not available

[1] In billion units.

[2] Through June.

Source: Can Manufacturers Institute.

Figure 2–2 Beverage can recycling.

Why don't Americans become more involved in recycling? Actually, Americans are becoming more aware of and enthusiastic about aluminum-can recycling, but for the majority of citizens to consistently participate demands that the process become commonplace, convenient, and simple. Busy people need to know that they can take their aluminum cans to a safe site nearby and receive compensation for them in a timely fashion. Groups, churches, and charities need the assurance of return for their collection efforts. The history of recycling has taken us from a single central but inconvenient location (usually in the roughest areas of town), where only the most persistent individuals traveled, to the large automatic recycling machines that were often dysfunctional due to maintenance problems or abuse. Dawning now is the genesis of widespread availability of recycling centers at key locations that actually cater to the needs and schedules of most consumers.

A Case Example: The Mobile Recycling Operation

A few years ago, a small mobile recycling company was formed by local businesspeople to bring 100 percent aluminum recycling to a local community in northern Ohio, and eventually throughout the United States.[2] The company's leaders worked within the recycling industry for six years, researching, experimenting, and inventing recycling equipment. Although their first machines were patterned after the large, automatic stationary units originally on the market, they discovered that the most efficient, dependable, and convenient units were not those at fixed locations but those that are mobile and continually manned. The unit that evolved they called a "Tow-About." Convenience and reliability for the public were the main focal points in developing the system.

Acceptance by the public was rapid. Can recycling volume reached over 5,000 pounds per week and by the first 18 months, peaks as high as 10,000 pounds were reached—a volume of 300,000 cans in a single week! By this time, the firm had become one of the largest independent recyclers of beverage cans in northern Ohio and was operating entirely without any form of public subsidy.

The system evolved around the simple philosophy that *convenience for the public would be rewarded by public support.* An example of how the concept works with the equipment involved is seen in Figure 2–3A, B, C.

The total equipment employed is a Tow-About Can Crusher and a furniture van. In the example, the truck has an 18-foot bed with an opening for blowing the cans into the van. As the van fills up with cans, the opening is sealed off. The Tow-About is a self-powered (16 H.P. gasoline engine), that crushes the cans, sorts the steel from the aluminum, and with a high-volume blower tosses the cans into the van.

When the bed is full (about 5,000 pounds), the Tow-About is dropped off at the garage, and the truck goes directly to the aluminum processor. Thus, a single handling of the cans is involved. The picture shows a boom with a digital scale

---

[2] Set up originally by CanQuest as a prototype to prove out the concept, the firm is now owned and operated by Annaco, one of the largest recycling and scrap operations in the United States.

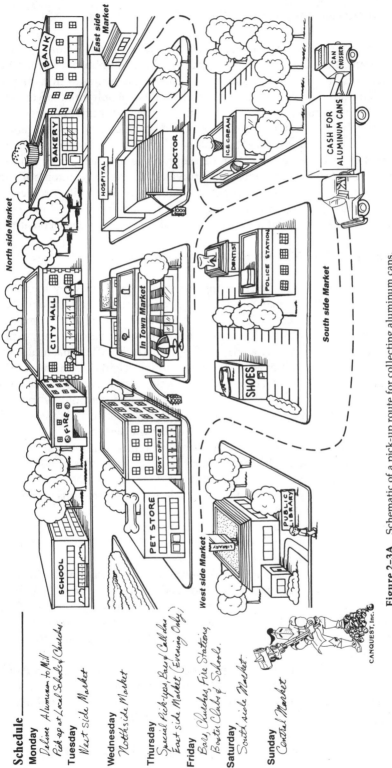

Schedule

Monday
Deliver Aluminum to Mill
Pick up at Local Schools & Churches.

Tuesday
West Side Market

Wednesday
Northside Market

Thursday
Special Pick-ups, Bars / Cellars
East side Market (Evening Only)

Friday
Bars, Churches, Fire Stations
Boosters Clubs & Schools.

Saturday
South side Market.

Sunday
Central Market

CANQUEST, Inc.

Figure 2-3A Schematic of a pick-up route for collecting aluminum cans.

In the neighborhood.

Figure 2–3B Making recycling convenient.

hanging from the rear post of the van. This scale, with a hook, is used to weigh the cans as they are purchased from the public.

As seen in the figure, the truck operates on a regular pick-up schedule. In northern Ohio, fire departments, schools, churches, clubs, and businesses collect the cans and place them in preestablished storage areas. When the bins are full, the firm is called and sends the truck to the pick-up site. Since the schools and fire departments operate on donated cans, the money they receive for these cans from the mobile operator provides a steady source of cash flow for pet projects. Bars also collect cans and use the money for personal needs. Businesses, such as General Electric, put the money in the employee Christmas fund or donate it to charities.

Because of the convenience for these collectors, they prefer to use this system rather than haul the cans in their personal cars or trucks. In fact, when the fire departments in the area collected the cans and hauled them to the scrap yards themselves, the volume per month was about 3000 pounds. But four months after the mobile recycling operation was set up to provide pick-up service, the volume climbed to 9,000 pounds per month.

Because the cans are dirty, buggy, and bulky, no schools in the area were collecting them. However, once convenient, on-site, pick-up service became available, over 20 schools joined the program the first year. The next year 217 schools were encouraged by local school boards to join the program. The Summit County Clean Committee, for example, sent a letter to the schools encouraging them to recycle and offered cash prizes to the schools doing the best job.

Even the mayor of Akron and the Summit County executive joined in the effort. See the proclamations, Figures 2–4 and 2–5. The fire departments in the program hold an annual dinner, with a trophy to the department collecting the most cans.

Analysis of the Program

This program probably works because it is based on the profit motive. No community-operated system in the area, for example, has been able to achieve similar results. In the systems we have worked with both in New Jersey and Ohio, for example, where state and local funding have been employed, aluminum can handling has become an expense.

Several recycling centers have failed in northern Ohio despite successive public grants. Many of these centers, supported by laws and restrictions on discarding waste, were unable to generate enough volume in aluminum cans in a month to match a week's volume at the Mobile Recycling Operation.

The problem seems to arise out of the failure to recognize that profit motivates human response. When communities mandate curb-side recycling, or set up recycling drop-off centers, they get what people do not want. The valuable stuff is rerouted to where the money is. This is especially true if the operation is also convenient. Even when people give to charities, such as fire department and school programs, they still want the cans to be converted into cash. Bars and

Proclamation

TO THE PEOPLE OF AKRON:

Whereas: *Recycling provides both environmental and economic benefits through the reduction of solid waste and the conservation of energy; and*

Whereas: *The protection of our environment through the recycling of aluminum cans aids in the overall preservation of vital natural resources; and*

Whereas: *Area merchants, distributors, fire departments, and numerous other organizations and businesses such as CanQuest Inc., are committed to finding solutions to the problems created by the amount of materials in our waste streams; and*

Whereas: *With the recoverance of a valuable resource, not only our environment but lives can be saved as aluminum donations are used to support the Burn Unit at Children's Hospital of Akron.*

Now, Therefore: *I, Donald L. Plusquellic, Mayor of the City of Akron, Ohio, do hereby proclaim the period from June 10 through June 20, 1990, as:*

"CANQUEST RECYCLING WEEK"

in the City of Akron.

In Witness Whereof: *I have hereunto set my hand and the Seal of the City of Akron, Ohio, to be affixed hereto this 1st day of June, 1990.*

Mayor
CITY OF AKRON

Figure 2-4   The city gets behind the recycling program run by a private operator.

PROCLAMATION

COUNTY OF SUMMIT
STATE OF OHIO

WHEREAS: AS LANDFILLS BEGIN TO REACH THEIR LIMITS, THE PROBLEM OF WHERE TO DISPOSE OF ALL OF OUR GARBAGE WILL BE A DILEMMA WE ALL HAVE TO FACE; AND

WHEREAS: ONE OF THE ONLY VIABLE SOLUTIONS TO REDUCING THE AMOUNT OF SOLID WASTE PILING UP IN OUR LANDFILLS IS TO RECYCLE; AND

WHEREAS: CANQUEST, INC., IN COOPERATION WITH LOCAL SUPERMARKETS, MAJOR DISTRIBUTORS, AND 22 FIRE DEPARTMENTS, HAVE SET A GOAL OF 100% RECYCLING OF ALUMINUM CANS FOR A 10 DAY PERIOD; AND

WHEREAS: IF THEIR GOAL IS ACHIEVED, OVER 500,000 POUNDS OF ALUMINUM CANS WILL BE ABLE TO BE RECYCLED; AND

WHEREAS: IN ADDITION TO THE SAVING OF SPACE IN THE LANDFILLS, ALL CANS BROUGHT INTO THE FIRE STATIONS WILL GO TO SUPPORT THE "ALUMINUM CANS FOR BURNT CHILDREN"; NOW

THEREFORE: I, TIM DAVIS, SUMMIT COUNTY EXECUTIVE, DO HEREBY PROCLAIM JUNE 10 - JUNE 20 AS

"RECYCLE WEEK"

IN SUMMIT COUNTY AND URGE ALL RESIDENTS TO RECYCLE ALL OF THEIR ALUMINUM CANS AND TO CONTINUE THIS PRACTICE THROUGHOUT THE YEAR.

IN WITNESS WHEREOF, I HAVE HEREUNTO SET MY HAND AND CAUSED THE GREAT SEAL OF THE COUNTY OF SUMMIT TO BE AFFIXED AT AKRON, THIS 8TH DAY OF JUNE, IN THE YEAR OF OUR LORD, ONE THOUSAND NINE HUNDRED AND NINETY.

COUNTY EXECUTIVE

Figure 2-5   Here, the council also shows broad general support for the operation.

clubs either want the money for themselves or to make personal donations. All of these incentives are lost when the community takes over and incorporates the cans into a standard waste program. Hence, when the community recycles, the bulk of the aluminum cans never makes it to the community center.

This implies that a recycling program must recognize these human desires and be designed to include them. It means either that the community must set up a workable buy-back schedule with corresponding conveniences, or it must accept the fact that the marketable recyclables are going to show up elsewhere.

REENTERING THE CONSUMPTION STREAM

There is an important lesson to be learned from the experience with aluminum: Aluminum gets recycled because it has value—used cans are cheaper to process than the raw material.

But what happens when used material has no value? How can we expect it to reenter the cycle? The fact is that we cannot expect this because when used material has no value, virgin material gets used because it is cheaper to do so. There may be several reasons for this. First, it may be cheaper to harvest than to gather up the waste; or it may be cheaper to process and convert into a finished product for a number of reasons which are seen later. These problems of getting the material back into the consumption stream are discussed in detail in the chapter on marketing, but let's look now at the problem from an economic point of view.

At this point it is sufficient to note that there is not always a market for waste products, and there *may never be one* for some goods. Hence, we have a double-edged sword in recycling that is not common to other types of human activity. We are in effect producing a large number of items with no known afteruse.

Setting up recycling programs such as curb-side recycling on a national basis will thus assure that the waste gets collected (and separated), but it will not necessarily force it back into the recycling stream. Isn't this really the classic economic example of pushing the string instead of pulling it?

Because the string bends when we push it, we solve the problem today by paying to have our waste taken away; we pay to get the paper mills, for example, to take our waste. In fact, the price for reuse at the mill may be so high that it becomes cheaper to pay expensive landfill charges and dump it. The string simply cannot be pushed!

Obviously, the work of a single community to create a recycling program has virtually no effect upon the total problem of recycling. Any one community can collect all the waste it wants, and the problem of disposal is only intensified. And the action of a lot of communities suddenly entering the arena merely exacerbates the problem by the size of the lot.

The desirable solution is to create a pull on the string; and this is not always easy or even, at present, possible.

The immediate solutions to this dilemma that come to mind are that we must either find markets for the waste, which will use the material in preference to raw material, or we must subsidize research to develop new, economic uses for old waste items. Much of this latter effort is in fact being done. Composting of leaves and lawn refuse is an example, in which the compost is resold to the residents as a usable soil builder.

The total approach to recycling being discussed here makes it clear how important it is to achieve nationwide planning to the problem, a point already made by Harkins and Baggs in the last chapter.

At the present time, however, *the reason aluminum cans get recycled so effectively is that they represent virtually the only string being pulled* consistently in the recycling milieu. Almost all other commodities have fluctuated from having a marketable value to having negative worth.

We can learn about the economics of plastics, glass, or paper by studying the conditions which make aluminum different from these other products. In the case of aluminum, there is a virtual shortage of raw material. There are only three principal countries that produce bauxite, the raw material of aluminum. Hence, recycled aluminum is needed to supplement the supply. In a very direct sense, recycled aluminum helps control the price of the raw material, and the shortage of raw material encourages the process of recycling.

On the other hand, the raw materials of plastics and glass are plentiful, and the raw material of paper is replenished every 15 years in the semi-rain forests of tropical America. These trees are farmed much like wheat, corn, or tobacco, and the costs of growing and harvesting them have tended to decline with volume.

It will only be when these raw materials become more expensive to the converter that we can expect them to be recycled in a way similar to aluminum. Only if pulpwood, for example, becomes either very scarce or very expensive will the string be pulled in a natural market process, causing wastepaper to enter the recycling stream without the use of artificial economic devices. Then, at last, dumping in landfills will end for every such product!

In a natural market economy for recycling, the vacuum cleaner begins at the converter. Here is where the string is pulled. Here is where the waste is pulled back in a chain beginning with the end user, through the scrap dealers and recyclers, and ultimately all the way back until it reaches the plants that reuse it for new products. If the plant doesn't want it, there is no pull on the string. The vacuum cleaner has no suction. The landfills fill up.

As with aluminum, to increase demand for the waste product, we must increase the cost of the raw material to the converter. We can start by eliminating subsidies which encourage excess raw material production. A second step could result from instituting "sin" taxes on any raw material that will eventually end up in a landfill. A stiff penalty on the use of virgin pulp, for example, could play a major roll in sucking up excess old newsprint, which is now stored in warehouses or being dumped.

This of course is a national decision, but then isn't recycling a nationwide problem? We have already seen that recycling from a local viewpoint has limitations. Believe me, Wellington, Ohio, or Emporia, Kansas, or all the other cities acting alone are not going to solve the total problem! They are merely going to push the dirt from one place to another until we get a unified handle on it.

SUMMING UP

From the foregoing arguments, it is clear that any system, private or public, that handles the community's recyclables must allow for the fact that many problems remain to be resolved, and that changes are going to take place over time. As we have seen, much of the valuables will not enter the system, and much of the materials collected will have little resale value, if any. (In fact, if we pay someone to take our waste, we may find that it is merely being hauled to another landfill in another state. As an example, New Jersey used Ohio as a dump for years after mandating a reduction in landfill. This continued, in fact, until one of the dumps exploded, causing a death.)

Furthermore, when most of the communities in America are separating their waste and having it hauled out of sight in separate containers, we will most likely find that we have gotten the cart before the horse, that is, that we are getting separation but not recycling. It may be some time before we begin to concentrate on working the other end of the string. This will of course happen, and when it does, the whole program will begin to function as it should and the pieces will fall in place. At that time recycling will no longer be a cause for concern but will be a source that attracts people to it, as other activities do.

Community recycling is still a premature concept because it has not yet developed into well-defined procedures. In fact, I personally feel that the correct sequence in which to undertake recycling is to begin by pulling on the string first, and then letting recycling systems spring up spontaneously within the infrastructure, as happened in the industrial revolution or other commercial developments, using local, state, and federal government, to provide the incentives and vision.

3

Separation Systems

The first problem in recycling is one of collecting the discards. (See Figure 3–1 for a typical community waste analysis.) Should we separate the items before or after pick-up?

Here again, convenience and costs are the main considerations. As Meg Lynch points out in the October 1990 issue of *Resource Recycling*, "Many people in the recycling industry are convinced that co-mingled recycling and processing systems are overwhelmingly better than the systems based on complete separation by residents. This belief may, in fact, rely more on myth than actual experience."[1]

In other words, the jury is still out and we don't know the final answer. We know that costs change with the type of equipment available, the type of waste generated by a community, the type of community itself, and the overall program, so that we may learn a definitive answer only by studying any given set of conditions. We look at several types of systems in the remaining part of this section.

CURB-SIDE SEPARATION

Picture yourself an apartment dweller or homeowner in suburban America. You have a small kitchen with a breakfast nook, and a dining room for the average-size family.

---

[1] Meg Lynch, Editorial Perspective, p. 4, Portland, OR.

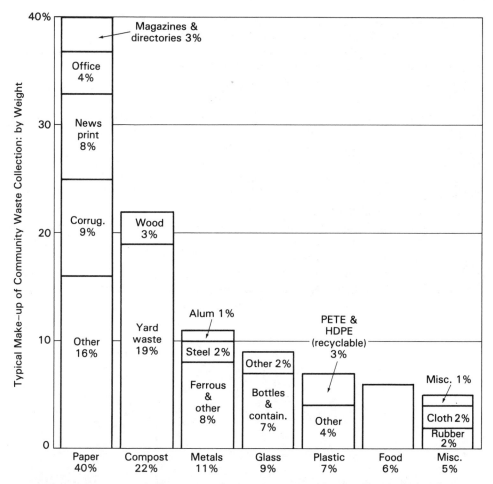

Figure 3–1 Graph indicating the make-up of community waste collection by weight.

At the present time, you have a trash container with a foot pedal to open the lid, and you dump all your solid waste into the canister. (Garbage goes down the drain via the electric disposer.)

Or, instead of a trash container in the kitchen, you may have a chute (like a clothes chute) into which you can drop the trash and it falls down a metal tube into a container in the basement.

This is the way it was done, and it may well be the way of the future.

For example, if you live in a community that mandates curb-side separation, how will these rules affect you?

Mandatory separation usually involves separate containers at the curb side for garbage and trash, beverage cans, paper, bottles, and plastics—perhaps as many as five distinct containers in all. These containers may be plastic bags or plastic drums, each a different color, or labeled with the contents.

The question is: Where does this separation take place for you as the home-owner? Do you set up five separate containers in your kitchen, so that as you create the waste you deposit it in the correct container (hopefully, without error)? Or do you carry the trash into your garage even in the dead of winter and separate it into its correct containers in the garage?

What about the extra space needed for all these containers? Will all homes be eventually designed to have a set of compartments along the garage wall to hold these separate bits of waste?

If it's all kept in the kitchen, what about bugs and mess? Normally, the trash collected in the bag in the kitchen goes to the garage each day. But five separate bags in the kitchen will tend to lay around for days before each is filled. Obviously, for the homeowner separation is not just a nuisance, but it poses special problems and concerns about health and sanitation.

At the curb, it poses new problems. Picking up five separate bundles of material and keeping it separated adds time and cost. Special trucks and equipment are needed to maintain separation (see Figure 3–2A, B, C). In such equipment, ten large bags of cans (from a neighborhood party) will fill the bin for cans. Then, with all the other bins still being empty, the truck is forced to head back to the transfer station (recycling yard) to unload before proceeding on to

Figure 3–2A Here a truck driver is working his neighborhood pick-up route. The truck has six compartments for storing different recyclables such as plastic, cans, paper, glass, and co-mingled waste. One driver services from 214 to 438 homes per day depending on type of neighborhood. (*Used by permission of Steven Flight, Recycling Coordinator, Copley Township.*)

Figure 3–2B Truck design permits driver/loader to enter from right side for quicker, safer operation on busy streets. Steering and all operating controls are dual, so truck can be driven from right or left side of truck. (*Used by permission of Steven Flight, Recycling Coordinator, Copley Township.*)

more pick-ups. This is obviously inefficient and cost intensive. An alternative program is to throw all the bags in the back of a large truck and then separate the bags at the transfer station.[2]

A third method is to use several trucks, each picking up certain items to maintain separation, and filling up the truck before returning to the transfer station. A fourth method is to do all separation at the transfer station. This is an extension of the method in general use today; namely, all garbage is comingled and goes into the trash hauler.

Actually, even when we have curb-side separation, additional separation is needed at the transfer station. Glass, for example, must be separated into the basic colors of brown, green, and clear. Paper must be separated into corrugated, newsprint, office paper, and so on. Let's see what happens at the transfer station.

---

[2] Also called MRF (pronounced "murf") for Material Recovery Facility.

Figure 3-2C   When storage compartments are full (sometimes three times per day), the truck is brought into the collection yard (transfer station) where each compartment can be emptied individually by tilting the bed, *a la* a dump truck.

AT THE TRANSFER STATION

As we have seen, much separation takes place at the transfer station. Hence, the transfer station requires large storage areas, or bunkers, for holding separated materials of many types. In this way, each can be collected into economical quantities, processed, and shipped in trailer-load lots to the processing or conversion mills.

These bunkers are usually made of concrete blocks and look like unfinished basements with one side open for access by front-end loaders and other equipment. They may be 25 feet deep, 20 feet wide, and 6 feet high, as an example. At the minimum, they must be at least as large as needed to hold a whole trailer load of material for economical cross-country shipment. The floor should be paved to allow front-end loaders to enter and scoop up the material for loading on to trailers or railroad cars. This paving also helps avoid contamination of the material. Dirt in aluminum or glass is a serious problem and can cause the whole load to be rejected at the mill. Mixing colors of glass is also a problem and reduces its value.

Waste brought into the station by pick-up trailers or trucks is unloaded at the conveyors (see Figures 3–3 and 3–4 for two examples). Here it is separated into as many as ten or more separate recyclables. As seen in the sketches, a number of operators are employed to manually do the separation. Standing on a platform, for

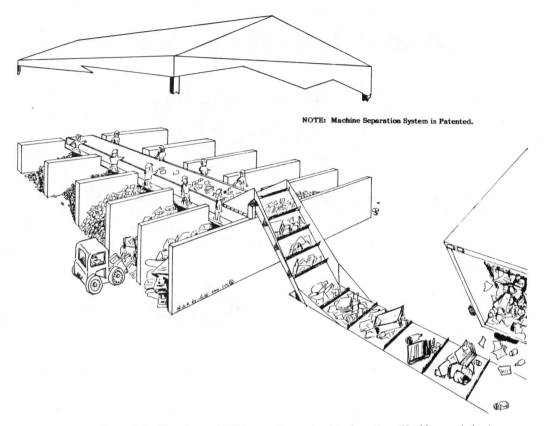

NOTE: Machine Separation System is Patented.

Figure 3-3 Showing an MRF (separation system) in operation. (*Used by permission.*)

example, employee A's job may be to remove clear (flint) and green glass. He or she takes the material from the moving conveyor, running down the center between the workers, and drops it into a bin to his or her left.

When the green glass bin is full, a front-end loader moves in and loads the glass into shipping containers, such as carboys or steel bins. Material such as cardboard or newsprint is taken by portable conveyor directly to a compactor, where it is baled for shipping.

In the meantime, all residual trash not separated manually on the platform continues moving to the right by conveyor. Then it is rolled off the end into a large storage box for final disposal, probably in a landfill. The systems as shown including shelter, costs from $100,000 on up, not counting auxiliary equipment, such as containers and balers.

Obviously, preseparation at curb side eliminates considerable manual labor, but operators' time is still necessary, as glass must be separated by color and crushed, types of paper have to be manually separated, and so on. Hence, the savings may be less than expected.

Figure 3–4   Material Recovery Facilities are designed to achieve separation in the fastest, cheapest way. (*Used by permission.*)

Processing at the Transfer Station

To really get a grasp on the details of separation, we need to know how the converter wants to receive the material. That is, in what kind of shipping package, and in what state or condition, will the converter accept the material? Even quantity is important because price is related to the tonnage delivered to the processor at a given time. Hence, a successful recycling operation must be planned so as to produce usable recyclables in economic quantities with efficient handling procedures for the converter. The better job we do in this respect, the higher the price we get and the higher will be the percentage of material that gets recycled. This latter consideration is important because I suspect that a lot of community recycling programs amount to little more than going through the motions. That is, they deliver the recyclables in such poor state of use that they not only get a poor price for their effort, but much of the material ends up in landfill anyway. An analogy here might help explain this point.

Wheat farmers, for example, get docked a certain number of points from the quoted price, based on moisture content, contamination (such as rat droppings and dirt), and so on. Hence, two different farmers at the same granary will get totally different prices for the same tonnage of wheat. The difference is *management*. It is, therefore, incumbent upon the manager of the transfer station to be fully informed of what constitutes superior performance so that he or she can command top dollar at minimum effort. Stated another way, the transfer station must be operated in such a way as to produce the highest percentages of recyclables possible, resulting in a minimum of recyclables in the landfill.

A case in point involves the glass collection program in Delaware County, Pennsylvania. This is a glass-making center. One day a load of waste glass from the center was delivered to the processor, who rejected it because it was contaminated by ceramics. They notified the center, which acted immediately to educate the public. They have not had the problem since.

Obviously, the goal is not quantity, but usable quality. Useless separation ends up in the landfill. Let's look at these recyclables from the standpoint of the processor.

Aluminum Beverage Cans

We have already seen that over 60 percent of aluminum beverage cans are being recycled. In addition, the aluminum may be used over and over with virtually total recovery. Furthermore, aluminum, which melts at about 1,200°, is self-sterilizing and is safe to reuse for foods.

Beverage cans are generally mixed in with other materials and are themselves often produced either of 100 percent aluminum or as *bi-metal* cans. Bi-metals are beverage cans with steel bodies and aluminum lids. Since steel is cheaper than aluminum, the beverage industry has shifted back and forth between aluminum and bi-metal cans, depending on the price of the sheet aluminum. It was estimated, for example, in 1989 when aluminum sheet was at a premium, that shifting to bi-metals by the big two soft drink producers would save each of them about $4,000 a month on shipments in Ohio.

Bi-metal cans have a value. About 17 percent of the can by weight is aluminum. Hence, if aluminum cans are bringing 50 cents a pound, bi-metal cans will bring about $8^{1}/_{2}$ cents a pound. In other words, it's worth its aluminum value. Unfortunately, for groups such as charities and other volunteers, the return is so low that the economic incentive is lost. In fact, many commercial recycling operations do not buy bi-metal cans. They accept them as a courtesy, but the costs of handling them may exceed the income.

Bi-metal cans are generally used in making high-grade steels. They are combined with other compounds and molded into pellets. The pellets are used as a Di-Ox, and are fed directly into the molten steel. At high temperatures Di-Ox burns violently. (Aluminum oxide was the main component of the incendiary bombs dropped on Hamburg and other German cities in World War II.) In doing so, it burns out the oxygen from the molten steel. The steel in the can, on the other hand, being very thin, oxidizes and burns up as a cinder or ash.

The transfer station that processes these bi-metal cans thus has a market, for them, but its costs may offset any income. The result is about a trade-off.

To separate steel cans and bi-metal cans from the aluminum cans, all cans are passed over a magnet. Usually, this magnet is on a drum which is part of a conveyor system. The cans are dumped into a large hopper at the foot of the conveyor.

The conveyor itself is nothing but a wide rubber belt with cogs at approximately 15-inch intervals. These cogs help move the cans to the top and dump them over the magnetic pulley. Because a single magnetic pulley only removes part of the steel, it is usually necessary to pass the cans over as many as four magnets, each of which removes some of the steel. Even after four separations, the cans may contain a fairly high percentage of steel. Alcoa Recycling in Cleveland, Ohio, which proc-esses millions of pounds a year, uses four separations, and the cans they get have already been through at least one previous separation over a magnet. In fact, the cans Alcoa receives from some recycling centers are so poorly separated that they are almost worthless as aluminum.

The system shown in the example may employ several magnetic separations. As shown in the diagram, steel cans go into one bunker, and aluminum goes into another after they pass through the magnetic separators.

As we discussed with wheat, dirt and contaminants also affect the value of the aluminum. Wet aluminum can weigh several times the true value of the pure material. When wet cans are delivered to the mill, a sample is taken and dried in an oven. The weight loss is then deducted proportionately from the whole load. Excessive dirt and other contaminants may cause the whole load to be rejected by the mill. It ends up in a landfill, and all the cans and effort are lost. Often the public throws cigarettes or pebbles in the cans. The amount of this type of contaminant is deducted as a percentage of the total aluminum weight by the mill. Loads of muddy cans may be useless for everyone, becom-ing landfill.

Many of these problems suggest the value of training the public in the "etiquette" of recycling. It is not enough to support the idea of recycling. Each person must also be concerned enough to understand how little things done in the home or at a social event can greatly affect the quality of recycling.

I just recently attended a recycling convention which illustrates the prob-lem. Here two containers were placed at a refreshment table, one marked *trash*, the other *Aluminum Cans Only*. When I inspected the *Aluminum Cans Only* con-tainer, it was *mixed* with every other type of trash.

COMPACTING FOR SHIPMENT

Cans have to be compacted for shipping. A 16-foot van, for example, will carry about 600 pounds of uncrushed cans. That same truck carrying a load compacted by a Tow-About (discussed earlier) will handle a 4,500-pound load. The same cans compressed by a baler become even denser (weighing up to 1,100 pounds per bale), and those run through a Mosely Densifier will weigh perhaps three times that figure. Obviously, shipping costs are important. A load of 600 pounds, for example, shipped by truck from Akron to Pittsburgh (including return trip) would cost over 50¢ per pound. The same truck carrying 4,500 pounds would cost only 7¢ per pound. And the same truck carrying densified cans could bring the shipping costs below 2¢ per pound.

These economies affect other decisions, as well. Annual volumes of aluminum and sizes of loads need to be known when buying auxiliary equipment. A low-cost baler or Tow-About is adequate for handling small volumes. Large volumes may justify the purchase of a densifier at much higher initial costs.

The converter (processing mill) almost always wants the cans prepared in a specific way. Mills often pay a premium if the cans are prepared and delivered as per specs. Some mills do *not* want shredded cans, for example. Hence, the cost of a shredder and the labor involved in preparing the load for shipment actually reduce the value of the shipment. On the other hand, a mill in another area of the country may prefer to receive them shredded and pay a premium. The Reynolds Mill in Alabama, for example, is designed specifically to process shredded cans and pays a premium of up to 2¢ per pound.

This means that in designing the system and in selecting the method of preparation for shipment, the first step is to talk to the mill and find out what it wants, how it wants it, and in what quantities. This is true, of course, not just for aluminum but for all recyclables.

Hence, system design must incorporate efficiency of handling and operation, proper preparation of the product, a knowledge of shipping procedures and costs, and a knowledge of what form of packaging brings the highest dollar.

Plastics

Plastics are the second most valuable waste in community recycling. Despite our increased usage of plastics for food, autos, and other products in the home, only 1 percent of the plastic is returned for recycling (out of over 10 million tons produced). In the past 25 years, plastics in the waste stream have increased their share from 1 percent to 5 percent.

The problem is not so much a lack of ability to reuse the materials, but that so many varieties exist, consisting of many different chemicals and physical properties. Many of these compounds have the same appearance but are not interchangeable. At the present time, there are two main recyclables. One is polyethylene Terephthalate (called PETE), which is used in the two-liter plastic beverage bottles found in the soft drink section of stores. The other is high-density polyethylene (called HDPE), which is used to produce containers for milk, juices, water, detergents, and oil, as well as some other liquids.

Most plastics are light in weight but bulky. As a result, plastics constitute 7 percent of waste by weight produced in the house, but 30 percent of its volume. Like cans, much of the volume is trapped air. Generally, the first step in processing plastics at the transfer station is, therefore, to shred them into chunks that can be easily and tightly baled for efficient shipping.

At the processing plant, the plastic is ground up into pellets. Then labels, dirt, and metal caps are removed. Here, again, contamination or poor preparation at the transfer station may cause the materials to be unusable.

Until recently the plastics used in beverage containers melted at low temperatures and began to degrade as temperatures rose. Therefore, they could not be reused for food because low temperature will not destroy bacteria. (There has been some success by beverage container producers in overcoming this problem.) However, because they do melt, they can be remolded (at a loss, however, in quality) into a number of useful items. At the present time, these old food containers are being converted into floor mats, trash containers, rope, scouring pads, filler and fibrous materials, lumber, fence posts, and furniture. Some of these molded products in furniture look like natural wood and are harder to mar and deface than the true product. As fence posts, the lack of biodegradability is a major advantage. These posts will outlast either steel or treated woods. They are truly the farmers' friend because their great-grandchildren will still be benefiting from them. Civilizations 10,000 years from now may well have them on display in museums, as an example of twentieth-century culture.

Paper

Paper is the major component in community landfills. It represents up to 50 percent of the total, as we have seen. Besides saving trees, recycled paper cuts water pollution by as much as 35 percent and air pollution by 65 percent. The quality of paper is related to the length of its fibers. These fibers come from the wood pulp used in the original paper slurry. The longest fibers usually make the highest grades. All fibers tend to break down with reuse. (Almost 20 percent of the fiber is lost each time.) But many common types of paper can be recycled. These include shopping bags and envelopes, cardboard boxes, office stationery, and newsprint.

The first step in recycling is to sort the paper by grades. These grades are based on the quality of the paper (its type) and the amount of dirt and residue in the material, such as paper clips, coatings used in original manufacture and printing, and other contaminants. As with other products, clean paper with long fiber content brings the highest price. Dirty paper may have no value.

The actual recycling process at the mill repeats many of the processes performed in converting wood pulp to paper. First, the paper is reduced to a water slurry using chemicals and beaters. At this time, metals and any dirt not removed earlier are skimmed out. Inks and coatings are processed out at this time. The new product then can be either used directly to produce paper, or it can be mixed with a wood-pulp slurry to make a higher-quality product.

Newsprint is an excellent product for recycling, if it is clean and all coated inserts have been removed. For one thing, it can be recycled directly back into newsprint, or used for insulation or matting material. At one time we did a better job with newsprint than we do today. In the past, Boy Scouts or other groups went from door to door and collected clean, bundled papers from each home. Residents saved these papers and welcomed the chance to participate. Today, we see little direct collection, and the newspapers get dumped in with all trash, making it a costly separation process and reducing the paper's value.

Supermarkets and stores actually do a better job with corrugated paper than the rest of the public. For stores, corrugated paper constitutes a major disposal problem. Almost all large stores today have compressors and balers. As the boxes are emptied, they are dumped into the baler. At regular intervals large, heavy bales of corrugated are produced, usually at the rear of the store. Actually, corrugated paper from businesses is the largest source of recycled paper in America today, and corrugated paper is a high-grade, long-fiber paper.

The office has also become an increasingly important element in the paper waste stream. The development of modern, low-cost printing presses, high-speed computer printers, office copiers, multicopy forms, and other paper-using devices have enormously expanded the volume of paper used per person since the depression. (The steel industry as long ago as 30 years, for example, used to quip: "one ton of paper for every ton of steel produced." This emphasizes the growth of bureaucracy and recordkeeping that had evolved.) Similarly, home use of paper has exploded. Home use includes disposable diapers, napkins, paper towels, toilet paper, facial tissues, greeting cards, stationery, plates, cups, and molded containers. Almost all of these are post-World War II products, many of which can be made from low-grade recycled paper, if it reaches the converter. Too often today it fills our landfills, and as we have seen, it is slow to decompose.

Steel Cans

We may do ourselves a disservice when we bury our cans and perhaps also our papers under an earth covering. Exposed to the air and the elements in the eastern climate of America, a bi-metal beverage can will rust away in as little as three months, leaving the aluminum.

Steel cans ("tin" cans) used for food contain much thicker steel walls. And the steel casing is coated on the inside with a microfinish of tin to prevent rusting and protect the food from contamination. All of our supplies of tin in America are either imported or obtained by removing this thin coating and reusing it, in a process known as detinning. (The residual steel is also usable, by introducing special controls at the furnaces.)

As with aluminum cans, or bi-metals, the first step begins at the transfer station. Here the cans are flattened and baled for shipment. In fact, even before this, at the home or point of first use, the cans must be washed and cleaned to eliminate food contents. This is not common, but some local community recycling systems now require it because food left in the cans can cause negative chemical reactions in the process of extracting the tin.

Obviously, a great deal of public support and commitment is needed if we are going to prepare our food cans properly for recycling. First of all, we are doubling the dishwashing chore of the housekeeper. This may not be significant to everyone, but for a restaurant this results in higher labor costs. Second, washing all cans means a considerable increase in the use of water. In California, for example, during drought periods local communities have in the past limited the practice of providing drinking water to customers at restaurants. Drinking water became available only on request. Washing dirty cans exacerbates the water problem.

Here, again we are facing trade-offs which make it evident that considerable thought must go into any local program before adopting it in the community. We are often in fact on the horns of a dilemma where we do not like either choice.

Glass

Glass is another major landfill item. Today over 5 billion bottles and glass jars are recycled each year and are used mostly for making new bottles. Recycled glass is now being used by 86 major glass manufacturers and the recycling of glass has grown almost five times in the past decade, helped in part by deposit-return laws and new uses. As a rule, most glass can be recycled, but some glasses have better uses than others. Like paper or plastics, downgrading often occurs. For example, window panes, pyrex, and ornamentals can only be used to make products such as roof shingles, fiberglass, and reflectors, in which light distortion or purity is not a problem. The major component in a community recycling system is, however, container glass such as jars and bottles. These make up almost 80 percent of all glass found in the community system.

As we discussed earlier, these glass containers must be separated into the three basic colors of brown, green, and clear, and then crushed. Crushing is done by a low-cost hammer-mill at the transfer station to reduce the bulk. The crushed glass is then stored in large (4' × 4' × 4') cardboard containers for easy handling and stacking by fork lifts. This process makes for economical truckload shipment to the converter.

In the example shown in Figure 3–4 each color of glass has its own bunker, so that separation occurs in the initial stage, when the glass is dropped down the chute. Crushing, however, takes place after the bunker is almost full, so that a complete truckload of glass can be crushed and loaded with a single set-up.

Naturally, colors get mixed even in separation by the operators. Mistakes are made, and glass gets broken before its initial journey to the curb, or on the way to the transfer station.

Lids, labels, dirt, and food add to the contamination. Much of this, however, can be dealt with provided it is not excessive. The biggest problem comes from the metal caps and miscellaneous dirt which can produce defective glass. As with other recyclables, both the price or even its complete rejection depends on the quality of the material being prepared at the transfer station. Once the glass reaches the converter, the crushed material is cleaned again and then pulverized into fine granules. Here it is mixed with other virgin glass-making materials and remelted to make new glass. The final step is to produce new bottles.

See Figure 3–5 for examples of some processing equipment used at transfer stations. The machines shown are used primarily for plastics, cans, paper, and glass.

Oil

Motor oil is our largest pollutant to streams, rivers, and underground aquifers. American cars generate about 1.2 billion gallons of used oil every year. Used oils are easily reprocessed and can be reused either as motor oil or fuel oil. Recyclers have developed exchange programs similar to those used by the auto parts dealers. Auto parts dealers, for example, sell remanufactured generators or other parts for

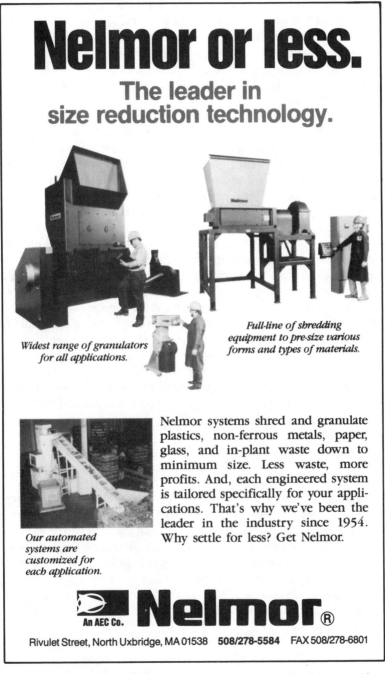
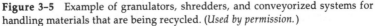
Figure 3–5 Example of granulators, shredders, and conveyorized systems for handling materials that are being recycled. (*Used by permission.*)

cars and give the purchaser credit for returning his or her old part. In the oil recycling business, the recycler may charge the service station for picking up the oil, say 10 to 15 cents per gallon, but in turn the recycler sells the re-refined oil back to the service station at a discount. Except for carbon build-up and other dirt which are filtered out, the re-refined oil is as good as the original product.

Tires

Less than 20 percent of old tires are recycled. Retreading has been the major reuse, but only 10 percent to 15 percent of old casings are suitable for retreads. Sears has a program worked out with Lakin-General, a major recapper based in Chicago, in which about 300,000 tires are recapped, returned to Sears, and sold with warranties up to 35,000 miles. Total tire sales at the 400 Sears outlets are almost 3 million a year. Of the tires not recapped, another 20 percent are used to produce muffler hanger straps and other rubber impregnated fabric products, such as mats or wharf bumpers. A program is under study now to use millions of tires to produce artificial reefs for fish beds, in island areas like Kwajalein. Tires have also been used to produce all-weather tracks in sports arenas, using ground rubber.

A number of states, including Ohio (once the producer of 95% of the world's tires) have banned tires from landfills. With over 60 percent of the worn-out tires having no present uses, some recycling firms have set up single-product monofils, into which the tires are stored. Once economic uses are found for these tires, they may be re-mined and put back into the market as oils (tires are rich in high-energy oils, and are burnt on both coasts by waste-to-energy programs) or other unforeseen products. Present taxes on tires are being used to fund research on new uses for these old tires. (A recent process-development freezes the tires at sub-zero temperatures, to break the materials into re-usable components.)

CONCLUSION

We have emphasized the need to prepare the recyclables for the converter. In a very real sense, every transfer station is as much a manufacturer (or perhaps more precisely, a miner) as any other type of factory.

As American industry has learned in competing with the Japanese, quality sells products. For at least the past 15 years, the United States has been losing market share in heavy industry, electronics, and even disposable diapers. In each case, the perceived reason for shifting to the Japanese product has been that of higher quality. Equally important, the market gain has been made by firms with lower total costs.

In fact, quality control experts such as W. Edwards Deming and J. M. Juran have long argued that higher quality leads to lower costs—because it reduces scrap, rework, and wasted effort caused by not doing the job right the first time. Deming is the American who was hired by the Japanese to help them after the war. He is now back in the United States helping America learn the same lesson.

Juran points out that the cost of poor quality can often run as high as 40 percent of the factory cost of the item. An example is Hewlett-Packard. Hewlett-Packard's experience was that poor quality in 1981 cost it 20 percent in sales, 25 percent in extra people, and 70 percent more in inventory—all caused by having to deal with defective parts.

Recognizing that these truths applied to them also, Ford began a quality drive in the 1980s. By 1986, it had cut daily expenses $12 million per day, and it went on to become the most profitable car company *in the world* that year.

Professor Dennis Karney, in a talk before the Economic Outlook Conference at the University of Kansas on October 9, 1987, said that the key to delivering high quality is to establish a customer orientation. "This can be as easy as having the worker" . . . talk to the customer to see how the product and its delivery can be fine-tuned. He stressed developing human resources: "Workers are assets, not liabilities." There has to be a recognition of the value of people to the operation. There must be a commitment to the brotherhood of man.

Karney showed that achieving high quality requires a systematic approach to the operation. The successful firm plans for the long haul. It intends to be in business for a long time. This means setting up training and educational programs for employees. This means anticipating changing conditions and customer needs.

Concern for quality also applies to the service industry. "Do not conclude," he said, "that the high-quality–low-cost phenomenon exists only in manufacturing. It applies equally well to services, both public and private." He cited examples and concluded, "Interestingly enough, higher quality in the public sector tends to reduce costs, resulting in either an increase in services, a decrease in the need for taxes, or both."[3]

Just one more word before moving on to the next chapter. Many of our present community recycling systems are not producing effective, or even acceptable, materials in quantity. As a result, recycling costs are higher than necessary, and the return on sales is lower than it should be. These operations become increasingly dependent upon community funds to make up for their inefficiencies. And as they become increasingly inefficient, they become more dependent on support. But the problem doesn't end here. The problem is that the purpose behind recycling itself is not being carried out as fully as possible. We are sorting materials so they can be recycled, but they are going into landfills either at home or across the border. Our need, stated precisely as possible, is to recycle *fully*, *effectively*, and *cheaply*!

---

[3] Professer Dennis Karney in a talk given at the Economic Outlook Conference, University of Kansas, Lawrence, KS, October 9, 1987.

4

Drop-Off and Buy-Back Systems

Whether separated or commingled, curb-side pick-up is the most common collection system in America. Another approach, now adopted by California, and also used extensively throughout the country is the use of *drop-off* stations. The Goodwill collection box standing in parking lots is an example. When the public gets paid for their recyclables, these drop-off stations become buy-back stations. As a rule these drop-off sites have tended to precede curb-side separation. When augmented by buy-back centers, curb-side recycling, and *transfer stations*, drop-off sites have resulted in a collection network that provides complete service to the public. Durham, North Carolina is a case in point. Here, curb-side pick-up gets about 40 percent of the recyclables and drop-offs get the rest. The drop-offs are the major outlets of bars and restaurants, following the trend discussed earlier, in the handling of aluminum cans.

HOW THEY OPERATE

The purpose of a drop-off station is to provide sites at convenient locations where the public can bring recyclables and leave them, or sell them. Many businesses, such as supermarkets and small communities, have used this approach to encourage the public to bring in their reusable goods. Supermarkets, for example, encourage the recycling of plastic or paper bags by giving a few cents credit on each bag furnished by the customer. These drop-off stations operate by providing bins or containers for dumping trash.

Drop-off containers come in many shapes and sizes. One approach is to set up a row of roll-off boxes with labels for glass, cans, and paper in a busy shopping area. People drive up and drop their waste in a predesignated container. In this approach, people are actually presorting by type of waste, such as glass or paper, much as we discussed earlier under curb-side separation. And as before, the materials are then hauled to a transfer station for further separation into colors of glass, types of cans, plastics, and papers.

THE CHANGING CONCEPT OF DROP-OFF

In fact, there has been a great deal of change in drop-off sites since the crude beginnings. The first sites used 55-gallon barrels, which were discards (recycled!) from some other use. These barrels were cheap, but they were seldom efficient, and definitely not attractive.

The next step was to design the containers to increase efficiency and reduce costs. Thus, containers such as dumpsters evolved that could be loaded by heavy equipment. These containers hold large volumes of material and are handled by special hydraulic arms on large trash trucks. They are found today behind all offices and stores. Larger containers evolved into roll-offs that fit on the backs of large flat-bed trucks. These are dropped at collection sites (see Figure 4–1).

Some of these units were later subdivided into smaller bins of two to three cubic yard capacity for separating the materials as discussed earlier. Now the trend is to even larger compartments, some holding up to 40 cubic yards of a single material.

At the same time, the trend is toward improving the attractiveness of these containers. Recently, for example, domed igloos or bells have begun to appear at sites. Shohomish County, Washington and Waukeska County in Wisconsin have pasted decals on the igloos transforming them into interesting gremlins, elfs, and monsters which attract children and parents. Emphasis is on making recycling fun for everyone. These igloos are an import from Europe, and besides offering an attractive, interesting appearance, they are designed for efficient handling. However, these igloos take longer to unload than conventional systems because extra steps are required to unload them. Like the dumpsters, they can be handled by the truck driver who uses equipment to pick them up and empty them automatically.

LIMITATIONS TO DROP-OFF

The unfortunate problem with these programs is that they require direct action on the part of each individual. If a person is inclined to be passive or has an extremely busy schedule, he or she may want the waste to be picked up.

Figure 4-1 This unit is called a roll-off box. It is kept behind city hall for residents to drop-off large units such as refrigerators and water heaters for recycling. The township gets one cent per pound for these items. Residents save as much as $20–$30 per unit by not having to pay to have them hauled away to a landfill. (*Used by permission of Steven Flight, Recycling Coordinator, Copley Township.*)

Furthermore, many individuals may not want to contend with the messy, dirty, sticky, cans and plastics.

Twenty years ago, for example, St. Petersburg set up 90 convenient drop-off sites to collect glass, cans, and newspaper. After an initial burst of enthusiasm the program failed and was closed down. Although vandalism was involved, that was not the problem. The program has now been reestablished, as a part of the state program on recycling.

Waukeska County, Wisconsin with a population of 300,000 and considered to have an effective drop-off program supports 13 drop-off centers and collects about 400 tons of recyclables. Since the American public produces over a ton of waste per capita, this figures out to a recycling rate of about 0.1 percent.

Hence, voluntary programs tend to have minimal success. And this may explain why the large waste haulers have moved so slowly into the field. It was once thought that they would dominate the drop-off market, but that trend has never developed. The private haulers have tended to stick to conventional collection systems leaving drop-offs to communities.

Once again, a look at the economics explains why. Most of these programs are operated either as public programs or by nonprofit groups. In Columbus,

Ohio the land is provided by the state, which also underwrites 50 percent of the operating cost. Another 15 percent comes from donations (not counting donated labor). The balance is expected to be obtained from income from materials.

Several counties in Michigan have combined to use a nonprofit organization which operates 25 drop-offs. These counties pay the operator $80 per ton in credits on landfill avoidance. One county in Wisconsin provides grants of up to $2,500 per year to operate each drop-off center, all of which are run by the community. At an average collection of 30 tons per center, this comes to a cost of almost $80 per ton, not including volunteers and community costs. An exception to the rule on public support is found in Bloomsburg, Pennsylvania. Here participation in the program runs as high as 50 percent. The long-term trend, however, is generally downward after an initial surge. As we discussed with aluminum cans, the large volume handlers have a direct market for these items, so that only residual collections come to the stations.

BUY-BACK CENTERS

To offset these problems, some areas have set up buy-back centers. California, for example, has taken this approach throughout the state. These centers pay the public for their cans or other designated waste. To encourage the public to participate, the price at each center is supported by the state at a level designed to make the public respond. The jury is still out on the success of this program. It suffers from the problems of messiness and inconveniences mentioned earlier. Messing up one's car every week for the sake of a few pennies hardly induces enthusiastic cooperation unless one is highly motivated by other interests. These systems, however, do encourage the disadvantaged to scavenge the neighborhood, as seen in the following example.

In the inner city of Philadelphia, unemployment among young males has reached 40 percent. One third of the families are below the poverty line. In the heart of this area, the National Temple Recycling Center has been operating since 1983, providing jobs and income to the area. The center is a multimaterial buy-back operation. It is part of an economic development project to provide low-cost housing and create jobs. The center processes and remarkets about 25 tons per day of glass, papers, metals, and plastics. Almost all of the materials are brought to the center by private individuals. The center has a staff of 12, of which eight were formerly considered unemployable.

Because the work at recycling stations of this type is highly labor intensive but requires a low skill level, it is ideal for those who have had no opportunity or experience in steady work.

Because it is locally operated, the Philadelphia center hires local help and buys its materials from the neighborhood. The center then actually succeeds in recycling most of its funds directly back to the community.

Still, as we discussed with the problem of getting a pull on the string, the incentive may work better if it occurs farther up the line. Most people prefer to drop their trash at the curb for a few dollars a month, and give the separation job to the collector.

LOCAL RESTRICTIONS ON THESE TYPES OF OPERATIONS

One important factor, which may come as a surprise to those getting started, is that local ordinances and zoning may prohibit the establishment of sites. Even though "everyone" is for recycling publicly, it is not uncommon to find strong opposition to it in any given community. This "let George do it" syndrome is not just a political or elitist phenomenon. The owner of the grounds upon which the supermarket stands may refuse permission, even if the store owner is cooperative. Or the store owner may place large ads in the newspaper advocating recycling—sandwiched in between product sales ads—and yet he or she may not permit a drop-off station on the grounds. One of the largest supermarket chains in Ohio is a staunch supporter of recycling in the newspapers, and yet the vice president in charge of recycling argues that the store cannot participate directly in recycling because, as he says, "food and recycling do not mix." And yet, his competitor, a smaller chain, does precisely what he insists cannot be done. These attitudes have been changing, and it has become much easier in those communities which are actively engaged in recycling to get site acceptance. Many shopping centers are now seeking to offer these services to their customers. Even now, however, in the same county, there are communities that will not permit buy-back centers, even though surrounding towns have provided them.

Hence, we must not forget in designing our system that the bottom line comes out as always: We are still dealing with trash—messy, dirty, smelly *trash*! And although the public, the press, and the politicians, support and recognize the need to recycle, in truth, very little has changed in terms of attitudes, or in terms of people. The excitement wears off quickly.

SOME GENERAL OBSERVATIONS

Put in more positive terms, I am saying that the system must be designed to maintain momentum; and to be a success, it must deal with realities. People will help! They will support these programs! But *you* must work out the means by which these systems will succeed and not turn people off by asking from them what they do not wish to do. In our own experience, we have found that even the most dedicated environmentalists can become jaded when they are asked to deal personally and directly with waste materials. This also explains why it is so important to maintain a clean, healthy workplace, as suggested earlier, because the final equation involves people.

There are other problems: Unmanned drop-off locations are often the target of vandals, and the sites frequently attract unsightly litter around the area. People will leave trash they want to get rid of, and the drop-off station becomes a public dump. Even with a paid staff, the help may not be able to control this type of problem.

You will probably lose money. Most drop-off stations are supported by subsidies because they do not attract enough volume to cover their costs. Delaware County, Pennsylvania, for example, pays collection centers $20 for every ton of glass taken in.

Offsetting many of these disadvantages is the fact that in lower-income neighborhoods, as in Philadelphia, these stations can be used to provide jobs to the handicapped and needy, who might never be employed otherwise. In fact, buy-back centers have a direct effect on the income of many needy persons, who walk the streets and vacant areas picking up cans and other recyclables to sell to the buy-back center. This is an important benefit to society, which may exceed the value of recycling itself. This income is generally "untaxed," and it represents a significant part of the underground economy for these entrepreneurs and bar owners.

Drop-off centers seem to perform best in sparsely populated areas, where homeowners are already hauling their own trash. No doubt this is so because these people have already been programmed to accept the inconveniences. For the urban dwellers, on the other hand, to haul trash, they must be provided with convenient locations—areas they frequent, for example, such as busy shopping malls. Unfortunately, these are also the areas that are least suitable from an aesthetic point of view. Any tendency to deviate from this convenience has a negative impact. Thus, studies show that there is a direct correlation between distance to the site (in other words, convenience) and the success of a site: namely, the greater the distance to travel, the lower the rate of recycling. This explains why Santa Monica has established drop-off sites within a third of a mile of every resident, with the result that 28 percent of its recyclables (cans, aluminum, paper, and glass) are collected. The decorated igloos mentioned earlier are also placed at school grounds. The main objection to drop-offs in quality locations is that they are eyesores.

Some success in overcoming such eyesores has been achieved by the decals discussed earlier, and by designing and displaying attractive signs, with clean, painted fenced-in areas that are well lit and safe for people to visit. Effectively done, these appealing, attractively designed containers make excellent subjects for field trips by school classes and club groups, building support in the homes for the program.

The signs should provide simple instructions, showing the public where to dump what. Most of these programs include an extra bin for trash that is not acceptable in the recycling bins, so that people who bring their materials can leave the recyclables in the proper bins, and the residue can be left in the trash bin instead of being hauled back or dumped on the ground.

Some of the unmanned sites provide a handy telephone to answer questions. Some use a tape recording which gives simple instructions or hours of operation. In fact, all drop-offs should display the hours of operation. Unmanned sites which are always open offer certain advantages to people who cannot conveniently visit the site during regular working hours. But as we said earlier, they also get a lot of trash and unusable materials cluttering up the area, because no one is on hand to control it. Unmanned stations are subject to pilferage and rougher treatment, so that they require heavier, stronger containers. The better-planned sites use heavy pipe guards or concrete pillars to protect the containers from vehicle damage.

Buy-back centers naturally do better in terms of volume, but labor costs and high insurance rates are important considerations. Cash-in-hand is a strong incentive to recycle, helping offset the trouble involved. Perhaps even more important is the psychological factor that money adds. Money takes the product out of the realm of trash and gives it a value. These centers can also be used to train young people in the mechanics of running a business, such as handling money, keeping records, and meeting the public. Having money on hand also introduces special problems. First of all, bookkeeping records and controls on funds have to be established. Workers have to be monitored and balances maintained. Paying money also imposes legal requirements, such as licenses and scale permits. It means owning accurate scales and cash boxes.

Perhaps one of the biggest advantages of drop-offs is the fact that they provide officials having no background in recycling with an inexpensive learning experience. Here's a chance to learn the realities and frustrations of recycling without spending a lot of money. These sites also train the public by building an awareness that something is happening in the community.

Drop-off programs have often led the way into recycling, introducing the public to the knowledge of which commodities can be recycled and how to prepare them. Plastic, as an example, was first collected by drop-off centers before it became a part of curb-side separations. Motor oil is another example. It is now being collected by igloo sites on the West Coast. In this respect, the various types of recycling, as we remarked earlier, complement each other. Their high visibility opens the door for the general public to the intricacies and the amount of energy required to do the job. Naturally, the public sees only the tip of the iceberg, but more important they become personally involved. They know that something is being done in their community. And they learn how to participate in the total effort.

5

The Basic Machinery and Their Uses at a Recycling and Scrap-Processing Center

Scrap-processing centers perform much the same function as the transfer stations we discussed earlier. They also combine many of the features of drop-off or buy-back centers, except that they usually are integrated into a single operation. They are usually privately owned and operated for profit. As a rule their main volume comes from large industrial producers of waste, although the public is encouraged to bring waste materials to the site as well.

The equipment and processes described here range from low- to high-volume handling, thus covering the general range of recycling operations. The products discussed concentrate on those covered earlier.

The equipment needed to operate a scrap-processing and recycling center varies from location to location and depends on the volume of the various types of material to be handled. Most of the items discussed earlier are processed, plus many items not suitable for handling at a transfer station. These other materials include sheet metal and cast material of ferrous and nonferrous types of materials. Typically in a recycling center these metal items consist of pots, pans, and other small metallic items that can be carried in the back of a car or small pick-up truck. Larger household items such as stoves and refrigerators are usually not handled in recycling centers, but go directly to commercial scrap dealers who are better equipped to handle the material and dispose of it in an environmentally acceptable manner.

PAPER HANDLING

To handle paper, there are several types of balers and shredders that can be utilized. In the typical small recycling center that may receive around 10,000 pounds per day, a *downstroke baler* would be used. (Figure 5–1) This machine consists of a ram on top of a metal structure which is used to compress the paper into a lower chamber where it is finally tied with wire and extricated from the box of the baler. The bale, weighing approximately 800 to 1,200 pounds, is then taken to a storage area until a truckload is accumulated. (See Figure 5–2 for an example of a paper shredder.) Shredding increases the ability to compact the material for greater weight per bale.

Larger operations might utilize a pit baler, called an *upstroke baler* (Figure 5–3). In high-volume situations, we might use a horizontal single-ram or two-ram baling press. Again, the large operations handling in excess of 20,000 pounds a day would utilize the *pit-type* or *horizontal-type* baler (Figure 5–4). These units are less labor intensive and have high productivity. With the downstroke baler, each individual piece of paper must normally be put into a charge opening and compressions made until a full chamber has been obtained.

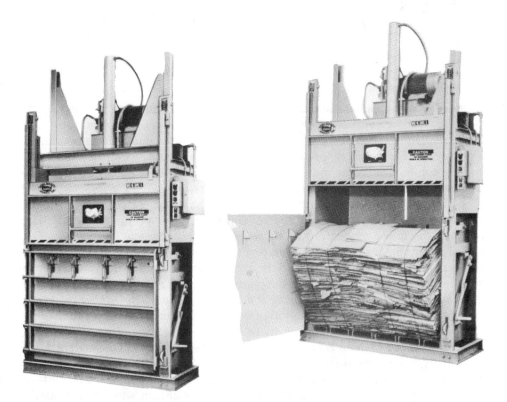

Figure 5-1 Downstroke balers sold by Counselor Engineering, Inc. (*Used by permission.*)

Figure 5-2   Paper shredders sold by Counselor Engineering, Inc. (*Used by permission.*)

PLASTICS HANDLING

In the handling of plastics, there are basically two methods available to the small processing center. The first is to receive the material, preferably separated by color, and then to bale it. Again, the downstroke baler could be utilized for the small volumes. Typically, in baling this material (consisting of plastic milk jugs and similar materials such as the two-liter soda bottle) the material is placed inside the downstroke baler and several compressions are made. When you are finally ready to tie off the bale, the door is opened and two or three wires are inserted into the slots to contain the compacted plastic jugs. One of the problems of handling plastic material this way is that air can be trapped and compressed inside the bottles. This can cause the bale to fall apart and have a rather ragged appearance.

For the larger volumes of plastic material, *plastic granulators* (Figure 5–5) are available which shred the plastic into fine pieces, usually $1/2$ inch or less, after which it is placed into gaylord boxes or other appropriate transportation containers, usually by conveyor. The material is then sold to consumers of plastic granulated material. The consumers of this material may further process the plastic by washing and drying it to remove residue from the contents and make it more acceptable for reextrusion into new plastic products.

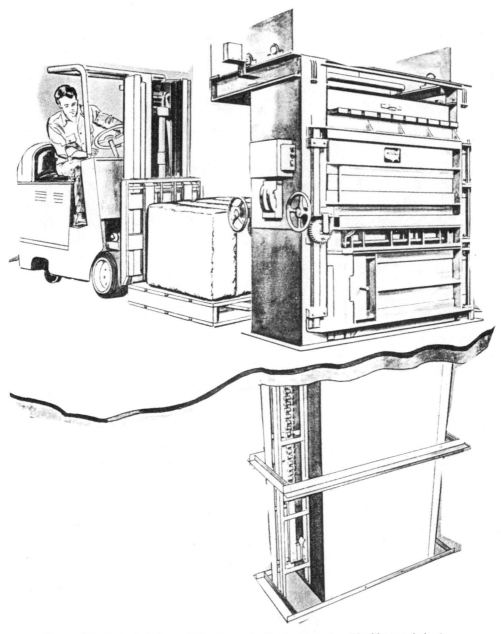

Figure 5-3   Upstroke balers sold by Counselor Engineering, Inc. (*Used by permission.*)

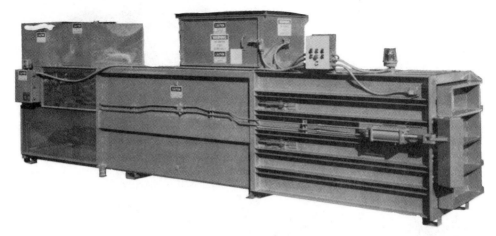

Figure 5–4 Horizontal balers sold by Counselor Engineering, Inc. (*Used by permission.*)

HANDLING ALUMINUM AND STEEL CANS

The handling of aluminum and steel cans can be done in a number of ways. In the small centers, aluminum cans are fed through *can flatteners* with magnetic separation devices, as described earlier.

In the *densification* process, (Figure 5–6) the cans again pass through a magnetic separator, and then they are compacted into bricks measuring approximately 1' × 1' × 8'' and weighing approximately 25 pounds. These densified cans are then loaded onto pallets, typically weighing 1,000 pounds. The material is then banded and loaded by forklift into trucks for hauling to the consuming and purchasing aluminum companies.

In processing sheet metal and cast-metal items, the downstroke baler is the least expensive method of handling this material. (See Figure 5–1.) Sheet aluminum, such as siding from houses and other buildings, is typically brought into recycling centers. This material is purchased on a per-pound basis and then processed into bales which are sold to consumers.

Any type of cast aluminum or other aluminum-type materials is purchased by the recycling center. In certain cases, the material is separated by grades, such as cast and sheet materials, all of which bring different prices. Segregating can improve the price obtained for this material.

In the case of other nonferrous materials, such as copper and brass, a similar situation exists. It often pays to segregate the cast and sheet-type materials to obtain better prices.

Another item that is purchased at the center is electric wire and cable which can be obtained by the dismantling and destruction of houses and during renovation work. This can be a valuable source of income. The wire is stripped of its insulation on a wire stripper and then usually baled in a downstroke baler and

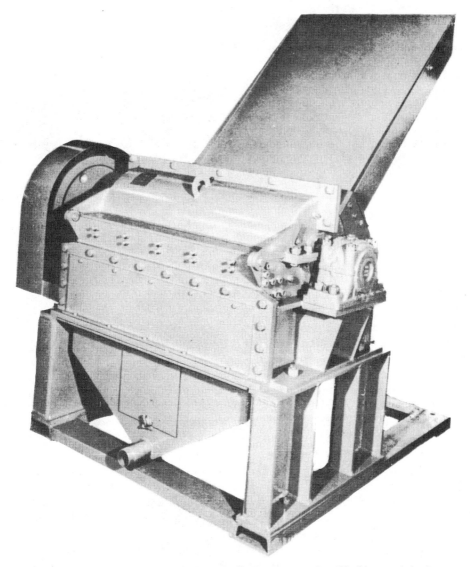

Figure 5-5   Plastic granulator sold by Counselor Engineering, Inc. (*Used by permission.*)

sold to people who recover copper and aluminum materials through granulation and other methods.

Cast iron and steel materials in sheet or cast form are also purchased by a recycling center. This material is usually the least desirable and least profitable for a small recycling center to handle. A fully equipped scrap yard is a better prospect for purchasing this material, but a small recycling center may be forced to purchase it in order to obtain the more valuable copper or brass from the same customer.

Figure 5-6 Beverage can densifiers sold by Counselor Engineering, Inc. (*Used by permission.*)

Glass, as we have seen, is usually purchased by color: clear, brown, and green. The *glass crusher* (Figure 5–7) typically pulverizes the material into approximately 1-inch pieces. Crushing the bottles results in a substantial volume reduction, making the load more economical for transportation.

Certain designs of a recycling center seem to work better than others. The most desirable approach is a "drive-through" arrangement, with adequate parking for the people bringing materials to the center. Often, especially on Saturday mornings which is one of the busiest days of the week, a number of cars may line up to gain entrance. If adequate parking is not available, this can cause dangerous situations and traffic congestion.

At the center, the typical car or pick-up truck enters the drive-through area and pulls up to a scale. The material to be sold is unloaded out of the vehicle and placed on the scale for weighing. It is recommended that an *electronic visible scale* be used. This gives the sellers confidence that they are receiving legitimate weights for their material. An appropriate purchase receipt should be issued, showing the various grades, quantity, and price per pound on the receipt.

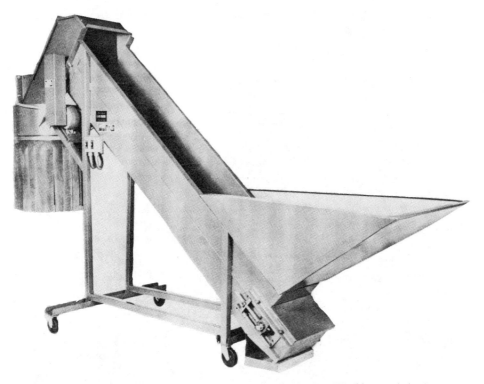

Figure 5-7   Glass crushers sold by Counselor Engineering, Inc. (*Used by permission.*)

After all the material has been unloaded, the sellers take their receipts to a cashier's window where they are paid the appropriate amounts. (This means that the sellers may have to drive out of the receiving area, park their cars and then walk back to the cashier to receive payment.) The material received by the center is then taken to the appropriate areas for processing into the most profitable form.

Numerous publications available for equipment source information and prices and other information regarding scrap processing and recycling are listed in the appendix.

6

Marketing

If the purpose of this book is to help develop a professional understanding and approach to recycling, then we must go beyond the system and the equipment and take a serious look at the problems of marketing.

We have hinted at this earlier when we discussed the fact that there may not be a market for your recyclables. But even when a market exists, you may not be getting the best price. For example, we ran into a community recycling operation in a fairly large town that was selling its aluminum to a local dealer for the same price as the public was getting. The community operation could have gotten almost double that price by shopping around. The best price could be obtained by going another 20 miles. Why did this happen? The people operating the station had no training in recycling and had no experience in running a business. (The center, by the way, closed after four years.)

Finding better markets does not require a great deal of experience. Primarily, it requires an awareness of the fact that commodity markets have many price tiers and to get the best price requires searching around, and talking to others in the field—say, a neighboring town. Recycling and waste management magazines are also valuable sources for learning about markets.

The real problem, however, is when no market exists at all. Then what can be done?

This problem is becoming increasingly important because today over 70 percent of the states have adopted some form of legislation requiring a reduction in landfill dumping of no less than 25 percent to 30 percent within the next few years. Some estimates now state that as much as 94 percent of the population must now comply with regulations dealing with recycling.[1]

Florida's mandate calls for 30 percent reduction by 1994. New Jersey, Ohio, Indiana, and Pennsylvania, to name a few of the others, all have inaugurated mandatory reductions.

For the most part, these laws have tended to reflect the urgency of the situation, and have created problems in compliance because of deadlines that must be met. New Jersey, for example, is way behind the deadlines set by the state, and at the present time only about 60 percent of the communities are approaching compliance.

New Jersey, in fact, is a case in point that can teach us all. New Jersey's Mandatory Source Separation and Recycling Act went into effect in 1987. Prior to that time, the legislature had passed a law (in 1981) that encouraged voluntary recycling. That law included large grants to communities to help them buy the necessary equipment and support systems. The new bill, which is much tougher, requires that designated materials be separated, collected, and processed. The bill wisely permits considerable latitude in the specifics among the almost 600 counties and municipalities. The bill is augmented by an Office of Recycling which provides direct guidance and technical support to the individual communities. This office also monitors the rates of recycling in the community and administers the flow of a recycling support fund which is augmented by a surcharge on waste dumping.

The New Jersey collection systems vary from publicly owned to privately owned. In some cases, one county will handle the collections for all communities within its jurisdiction. The county operates its own transfer station.

Or the county will assist in marketing the materials and provides a transfer station, while each community handles its own collections. Generally, in the larger communities, collection and processing at the transfer station is handled by private entrepreneurs, who rely upon the state for marketing help and for public support. Another alternative is where the community handles its own collections but relies upon a private transfer station to process and market the recyclables.

Because its long involvement in recycling places it as a front runner in the field there is a great deal of public support in New Jersey for the program. Nonetheless, there is also an undercurrent of resistance. Many communities have failed to achieve significant diversion levels for commodities. Apathy and resistance is strong in many areas. In the big towns, for example, it is difficult to get high-rise dwellers to separate their waste. Then too, where there are well-entrenched systems involving heavy investments in equipment and procedures, there has been a clear reluctance to making the necessary adjustments. These people have become experts in hauling and disposing of trash. They resist changing over to a whole new system with heavy new investments

---

[1] Richard Keller, *Recycling Today* (November 1990).

in equipment, buildings, and retraining. These transitions are coming slowly, even though most of those who have changed have been successful economically. Business is always a risk, and the safe way seems to be to keep doing what you're doing.

As New Jersey's system has begun to evolve, it has increasingly pointed out the problem of marketing. What to do with these materials is an enormous question. Until a few years ago, New Jersey was known as the state into which all other states brought their waste. It was the landfill area for its neighbors. But today, *over half of its waste is now sent out of state!* This highlights the problem: Where does it go?

Did it go to Michigan? Probably not, but they too are having problems. At Grand Rapids, Michigan, for example, where a number of drop-off centers have been operating for almost 20 years, it became necessary in 1990 to cut back on operations because *warehouses* were nearing capacity. Our nation's scrap-iron supply, according to a *Wall Street Journal* editorial is up to 20 years. Compare these comments to the following letter:[2]

> The April 30 Marketplace article on automobile recycling and the May 29 letter of correction from Michael Blumenthal may have confused recycling of scrapped autos with recycling of tires. The letter from Mr. Blumenthal appears to suggest that 75% of autos are landfilled or stockpiled. These data refer to tires, not scrapped cars.
>
> About 75% of each auto is now recycled, one of the highest percentages for any major consumer product. The remainder (the shredder residue, or "fluff") is landfilled. This represents 1.7% of total municipal solid waste. Automotive plastics, which account for a quarter of this "fluff," represent one-half of one percent of the total municipal solid waste that is landfilled. The other major components of automobile "fluff" are dirt and corrosion, glass, and rubber and fiber materials.
>
> LEWIS I. DALE
> Executive Director
> Industry Government Relations
> General Motors Corp.

With approximately 2,000 wastepaper dealers in the United States, we collected more than 22 million tons of paper in 1988. This represents about 29 percent of total paper production. However, in 1988, the United States recycled only 4.5 million tons of waste newsprint. Over 400 paper mills, here and in Canada, are now using old newsprint to make paper products such as boxes and recycled newsprint. In the corrugated field, usage has been increasing at the rate of 12 percent per year. Other grades have also shown steady increases over a ten-year period. But recycling capacity has not kept pace with supply.

---

[2] Letter to Editor, *Wall Street Journal*, June 25, 1991. Used by permission.

What the state of New Jersey has found is that mandatory separation has led to an overwhelming glut of recyclables, overloading the present market. *And*— equally serious—there has been a concurrent drop in quality. That is, much of the recyclables generated are in fact unrecyclable.

The drop in quality can be traced directly to the mandate requiring separation, with achievement goals. As we have seen, states across the country today are setting recycling (separation) levels of 25 percent to 30 percent, with no regard to where the materials are going to be used! Hence, New Jersey, which is in the vanguard, has focused on quantity rather than quality. And this is now the universal trend. Separation in volume meets the state standard—for example, by pulling glass out of the landfill—but it produces such poor quality, that the glass can't be reused.

Further exacerbating the problem is the establishment of higher dumping fees at landfills, while giving economic incentives for each ton of recyclables rerouted. Thus, since 1982, New Jersey has increased its rate of collection of recyclables by over ten times. Separation is working, almost with a vengeance!

New Jersey's example shows that the basic philosophy is sound, but that implementation poses serious problems. Well intentioned as the program is, it is only partially successful in achieving its real objectives: getting recyclables *recycled*. The quality problem can be resolved, as we have seen, with training and tighter controls—and at less cost for a better product. But marketing is less easily dealt with.

Marketing offers a unique set of problems not found in any other field of endeavor: It is the only business which produces a product without regard to demand. Furthermore, it represents a unique situation in which the consumer, not the manufacturer, bears the cost of disposal.

Read, for example, the comment by Alair MacLean, Vice President of Fiber Recovery Unlimited and Caroline Rennie at the Fels Center at the University of Pennsylvania. Writing in the June 1990 issue of *Resource Recycling,* they say, "As citizens obediently and enthusiastically sort their trash believing that it is being recycled and that they are helping the environment, recyclables build up in warehouses, or end up being burned or landfilled anyway. The reason: Industrial capacity to recycle has fallen hopelessly behind."[3]

One local official states it this way: "We began recycling without firm commitments from buyers and ended up with a well-organized garbage dump."[4] In resolving this dilemma there are only two possible solutions: We either quit making so much waste, or we create a market for it. Both are viable solutions. We look now at each, taking them in order.

---

[3] Alair MacLean and Caroline Rennie, *Resource Recycling,* June 1990.

[4] *"Why Waste a Second Chance,"* National Association of Towns and Townships, Wash., D.C., 1989, p. 15.

SOURCE REDUCTION: REDUCING THE AMOUNT OF WASTE

The trend in waste management, under urging by environmentalists, has been to replace nonrecyclables with recyclables. The best-known examples are in packaging. Here much publicity has been given to doing away with styrofoam and replacing it with paper. Of these programs, the best known is that of McDonald's, the fast-food chain. Unfortunately, much of this well-intended effort is self-defeating in ways that we are just beginning to realize.

In the first place, as we have just seen, the fact that a commodity can be recycled does not assure that it will actually be recycled. It is now recognized that wholesale promotion of recycling must be attended by a look at the total program of waste reduction.

And furthermore, as we shall see, uneducated emphasis that demands a wholesale shift to recycling—and therefore to recyclables—can create *more* rather than less waste in landfills or incinerators.

In fact, emphasis on using recyclables instead of other types of materials often actually increases the problem of disposal because it increases the production of those very products that glut the country. This in itself might not be bad, but frequently the displaced packaging material was the best option. Let me explain.

We all would have to agree that the best way to eliminate waste is to not produce it to begin with. Barring that, the next best choice is to produce the least amount possible. Now, if package-material A takes up one tenth as much landfill as package-material B, and neither is being recycled, then package-material A is definitely the better choice.

Unfortunately, because we now emphasize and even demand the adoption of recyclable materials (which are often not being recycled anyway), even when they take more landfill space than the material being replaced, we are actually *increasing* our landfill problems. Our solution has been emotional rather than well thought out.

Let me give an example:

Assume that our goal is total waste reduction at the landfill (or incinerator). This can be done several ways: We can either eliminate the package, for example, or reduce its weight or its size. Any of these will work. (We can also reduce toxic wastes, such as auto emissions, using the same approach.)

Now if a designer is given instructions to produce a package which will occupy the least amount of landfill, he or she will design one type of package. If on the other hand, the designer is told to use only recyclable materials, he or she will produce another type of package.

We have an excellent illustration of this principle in the packaging of coffee. The brick-pack (made of a foil of aluminum and plastic) takes only 15 percent of the space of a tin coffee can. If both materials are going to end up in the landfill, then the brick-pack is the necessary choice. Obviously, as we move toward more complete recycling of tin cans, a crossover will occur (actually at an 85 percent recycling rate for the can). A point will be reached when we should discard the foil-pack in favor of the can.

There are numerous examples of this type of potential savings. In many cases they are being utilized. The key, however, is to integrate packaging engineering into the legislative programs, so that we can arrive at the best solution to fit the situation and state of the art. We need also to get the word out to the public about the principles behind landfill management—that recycling is a long-term goal and may not be the best immediate solution.

CREATING A MARKET

There are several means by which markets are created, and it is not beyond the community to play a major role in this creation. A big first step is to establish collective marketing cooperatives. There's strength in volume. In New Hampshire, 65 towns formed a marketing cooperative to sell their recyclables. This gave them the leverage to guarantee large volumes at a predefined quality, which would meet the long-term needs of the recycling mills. Part of the problem for towns in the past has not been the lack of technology, but rather their inability to provide a sufficiently large, dependable supply to the mills in quantities that would support the costs of tooling up a recycling plant. Much of the lag in market development can be traced to these uncertainties in dependable supply. The New Hampshire story suggests that cooperative marketing may actually help create markets for recyclables. These cooperatives are also valuable in establishing price. For example, at another New Hampshire cooperative, a currently negotiated glass contract gets $25 per ton. This too is above market price.

Even when the supply is guaranteed as in New Hampshire, mills hesitate to move into expensive conversions because of sudden shifts in the products themselves, or for that matter a shift in the market.

Let's see what can happen.

SHIFTS IN THE MARKET

In every recyclable except aluminum the market tends to weaken over time. This is not surprising because supply has been increasing faster than demand. And when this happens, the result is predictable because it follows well-known experiences from the past in raw materials. In fact, economic law says that nations dependent upon raw material exports will increase their output when prices decline, thus causing further decreases in price. At the same time, user nations develop substitutes, which further reduce the need for these raw materials.

Rubber and silk are classic examples, their replacements being neoprene and nylon. A modern example involves the Japanese who are avid shrimp eaters. To obtain shrimp amidst rising demand and diminishing supplies, the Japanese developed shrimp hatcheries among the underdeveloped Pacific Islands. For the natives, this provided a large unexpected bonanza. But again, volume expanded rapidly, and the price began to plummet. This led to a further increase in production and still lower prices. What the Third World nations have experienced throughout modern history, recycling is experiencing today.

Glass, paper, plastics, and steel have all seen the bottom drop out. Aluminum, alone, offers a different picture. The situation here is unique. To date the total capacity to produce aluminum from both bauxite and recycling *has not* created a surplus. In fact, the trend appears to be headed in the other direction.

This can be seen in several sets of statistics.

First, it is estimated that beverage can production will be up 6.5 billion cans from 1989. Ninety-seven percent of these will be aluminum. There are also efforts to increase the use of aluminum in food cans. At 6 percent in 1990, it will reach 10 percent in just a few years. Some cheeses, sardines, and a few other items now come packaged in aluminum. Methods for deep-drawing heavier grades of aluminum (required for food cans) have also been worked out. Also new, smoother flowing aluminum alloys are coming on stream to make their uses for food cheaper and better. Hence, the immediate future for aluminum-can usage in America for beverages or food favors recycling. In fact, at the present trend, bauxite production has been lagging behind demand for aluminum cans.

Second, there has been an increase in the number of secondary smelters of aluminum in the United States. These secondary smelters convert the recycled aluminum cans into ingots and ship them to foreign markets, where they are used for a number of products other than cans. In 1989, overseas shipments climbed over 80 percent. Japan alone was up almost 300 percent in purchases of recycled aluminum from cans. Add to this the fact that the United States uses almost 94 percent of the world's aluminum cans, and we can see the unfolding of a vast untapped market.

Our own smelting capacity exceeds supply and we will not reach full potential at these mills until 1995. These new mills themselves represent a major shift in the aluminum market. Whereas at one time Alcoa dominated the price structure, today's prices vary by geographic area, offering excellent opportunities for arbitrage. Small mills in need of raw materials offer limited time premiums of 10¢ to 20¢ per pound to keep their mills running. The result is a segmented market, favoring the recycler.

A third point is that at the same time that demand has been climbing, quality of recycled aluminum has been declining. Part of this may be due to more rigid specs at the mills, but it is also due to the poor quality produced at some transfer stations. As we have so often pointed out, the sudden emergence of a nation of amateur recyclers "has adversely affected the ability to monitor and control the end items." *These are remarks made directly by one of the major users.*

For one thing, there is no clearly defined standard applicable to all smelters. Comingling operations have been a major cause for concern. Some smelters are particularly reluctant to buy from certain recyclers, for example, because of broken glass, steel, and plastics which contaminate the cans.

IS ECONOMICS THE ONLY ANSWER?

So far we have been describing the classic condition common to an undeveloped nation:[5] that supplies of raw materials will increase until they force the price down.

Two steps have already been taken to reduce the need for aluminum and soften its price. First, the thickness of the can has been reduced so that today almost 30 cans can be produced from one pound of aluminum. Compare this to the time not long ago when 23 cans weighed one pound.

Second, bi-metal cans (mentioned earlier) are coming on stream, using cheaper steel for the side walls and bottoms. Only the tops are aluminum, and the steel industry is doing research to produce an equivalent top. Hence, traditional economic down-pressure is surfacing in the aluminum-can market and can be expected to force it to go the way of all other recyclables.

But in today's world, at least as it applies to the problem of waste, the old rules may not apply. Recycling philosophy has a different perspective from that of business. Evolving in the last two decades, it has adopted an almost anti-economic attitude. For one thing, people concerned about the ecology place quality of life ahead of economic savings. They are willing to pay the price necessary to keep the world beautiful. There are times, I confess, when I wonder why we need this idealism—why we just don't dump all our trash in the Grand Canyon, out of my sight. It would probably hold all the cans, bottles, plastics, and papers we can produce for a few generations, and as long as I don't have to drive through Arizona, I can enjoy the rest of America quite well, thank you.

But these modern young people won't let me forget, and they tell me that the world is becoming one enormous trash heap. Through them and their perseverance we are being made aware *now*, in this last decade of our century, that our ability to annihilate ourselves is no longer limited to our creativity in warfare, but includes the great rubble heap we are making of the world. It is not the enemy without to be feared, but the enemy within. I remember the time as a kid when I peddled papers to a poor old black woman living on the edges of our society. She lived on the Firestone dump (in the middle, to be precise) in a shanty of slats and tin sheets. The dump was used to incinerate old tires, which burned with a black cloud of smelly smoke 24 hours a day. The dump also held junk and other solid wastes, and trucks came in each day dumping new loads. A bulldozer ran over it to keep it leveled. This desolate area was, sadly, this poor woman's home. I had her for a customer for as long as I had the route. She was always kindly and appreciative of my peddling that extra mile to get the paper to her. (I made 1¢ per paper those days, you see.) She was one of the few customers I had who paid on time. I do not even know if she lived alone, although I never met her family.

---

[5] The analogy may be accurate. Compared to the Industrial Revolution, recycling is in its infancy. It is fumbling and searching for a handle to hold on to.

If we believe the ecologists, this is our future home, too, because the world is becoming less and less beautiful. The degradation is often so slow that we cannot see the changes. Telephone poles and wires stretched overhead along the streets, for example. Billboards lining the roads. Trash scattered in the ditches and on the sidewalks. Litter strewn in the lonely desert where hardly a soul moves across the face of the earth or in the firmament.

Yes! I think I understand the story these young people are trying to tell me. Their dream and vision of the sanctity of nature we all need. But I believe they are making a serious mistake as well. The problem is that they are so swept up in their enthusiasm for helping me avoid the fate of that poor old black woman, that they may be pouring the baby out with the bath water. In our enthusiasm that's become a national commitment, we are attacking the problem with reckless disregard for the economics. "Economics be damned, and full speed ahead," as that great Admiral Farragut might say today if he floated down our polluted Mississippi River.

I do not wish to decry the value of the need to concern ourselves with the quality of life. I hope I have made this clear. But we must also not forget what can be accomplished through economic incentives. I believe that the most energetic and soundest recycling programs *will ultimately have to be based on finding an economic means* for achieving them. This has been made clear repeatedly in the preceding chapters. It's what I have called finding a way to pull the string.

Our newly-found appreciation for human values is not really new. It was in fact the general guiding principal in the Middle Ages, when forest and stream were brought under strict management by the nobility. Even today, we see it in the rivers of Germany and much of Europe, which are lined with cobblestones, while the forests are like a privately manicured estate. These features tell us what once existed, before the Age of Commerce and Industrial Revolution replaced a love of nature with the lust of accumulation. And yet, the tremendous increase in the well-being of humanity in better health and better standards of living shows that the old way was not best. On the other hand, the problems that we have brought upon Mother Earth show that hedonism also has fallen short of fulfilling all our needs.

Perhaps the benefit for humankind from all this sad pollution of the beauty of nature is that we can now see both sides of the coin. We can see that a balance must be achieved. We must indeed deal with the quality of life. But unless we fail to appreciate the value of economic motivation, our goals will simply not be achieved. We will fall short! I say this because, as we see in later chapters, it is not within the realm of human nature to achieve the optimum unless there is adequate inspiration. People need a motive—an incentive, or carrot out in front of their noses, to get them moving. And much as we love nature, the strongest pull still comes from economic benefit. The great dreams of beautifying nature will fade quickly, if we cause a reduction or stagnation in the standard of living.

ESTABLISHING A MARKET ECONOMY IN RECYCLING _____

There are four ways to put the economic incentive into recycling.

1. It can be introduced at the national or international level.
2. Each state has the means to create its own recycling economy.
3. The community has a great deal of opportunity to influence economic planning and decisions.
4. It can be achieved through private enterprise and public cooperation.

As with virtually any activity, the closer one gets to the grass roots, the more likely one is to achieve efficient results. This means that initial success begins within the community.

We have already discussed the effect that quality has on price. Knowing the market, on the other hand, can produce equally dramatic results. As an example, a ton of loose office paper is worth $30. Baled up and sorted by grade, that same ton is worth $150. Taken to the convertor, the paper is recycled for its high-grade fibers and produces a top-quality grade of printing and writing paper, for which the convertor gets $900 per ton.

To grasp the potential for this market, take a look at the raw material supply that is being generated by our offices. It is estimated, for instance, that Americans use more than one *million tons* of computer paper per year, not counting home usage. Of this, each ton not reprocessed creates three yards of landfill. With dumping fees of up to $80 per ton, the failure to find a market for this paper is losing money at both ends by failing to market it for $150, and paying an $80 tipping fee. With your own local paper recycling mill, you can earn as high as $1,000 per ton!

To explore this further, it doesn't take a large city to support local recycling plants. Muskogee, Oklahoma, for example, with less than 50,000 inhabitants has attracted a number of recycling plants. These include a paper recycling mill that also recycles phone books. It has steel recycling at another plant and is now reaching out to attract plastic recycling industries. The recycling plants already employ almost 2,000 workers and have greatly added to the local economy.

Towns that are enjoying the benefits of recycling have also learned that the products made at these plants are suitable for home consumption as well. Emphasis is put on local procurement and home use not only by businesses, but by the citizens and city officials. They have, in some cases, set up economic incentives such as tax preferences, reduced real estate and property taxes, and other means to favor those businesses engaged in recycling.

The success of these local programs is shown by the fact that it has now become necessary for them to restrict the flow of these valuable waste commodities, to assure the plants a continuous supply at low cost. Instead of searching for another landfill at some other place in the state, they have reached the point that they are beginning to import waste from neighboring towns. Instead of a liability, waste has become a resource!

The success of these local programs makes it clear that much can be done to enhance the spread of this type of leadership and enterprise. Some of the most effective methods are through training programs funded by states and through visits and tours to cities involved in this effort. These visits are priceless. They not only provide insight and encouragement but aid in the assimilation of ideas and experiences between communities who are in the vanguard.

Consultants are also an important means by which communities can bridge the gap because consultants not only understand the limitations and problems, but they also have the contacts needed to put the ball in motion. With less wheel spinning and fewer false starts, consultants who are qualified can get the job done more quickly and at lower cost than an individual with no experience in the field.

Financing is also a problem for small communities, which may have to issue bonds or obtain state financial support in order to attract businesses into the area. This may involve setting up industrial parks, with water and sewers, electricity and gas, and paved roads. It often involves tax credits. An Industrial Development Board may be needed to oversee the program and provide the enticements needed to attract recycling businesses. To be completely successful, the incentives must include guarantees of readily available, quality waste, and at least a partial market at home for goods produced in the plant. Finally, a dependable, enthusiastic labor force must be available at reasonable costs.

At least as important as all these steps is the ability to find and seek out potential reprocessors. This involves setting up and supporting a search committee with professional experience in recruiting potential reprocessors.

This defines a totally coordinated program with adequate funding and long-range commitments from the community. This is necessary because success is several years forthcoming and is often a continuing process over an extended period of time. The goal is not to seek a single recycler, but often to bring in a number of complimentary programs.

Since a recycling plant such as a sheet rolling mill or a paper mill produces goods far in excess of the needs of the local community, it follows that only a limited number of these plants can actually be established. It means that the competition for these plants between cities will be keen, and it will be tempting to offer excessive incentives which may not be sound financially.

The limited number of these plants also means that hubs will evolve around the larger communities, which will draw recyclables from the surrounding areas like spokes on a wheel, pulling the waste toward them like a string attached to a toy.

Obviously, we are describing a situation in which cooperation and coordination are fundamental. This means that the state must provide leadership and overall planning. While the state must provide support staffs and funds, it must be careful to avoid coercion through laws and regulations. This is so because efforts to force the natural processes of market development result in distortions and enormous waste. No example of this is clearer than the controlled market system of communist Russia. Effective incentives will produce creativity and enthusiasm, which will generate results far beyond the energy which coercion can achieve.

Hence, it is imperative that the states *and the communities* decide first *what the goals are—not how to achieve them—but what is to be achieved.* Then they must decide as carefully as possible (*study the works of other successful operations, for example!*) what incentives will encourage people to achieve these goals.

Then the goals and activities must be audited, and perhaps the incentives will need to be adjusted. Patience and understanding of the processes of human nature must be encouraged. At first, the projects will begin much more slowly than those that are mandated, but they will soon overtake them, and eventually they will far outstrip them. The laws of the marketplace apply to recycling. It is the incentives alone for which the community and state must provide leadership!

State Incentives

In 1973, Oregon was the first state to recognize the need to establish economic incentives to encourage recycling. In a series of programs as early as 1990, it provided almost $67 million to 83 recyclers. These included battery recycling, de-inking, corrugated, glass, and mulching facilities.

One of Oregon's programs allows tax credits of up to 50 percent applied against state taxes. A similar bill in New Jersey which began in 1987 allows 50 percent tax credits to recyclers that manufacture products containing at least 50 percent waste materials. New Jersey's program also includes low-interest loans of up to $500,000 for capital investment.

A number of states have instituted market development studies, but perhaps none has put more emphasis on the value of incentives than Pennsylvania. The Pennsylvania study is specifically directed at determining what types of incentives are needed by the end-user to increase the use of waste materials. Pennsylvania has aimed its study initially at glass, plastics, and paper. One result of the study has been the recognition that it takes a different type of incentive to achieve recycling in plastics than in paper or glass, for example.

There are a number of ways in which the state can provide incentives. As of 1990, for example, 41 states and the District of Columbia had recycled-content procurement laws in effect. Local communities often have their own regulations, and have in many cases taken the lead in establishing recycling procurement regulations. In fact these procurement laws in the community have helped encourage the growth of small recyclers in their areas.

A major problem with recycling-content laws is that they are as yet inconsistent and poorly defined. Like the list of ingredients required on food containers, the exact content is not listed in specifics as it would be in a recipe. We only know a certain item is included in the container, but not how much of it. Other confusing factors such as purchasing procedures and finding sources of supply can also reduce the effectiveness of these regulations. Then, too, recycled goods are often more costly, so that the community ends up paying a premium for what often is an inferior product.

Because mandated procurement laws on recycled goods are coercive, they have not been as effective as desired. For one thing, coercive laws do not enlist enthusiastic support. The enthusiasm that exists for recycling is because of personal commitment to the concept. It's recognized as needed and necessary. Unfortunately, coercion encourages evasion rather than cooperation, and this causes new rules to be added to the existing ones, until a plethora of rules comes into existence.

Thus, it is the nature of laws to multiply, so that in the United States there are an estimated 5,000,000 laws on the books. Many of these are obsolete and ignored. (Public kissing laws are no longer enforced.)

Fees and taxes, although they perform an essential function and cannot be avoided, are nevertheless punitive, or coercive. Thus, workers pay a tax (or fine) on their earnings. And the more they earn, the greater the amounts they pay to the state. Unfortunately, this sends the workers a negative signal about work. This is the Laffer curve, which says that as taxes exceed a certain level, income goes unreported to avoid the payment.

Hence, except for a few tax incentives, it is unfortunately the nature of legislative regulation to write laws that coerce and penalize, and the result is that public goals are almost never fully achieved. This happens, unfortunately, because legislation is a reactive process. It deals with omission and oversights. But as each situation breaks through the legal net, a new set of rules is written to close the hole.

The same is true of procurement laws. Unless the law is specific, it provides enormous loopholes for evasion. For example, if a regulation mandates the use of recycled computer paper in public offices, what percent must this be? Is paper that contains 50 percent recycled paper and 50 percent virgin pulp acceptable? Must it be 100 percent? What if 100 percent recycled paper is impossible because quality cannot be maintained? Obviously, the standard will vary. Napkins could be 100 percent, Kraft paper might be only 25 percent, and so on. What if recycled paper isn't available from the local mill because the mill has completely exhausted the available supply and is forced to import virgin fibers? What about quality? Do we not also need to set up specs on these too?

Are we going to write laws to cover all these contingencies? Are we not going to have to do this for all types of products and waste materials?

Let me be specific! This is now being done. The Environmental Protection Agency, for example, has set minimum standards for government purchases of recycled paper. These range from 5 percent recycled content for brown paper to 40 percent for newsprint, and 50 percent for the better grades, such as writing paper. But at the same time, various government agencies have upgraded brightness specifications—and greater brightness is contrary to the concept of recycling. As paper specifications call for a brighter finish and tone (which incidentally are subject to glare and eye fatigue), the standard becomes increasingly difficult for recyclers to meet. Thus, this effectively restricts the use of recycled paper.

San Francisco goes even further. It has laws on the books which prohibit the purchase of recycled papers altogether. In fact, so many states and communities have prohibitions and restrictions on recyclables, including paper, that review boards have sprung up to eliminate and rewrite these specs. The federal program is already three years behind schedule.

Unfortunately, the program to rewrite these specs to make it easier to procure recyclables causes the specs to become increasingly bureaucratic. In his study of the government, Peter Grace (Grace Commission Report to President Reagan) reported that the procurement regulations in a single government agency totaled more than 30,000 pages. "This," he says, "goes a long way toward explaining purchases of $435 hammers, $659 ashtrays, $640 toilet seats and $7,400 coffee makers."[6] The federal specifications for "a rodent elimination device" (a "mousetrap" to the laymen) run 102,000 words, covering 200 pages. The four-pound document itself is weighty enough to kill the average mouse. Heaven forbid that it be rewritten again. Attempts to rewrite it to simplify it might be dangerous to the economy. A similar example was given to me by a bank president, having to do with federal bank regulations. One paragraph created so much confusion among banks, he pointed out, that it was rewritten. The "simplification," as it was billed, ran 15 pages long!

Problems of this type are exacerbated by the fact that each community adds its own specs on recycled paper, often ignoring the works of others. The result is enough to give the paper manufacturers gray hair trying to produce a plethora of products with costly short production runs. For local users, not only is it difficult to get what they want, but costs are higher than using better grades of paper.

Let's consider an alternative approach. Instead of the stick, suppose we try a carrot.

People are like rabbits. They love to go after that carrot. What we need, then, is to figure out an incentive that will encourage recycling, rather than demand it! To pull the string we must start at the mill. We meet with the manager of, say, a paper mill.

"How much recycled paper do you use?" we ask.

"None," he replies. "We tried some a few years ago, but it did some expensive damage to our equipment and we discontinued it."

"Couldn't you set up a quality acceptance program and check the quality before you accept the material?"

"We did that too," he replies, "but the material was so bad we couldn't depend on it."

"Well," we reply. "If we set up a quality assurance program and guarantee both quality and a steady supply, would you be interested?"

He thinks a minute. "I'm not sure. We use a lot of paper here and we have a good reputation. We can't take a chance with our customers who depend on us. If we ship inferior grades to the converting mills and their slitters break down, we would lose them. This is a highly competitive business and we must maintain delivery and quality."

---

[6] J. Peter Grace, *Burning Money,* Macmillan Publishing Co., New York, and summarized in a draft report, June 6, 1988, "A Grace Commission Progress Report" from *Citizens Against Government Waste,* Wash., D.C.

"But could you use the paper if we supply it as you want it?"

He pauses again, and shakes his head. "I don't know. Our costs are higher. It actually costs more to reprocess some papers than to buy the virgin pulp. We have the trees and the land that we need. We really don't need your wastepaper."

We think to ourselves: *Now, we're getting somewhere!*

"How much would it cost you," we ask, "to use the wastepaper we supply, and not use your trees?"

He looks at us suspiciously. Then he crosses over to a file cabinet and opens a drawer. He pulls out some accounting sheets (printed, by the way, on computer paper). He rubs his chin, and studies the figures.

"Well, it looks like it costs us $8.00 per ton more to use wastepaper than to use virgin material." (Because recycled paper may cost more than virgin paper, states like New York and California have set aside premiums of as high as 10 percent over standard prices to encourage mills to shift to recycled paper.)

"If I pay you $10, guarantee quality and minimum quantities delivered to your door do I have a deal?" [After all, the tipping (dumping) fee on paper is costing us $50.00 per ton and we produce many tons of wastepaper! So this is a great deal for us too! And furthermore, business incentives are not new. After all, tax incentives have always favored resource development at the expense of reuse. Perhaps now we can reverse the process.]

"Well, maybe," he answers cautiously. "You see, if we get set up to process large quantities of your waste material we're going to need special equipment, which means a sizable investment over and above our present operation."

"We can help you there, too," we answer, gleefully. "We have an Industrial Development Board which can provide you with low-interest bonds." Then we sweeten the pot even more, by adding: "We will also publicize the conversion to our community and encourage everyone to buy from you."

Now, if the mill can make more profit by running recycled material and can hold its original customers as well, the mandatory procurement becomes unnecessary. Furthermore, we can subsidize the mill's use of recyclables up to the tipping costs we are now paying at the landfill. These costs, as we have seen, run as high as $80.00 per ton. (This hypothetical approach can be run in reverse, producing excellent results. For example, a paper recycler in Missouri contacted the *Columbia Daily Tribune* to encourage them to use recycled newsprint. The newspaper accepted the proposal on a test basis and soon was using 50 percent recycled paper. Present plans call for going to 100 percent recycled paper.)

Naturally, this is just a hypothetical example, but it is based on personal experiences. The profit motive drives business. And it follows that the higher the subsidy, the more complete the use of waste materials becomes because marginal conversions become profitable at some point. Here, I can give an example familiar to everyone. In the United States a number of gold mines became unprofitable when the price of gold was pegged by the government at $35.00 per ounce. But after President Nixon permitted the dollar to float against gold, gold soared to over $400 per ounce. The immediate effect was to open the old abandoned mines and put them back into production. Furthermore, they will continue producing as long as the price of gold exceeds the costs of mining. Oil wells, too, have had the same experience. When the price of crude oil soars, abandoned wells go back into production.

There are problems with this scenario, however. Why should Atlanta, Georgia pay a paper mill in Florida, for example, to use recycled paper? The answer is the same as for the mill: So long as Atlanta saves more in tipping-fee avoidance than it costs to get the paper recycled in the Florida mill, both parties gain.

Naturally, Atlanta's alternative is to find a cheaper landfill, somewhere in another unlucky state, that costs less than the amount the mill charges. There is an actual example of this type, involving the *Chicago Tribune*, which has a de-inking mill in Ontario, Canada. This mill makes recycled newsprint that is sent to Chicago. But the waste newsprint is *collected from Canadian residents.* Hence, the Chicago paper, even though recycled, is not processed in Illinois. In fact, the curb-side program introduced into Chicago as a test program did not even provide for collecting waste newsprint. If it had, it might have used the *Chicago Tribune* as a market. The Atlanta example indicates the limited ability that any community or even state has in achieving control of the process without cooperation among states. Perhaps federal laws that prohibit waste from being transported interstate are needed unless it can be verified that it is being recycled. (The *Chicago Tribune's* material was being recycled.) We have such laws today, for other reasons, which prohibit interstate transit of certain types of materials without special permits or licenses.

Historically, the pattern until the mid-1980s has been to produce legislation that focused on collecting materials and sorting them out with the hope of being recycled. Now, we are beginning to see beyond the mountain of trash and recognize that we need to concentrate on the reprocessing stage. As we have seen, this stage can be entered into by mandatory laws that will no doubt produce an upswing in recycling but which will never obtain optimum results unless there is a sincere interest on the part of the recyclers themselves. Recyclers must be encouraged to function in a competitive environment. This can only happen where true incentives which have been carefully thought out control the marketplace.

First, we need to encourage the development of new recycling technology. Plastic is a good place to begin, but many other commodities and wastes need to be brought under this umbrella. And again, I do not believe incentives should originate with the legislature. They need to be worked out by people in the field who understand the needs and processes involved. Then they can be brought to the legislature for review.

Second, we need to encourage the development of small satellite reprocessors at the community level. We need to supplement and foster their growth and success by means of Industrial Development Boards or small business incentives.

Third, we need to work on waste reduction programs (discussed earlier), such as use of substitutes, or less space-consuming items. Incentives may help here, too.

And finally, if recycling is to succeed in the American way, using the ingenuity which built this country, we must develop and train an efficient and competent labor force so that we can get the job done right in the first place—*at minimum total cost.*

As a final point, consider the possibility that if old gold mines sprang into operation at $400 per ounce, what would happen if all tipping fees went to $1,000? How long would it be before everyone went into the recycling business for a piece of the pie? How many laws would we really need then to encourage recycling? Wouldn't it be automatic?

THE MARKET SYSTEM: PRICE NEGOTIATION

The key to finding outlets for your products is to determine precisely how much of these items your community generates, and how the market operates. To avoid the shotgun approach, it is necessary to be selective in your search. You must learn who buys what and why. This means that you must do your homework before you begin your program.

Because communities are dealing in high-volume, continuous production of a given waste, the specifics of negotiating a price need to be considered. There are several approaches used. First, a noncontract, open-market type of sale works well when a market exists and there are several buyers in the area. The advantage is that open pricing offers an opportunity for competitive marketing and a chance to get a higher price. On the other hand, if the price falls and the market suddenly shrinks, you may have no buyer at all. This problem has happened numerous times with paper, the price of which is highly volatile with great swings in demand and price. Even when the Japanese moved in and bought up large quantities, the price still fell because of the glut which recurs in the collection centers.

For the waste collectors to operate on an open-market program, they need to know and study the market price patterns over a period of time. They then become commodity speculators. Hence, the people who deal in this type of marketing generally have considerable storage space so they can hold out for a better price, and they have the financial wherewithal to withstand the loss of cash flow.

For these reasons, most community systems including private collectors prefer to lock in a price. Their objective is to move the waste out of the area, not to hold it on speculation. As a result, they often get less, but they do not risk major setbacks because of lack of experience in speculation.

Should you prefer the contract type of agreement, you will be expected to maintain dependable volumes and to meet minimum quality standards, as defined in the agreement. You, in turn, will have assurances of a market and a price. Some of these contracts allow for price fluctuations within certain defined limits.

The contract itself will define the material, its grade or quality, and specify delivery arrangements. It will set specific limits on acceptable levels of contamination, and how the material is to be prepared, that is, baled, crushed, in special containers, and so on. There will be nonperformance penalties, which apply to your operation, and a pricing scale to determine price variations, if applicable.

A CASE STUDY: THE MARKET POTENTIAL
OF RECYCLING

Turtle Plastics in Cleveland was founded in 1980 by Tom Norton. Mr. Norton, who has his bachelor's degree in History, spent 25 years with his brother in the lighting equipment business. But his life-long hobby had been an interest in environmental problems, so he sold out and began pursuing these interests in earnest.

Turtle Plastics is a classic example of the potential that exists for the entrepreneurial recycler. It also illustrates a point we will discuss later, that most breakthroughs in technology occur, *not in high tech firms,* but with entrepreneurs who see a need and find a solution.

Mr. Norton began by collecting waste plastics and grinding it into pellets. As he points out, he ran into "resistance to get it accepted" as a source material for products. So he decided to produce his own products and market the end product using the pellets. That's when he founded Turtle Plastics.

The first product was a fatigue mat, produced about 1985. These mats are used as safety walks in shops, for fatigue mats at work areas, and to maintain safe working areas where oil and other liquids could cause slippery footing. Some mats use ground slag from steel mills to produce a gritty, non-skid surface in oily work areas.

The mats are made with cross linked holes and have interlocking cleats for joining them together. As Mr. Norton points out "the quality of the mat is better than those made from virgin plastics. They are twice as thick and cost 30% less," because as he says "the material costs me nothing!"

A major market for these mats is in fire trucks and emergency equipment. Every emergency vehicle stores equipment in steel cabinets. These objects tend to slide about on the steel painted surface and get wet from rain and firehose spray. The mats, which are about 3/4'' thick, keep the equipment up out of the moisture and keep it from sliding.

It takes about 20 of these mats to line the bottom of a typical storage bin, and about 10,000 vehicles are produced each year, each using about 100 pads in all. The pads outlast the emergency vehicle.

As his capacity grew, Mr. Norton searched for more products to make. He noticed that there are hundreds of thousands of urinals in America and that each urinal uses a plastic deodorant screen to stop cigarette butts and waste from clogging the drains. These screens had to be replaced each month as the deodorant faded.

He tried to enter the market with black screens, using the material he was using to make mats. But he found out that all government specs (as well as many others) on urinal screens specified that they must be blue. Since it would take years to rewrite the spec, he decided to find a source for blue plastic waste. He noticed one day that swimming pool liners came in blues. Furthermore, they are replaced every five years or so. They get dirty and wear out. The sun-belt was an obvious source for these raw materials, so he contacted the big pool maintenance firms in the Southwest and set up a supply chain. He thus solved a major problem for himself and a disposal problem for the pool maintenance people.

The liners come in to his plant in truck load quantities where they are washed automatically and then shredded, rewashed and cleaned. Then they are prepared for molding into urinal screens, which are marketed under the name "Oui Oui Screen."

The next step was to produce license plate covers commonly seen on most cars. Turtle Plastics even produces its own brand with the slogan "Recycle Now!"

Other products came quickly out of the creative head of Turtle Plastics' founder.

Today, these include fishing rod handles for Shakespeare, one-piece shoe soles for Nigeria, molded rollers for relaxing and massage equipment, and pellets for other manufacturers.

This latter represents an interesting case of how ideas begin to take root: For example, Eastman Kodak receives millions of film cartridges from hundreds of processing centers. These are made of plastic cases, with steel reels and have labels pasted on them. Eastman came to Turtle Plastics to see if Turtle could work with them to develop a recycling-chain for these units. He did.

Today, the empty cartridges come into the Turtle plant in truckloads and are dumped in a hopper. Then by means of special machines, designed by Mr. Norton, the cartridges are crushed, the steel removed by magnets, and the paper removed by soaking. The plastic is washed and pulverized into pellets. Then it is sent back to Kodak for remolding into film cartridges. The steel reels are sent to Weirton Steel to be melted down, rolled into sheet, and stamped into new reels.

The process at Turtle is completely automatic involving a minimum of labor. It is an amazing example of automated manufacturing in reverse—de-manufacturing so to speak. Instead of automatic assembly, such as occurs in making the cartridges, it is automatic de-assembly! Moreover, it is an example of entrepreneurial genius by a man who is neither an engineer nor a chemist, but a historian by degree. It is an example of a man who gets things done by solving problems creatively.

The SMRF

The first source material used at Turtle was plastic auto trim, which Turtle Plastics pelletized and made into mats. This meant that a market was found for a product where virtually none existed. In the next step, a raw material had to be found to meet a specific color need. Both of these represented commercial examples of recycling, but they did not come to grips with the more widespread problems of community, or residential recycling.

Mr. Norton dived into this problem also, employing the same enthusiasm and creativity he had displayed earlier. He designed his own material recovery facility which he calls a SMRF, *S*mall *M*aterial *R*ecovery *F*acility. This system uses the same principles discussed earlier, namely to reduce labor to a minimum.

Working with nine communities representing 135,000 persons, the system requires no special equipment by the community, nor does it require any special efforts by the residents. All recyclables are placed in a single standard trash bag at the curb. (See Panels 6–1 and 6–2.) The bags can be any color and size. Glass,

Panels 6-1 and 6-2   These panels are the instruction sheets provided to each community participating in the recycling program.

THE ONE BAG SYSTEM
(A COMMUNITY RECYCLING PROGRAM)

THE BAG
YOUR COMMUNITY WILL FURNISH YOU WITH A CLEAR SPECIALLY MARKED PLASTIC BAG. IN THIS BAG YOU SHOULD PUT ALL YOUR RECYCLABLES FOR THE WEEK. EVEN THE BAG WILL BE RECYCLED INTO NEW BAGS. YOUR WILL NOT HAVE TO SORT MATERIAL INTO 2 OR 3 CONTAINERS.

THE TRUCK
COMMUNITIES CAN PICK UP THE BAGS WITH THEIR OWN TRUCKS OR HIRE A PRIVATE HAULER. A PACKER TRUCK, DUMP TRUCK, OR STAKE BED TRUCK, CAN BE USED. BY USING A BAG, MATERIAL DOES NOT HAVE TO BE SORTED AT THE CURB. THE TRUCK ONLY LEAVES THE ROUTE WHEN THE **WHOLE** TRUCK IS FULL, NOT **ONE COMPARTMENT.**

THE PLANT
LOCATED ON CLEVELANDS EASTSIDE, THE MATERIAL WILL BE BROUGHT TO OUR FACILITY WHERE ALL THE RECYCLABLES WILL BE SEPARATED USING EFFICIENT CONVEYERS, MACHINES AND PEOPLE IN SORTING LINE. ALL OF THE MATERIAL IN THE BAG WILL BE **RECYCLED.**

CLOSING THE LOOP (....or what it means to really recycle)
UNTIL **YOU** USE PRODUCTS MADE FROM RECYCLED MATERIALS, YOU ARE NOT RECYCLING. ONLY WHEN PRODUCTS HAVE BEEN MADE FROM RECYCLED MATERIALS, HAS THAT MATERIAL BEEN RECYCLED. OUR TWO COMPANIES, CLEVELAND RECLAIM AND TURTLE PLASTICS DO BOTH. THE FIRST RECYCLES MATERIAL AND THE SECOND REMANUFACTURES PRODUCTS FROM 100% RECYCLED MATERIALS.

WHAT YOU CAN PUT INTO YOUR BAG

GLASS	METAL
GREEN BOTTLES AND JARS	ALUMINUM CANS
BROWN BOTTLES AND JARS	BI-METAL CANS
CLEAR BOTTLES AND JARS	TIN FOOD CANS

WHAT YOU CAN DO NOW
*CALL YOUR LOCAL NEIGHBERHOOD LEADER AND INSIST ON A CURBSIDE RECYCLING PROGRAM.

*CALL YOUR MAYOR AND CITY COUNCIL AND INSIST ON A CURBSIDE RECYCLING PROGRAM.

*WRITE A FOLLOW UP LETTER TO THESE PEOPLE.

*FORM A CITIZENS ACTION GROUP TO WORK WITH THE CITY. IF YOU ALREADY HAVE ONE, GET INVOLVED WITH IT.

REDUCE THE AMOUNT OF PACKAGING YOU BRING INTO YOUR HOME.

REUSE AS MANY ITEMS AS YOU CAN.

RECYCLE-TAKE MATERIAL TO DROP OFF LOCATIONS, PARTICIPATE IN A CURBSIDE PROGRAM.

COMPOSTE YARD WASTE AND FOOD SCRAPES.

BUY RECYCLED PRODUCTS RATHER THAN VIRGIN PRODUCTS.

PLASTIC

IDENTIFYING HDPE

HDPE Containers **are never clear like glass**. HDPE is either colored (i.e., detergent bottles) or opaque (i.e., dairy bottles) with a dull surface finish - not shiny - and will float in water.

CLEAR (Opaque) HDPE CONTAINERS

Dairy and water bottles gallon and half gallon milk, distilled and spring water, orange juice and punch/drink containers.

COLORED HDPE CONTAINERS

Liquid laundry detergent, fabric softeners and liquid bleach bottles, dishwashing and automatic dishwashing detergent bottles, skin lotion, baby lotion, bubble bath bottles.
Automotive: Motor oil, antifreeze, windshield washing fluid.

PETE

PET (Polyethylene terephthalate) is clear, not opaque. Sinks in water. Examples are clear or green tinted, 2-litre beverage bottles.

Panels 6–1 and 6–2   These panels are the instruction sheets provided to each community participating in the recycling program.

plastics, and metals are all thrown together. Paper is excluded at present.[7] The bags are picked up by standard trash haulers. Because the bags contain glass, the truck drivers are instructed to compress the load to a two-to-one level rather than full compaction, such as used with garbage. (Some glass is broken in handling and hauling but this amounts to about 5% of the total, and these shards are later used for roadbed and other items.) The load is brought to Turtle Plastics and dumped into a hopper with a large auger. This auger, which has screw blades about 3 feet in diameter, turns slowly, gently breaking the bags *but not the glass,* and augering the contents up onto a conveyor belt.

At the belt, five workers remove glass by color, plastics by type and other materials, throwing them into small side conveyors, which haul the separated materials up into hoppers, where the glass is crushed, the plastic shredded and the metal flattened, and stored in bins for further processing.

Further processing is to pelletize the plastic and produce Turtle's own products, or ship the pellets, such as HDPE and PET to container manufacturers. The glass sorted by color is sent to glass plants. Aluminum cans go to the mills and are used primarily in making new aluminum sheet for future cans. Other items go off the end of the conveyor and represent about 10% of the total load coming in from the communities.

The communities pay Turtle Plastics an average of what they save in typing fees. Hence, landfill of recyclables is practically eliminated by the process, and the system is a cooperative effort between private enterprise and a number of small communities, with a surprisingly happy and beneficial marriage.

The Turtle Plastics story illustrates that the real solution to efficient recycling may rest in the emergence of a group of entrepreneurs who take the lead in bringing small communities together as a cooperative enterprise, in which each community becomes a raw material source for a "reverse-manufacturer" and market-maker for their products.

Furthermore, the organizational effort needed to bring a number of communities together with an entrepreneur will almost certainly originate in the private sector since individual small communities cannot be expected to provide the expertise or organization needed. A good background for this type of leadership are people who know both manufacturing processes and the recycling business.

One or two points of further interest are that the whole operation at Turtle employs 23 people, and the SMRF requires 3000 square feet of building to house the whole operation. (For a pictorial account of Turtle Plastics see Figures 6–1 through 6–17.)

SPREADING THE WORD ON NEW BREAKTHROUGHS

The field of recycling is developing so rapidly, as we have seen, that many good ideas are being tested and used, which need to be known by others getting started.

---

[7] Mr. Norton is working on methods for adding paper to his product line.

Figure 6-1 Bags of recyclables arrive at Turtle Plastics in large trash haulers, where they are dumped into a large hopper. This hopper is about 15′ wide and 25′ long and forms a "V" at the bottom. At the bottom of the V is a large 3″ diameter auger, which moves the bags up onto the conveyor, breaking the bags open as they move along. (*Used by permission of Tom Norton, owner, Turtle Plastics Co. Photo by Ray Blesh.*)

Figure 6-2 This is a view of the end of the feed auger, showing broken bags of materials being dumped onto a wide conveyor. The blade of the auger is visible over the conveyor. (*Used by permission of Tom Norton, owner, Turtle Plastics Co. Photo by Ray Blesh.*)

Figure 6-3 This is a view of the conveyor showing recyclables spread out for the operator to sort. The operator removes the recyclables and dumps them into a side hopper such as that shown on his left. (*Used by permission of Tom Norton, owner, Turtle Plastics Co. Photo by Ray Blesh.*)

Figure 6-4 Here we can see the operator removing a bottle which he will toss into the proper hopper behind him. The hopper is not visible in this picture, but two auxiliary conveyors running under the hoppers can be seen behind the operator. (*Used by permission of Tom Norton, owner, Turtle Plastics Co. Photo by Ray Blesh.*)

Figure 6-5 Here is a close-up of an auxiliary conveyor hauling materials up to a crusher. (*Used by permission of Tom Norton, owner, Turtle Plastics Co. Photo by Ray Blesh.*)

Figure 6-6 Here we see the other end of that same auxiliary conveyor and a load of crushed cans ready to load onto a truck. (*Used by permission of Tom Norton, owner, Turtle Plastics Co. Photo by Ray Blesh.*)

Figure 6–7   This is a long-view of the main conveyor showing five operators removing recyclables. Each operator has his own commodities to sort and put in side-hoppers. Signs over each auxiliary conveyor tell which commodity goes into which hopper. See Fig. 6–3 for two such signs. (*Used by permission of Tom Norton, owner, Turtle Plastics Co. Photo by Ray Blesh.*)

Figure 6–8   Here are car-boys of crushed glass. The glass crusher is visible behind the two car-boys. (*Used by permission of Tom Norton, owner, Turtle Plastics Co. Photo by Ray Blesh.*)

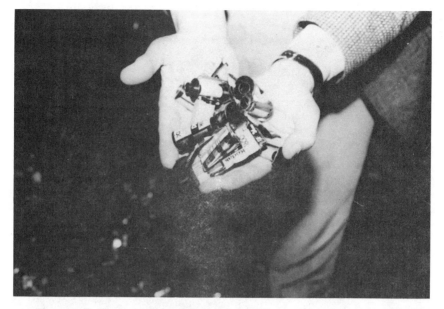

Figure 6-9 These are the empty film cartridges as they are received from Eastman Kodak. (*Used by permission of Tom Norton, owner, Turtle Plastics Co. Photo by Ray Blesh.*)

Figure 6-10 Turtle Plastics handles large volumes of these cartridges. This view shows excess cartridges that have fallen on the floor while loading the hoppers with a front end loader. This operation is the beginning of the de-assembly operation. (*Used by permission of Tom Norton, owner, Turtle Plastics Co. Photo by Ray Blesh.*)

Figure 6-11   These are washing machines for cleaning the crushed cartridges and dirty plastics during the process of preparing the material for re-use. (*Used by permission of Tom Norton, owner, Turtle Plastics Co. Photo by Ray Blesh.*)

Figure 6-12   Another view of the washing machines for cleaning the crushed cartridges and dirty plastics during the process of preparing the material for re-use. (*Used by permission of Tom Norton, owner, Turtle Plastics Co. Photo by Ray Blesh.*)

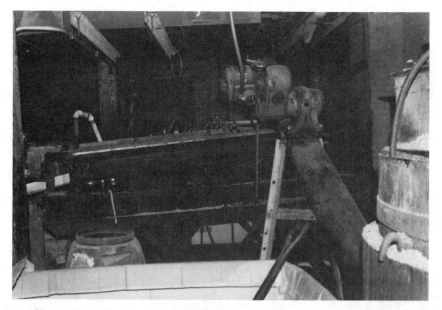

Figure 6-13 The slanted bed shown in the center of the picture is a conveyor that vibrates and washes the plastic chips, one more time, to clean out grit, paper and contamination. (*Used by permission of Tom Norton, owner, Turtle Plastics Co. Photo by Ray Blesh.*)

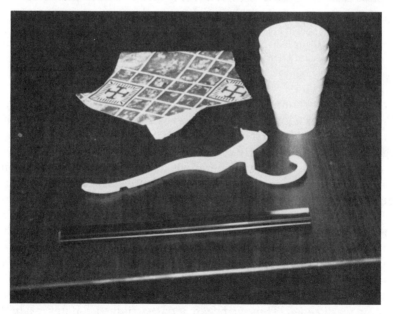

Figure 6-14 Recycling begins with determining what products are being collected, either curbside or from commercial waste, and how they can be processed into new, usable items. Here are four typical "raw" materials used by Turtle Plastics: Clockwise: Polystyrene cups, car trim, broken coat hanger, and a piece of swimming pool liner. (*Used by permission of Tom Norton, owner, Turtle Plastics Co. Photo by Ray Blesh.*)

Figure 6–15 Here are two plastics ready for remolding into products. On the left are cleaned, shredded pool liners to be made into urinal screens. On the right are pellets ready for molding into fatigue mats, fishing rod handles, shoe soles and rollers. (*Used by permission of Tom Norton, owner, Turtle Plastics Co. Photo by Ray Blesh.*)

From the first seminar we gave on Community Recycling in conjunction with the Institute for Global Action, we were made aware of two major needs in community recycling. The first of these was that the people we were dealing with, although they were usually fully committed and dedicated, had with few exceptions almost no formal training in operations management. Their backgrounds, as I described earlier, were in such fields as furniture sales, supermarket assistant management, professor of political science, equipment sales, insurance sales, and so on. Secondly, the magazines that were on the stands for people to read on recycling, although doing an important job, tended to split their interests between the public and private sectors. This left a gap in the important field of management and creativity for the public official. Subjects such as strategic planning and creative marketing, and subjects such as the one outlined above are examples.

The seminars, from the first made it clear that some type of follow-up information was needed. Thus we began at once to issue up-dates, examples, and news-ideas to fit their needs to past attendees.

This evolved in natural course into a regular news report, which we called *The Community Resource Report*. This paper, we felt, could serve as the nucleus or focal point for bringing communities together in a form described in the Turtle

Figure 6-16 Typical recycled products: Clockwise: Urinal screen. Back roller for contour chair, shoe sole, fishing rod handles, fatigue mat. (*Used by permission of Tom Norton, owner, Turtle Plastics Co. Photo by Ray Blesh.*)

example—to serve as a clearing-house for inquiries and requests for help. It offered an organizing program for the communities to work with, as they began to respond to public needs.

Covered in these reports are current trends in market developments, management skills and training, innovative breakthroughs (such as creative marketing and processing) and financial planning. Examples are taken from actual case studies of the type just given, showing how others have solved a specific community recycling problem. The papers are distributed only to community officials, educators, libraries, those at the seminars, and qualified persons.

For more information write The Community Resource Report, PO Box 677, Bath, OH 44210.

Figure 6-17   Fatigue mats linked together to form a large work area. Top of the mat is impregnated with steel slag to create a non-skid surface. The design and thickness of the mats allows drippings such as oil and water to drain through so that the worker stands on a dry, spongy surface, to reduce fatigue and improve safety. (*Used by permission of Tom Norton, owner, Turtle Plastics Co. Photo by Ray Blesh.*)

7

Private versus Public Operation

Privately-owned, profit-oriented recycling versus public operations is an issue which must be considered. Each has a large part to play in the future of recycling.

To understand the differences in philosophy between private versus public (or profit and nonprofit), one must understand what recycling means to each sector, because each has a different view of the problem and how to solve it. This point is illustrated by the following example: Visiting a local scrap dealer, I had the chance to hear his opinion on recycling. We were talking general business, when he told me he had received a call some weeks before from a recycling "idealist." (Maybe it was the local paper?) Whoever it was, the caller really boiled his kettle. They asked him if he was going to do anything special for Earth Day. Well, I guess he chewed the person out. After all, he had been in the recycling business for 50 years!

There are many ways that I have found to view recycling. I once thought it to be the reuse of products, materials, packaging, and other waste. That was it! All we had to do was keep using the same materials that we manufactured, and we would never have a landfill or pollution problem again. Today, a lot of people feel that way, but what they do not realize is that the waste we create is a disease with no easy cure. It takes more than *desire* to solve the problem.

As we get more and more deeply involved in the direct, day-to-day operation of recycling systems, these differences become increasingly apparent. In my home county, as an example, there are over 20 recycling facilities. From city halls to scrap yards, every one is recycling, but are they doing it for the same reason? Do they have the same objectives? What effects do these diverse and often conflicting approaches have upon the overall result? Many wholesalers, retailers, and distributors publicly support recycling, as we saw earlier, but do they really get involved? Even with the most efficient recycling facilities, is there a way to achieve 100 percent recycling? Why does the government pass bills which do not provide real benefits to citizens who try to recycle? Where do we turn for help? Profit-seeking recyclers want to recycle the valuable materials, but they ignore the rest of our waste because it has no value. Nonprofit recyclers, on the other hand; are not goal or incentive oriented. How do they expect to make a difference? These are quite a few questions for what seems to be a very simple industry. This is a much bigger picture of recycling than just "reusing products and materials," but it is a picture that everyone getting involved in recycling should seek to understand. Properly understood, this broader viewpoint will help both the private and public sectors better understand the symbiotic relationship that necessarily must evolve between them.

Over the years, I have visited many different recycling centers. (I define *recycling* as any effort to lessen the burden on our landfills.) These include scrap yards, community programs, and specialized collectors. All of them are *recycling centers*, and all need full community support. Each of them must work together for the common cause. Unfortunately, there are many barriers between the different types of recyclers. And yet, if we stop and look at what each is doing, we realize that they are all doing the same thing. *They are keeping waste out of landfills.* Isn't that our final objective? Why, then, don't we work together as a team?

Besides the profit motive, there are great differences in the capabilities of these diverse groups. For example, when is the last time you saw a car sitting in a landfill? Most likely never, because most community systems are incapable of handling large trash. Curb-side pick-up trucks are designed to handle neighborhood waste in small drums or barrels. But scrap yards, on the other hand, can handle cars, and an old car is worth money. Hence, the car gets recycled, and the yard is happy to recycle it. The difference is not just motive but capability and equipment. Communities do not have the specialized, expensive processing equipment, so that it is not economical for them to recycle many products. Thus, both the scrap yard and the community recycling program have important roles to play in our cities and towns. To achieve 100 percent recycling, each must work together. In this way, we can learn from each other.

Another lesson those who enter the field learn is that recycling is not for the fainthearted. Recyclers work hard with little reward. They take our waste which is dirty, wet, and smelly. Then, because of the dirt, the materials being recycled destroy the best-built machinery in a short time. After a week of use, new machinery looks like it has been through a war. No matter if the operation is for profit or nonprofit, you will have dirt under your fingernails at the end of the day. For employees, recycling is the great equalizer.

The United States has a free market economy, which encourages competition and promotes accomplishment. The strong survive, or should we say, the ones who have accomplished what they set out to do survive. When you run your business, always watch what your competitors are doing and work with them if possible. Everyone knows something you don't, and you can learn from each other. Remember, someone is most likely having the same problems you have or will have. Hence, there should be no lines drawn between the sectors of the economy, other than good-natured competition, with a single goal for both.

Here is an example of how cooperation pays off: One community recycling center I visited in New Jersey was run with very little supervision. When they found out they had to recycle, they went to local buyers of recyclables and planned a pick-up schedule for the materials they collected. They did not have to buy any equipment, except a vehicle to do the curb-side pick-up. This community felt that the more they could get local recyclers involved the less taxpayers' money would be needed—because it cost less to run the program! It also created jobs for the independent recyclers due to increased business. This approach may not work with every community because of lack of local recyclers, but it gives us an example of what can be done if we work together.

In an earlier section, we discussed the mobile recycling unit operation for cans. This firm has built its business on convenience. This means it tries to make recycling of aluminum cans as easy as possible for the public. The whole income of the business is derived from the aluminum cans, which gives it a real *incentive to collect as many as possible*! Schools, bars, homes, stores, communities, corporations, scrap yards, and charities all work with them. The Summit County Building, which houses all the county-related activities, located in downtown Akron, recycles with them. The mobile unit gives Summit County a service which it cannot refuse: convenience. As a result, it is much easier for Summit County to work with an independent company than to try to do the job themselves.

The city of Akron also works with this firm. In the summer of 1990, for example, it proclaimed a "CanQuest aluminum can recycling week," even though it has its own successful curb-side pick-up program, and a recycling energy plant. The city of Akron recognizes the advantages of working with an independent recycler. Again, the overall goal is to reduce solid waste going into the landfills.

COMPETITION _____

And yet, I have run into a lot of negative reaction to a private individual who makes a living by recycling our waste materials. This resentment probably arises because of the competition for the valuable commodities. A lot of community recycling programs, for example, need this income to support their overall operations because the majority of communities recycle everything collected or brought to them. When competition is present, the valuable materials flow away from the nonprofit recycler to the highest bidder, although this need not be the case. Well-run community programs can compete in the open market for these goods, and they have certain advantages in terms of public support on their side. In addition, tipping fees, credited to people who recycle, plus government incentives can help divert products that are not economical to recycle out of the landfills and into the recycling market. This again shows that a well-planned program can be designed to work for everyone.

Another way to achieve economic results is through a bag program. In these programs, a community purchases large marked plastic bags which are put in the local stores. The community makes use of the bags mandatory. The residents use the bags to store recyclables, and once a week the bags are picked up and taken to the community recycling center. The program, in theory, is supported by the sale of the bags. The bags cost more than an average bag, but the price is set to cover the cost of the pick-up service. The nonrecyclable garbage goes straight to a landfill, bags and all. These communities must still deal with the costs of opening the bags, separating the commingled materials, and processing them for shipment to buyers. These programs have been operated both privately and by the public sector.

REFUSE SERVICE RECYCLING

Present curb-side systems in use now can be integrated into the communities' plans to begin separating their waste. In many communities, local refuse services (garbage collectors) have a contract with the community to collect the trash. With higher and higher tipping fees, it is becoming increasingly necessary for the refuse services to go into recycling. Most of these companies contact their customers to inform them of the new recycling service and ask them to participate. There is usually a monthly fee. Some of the refuse services provide containers at no cost to their customers. These refuse services make their living handling our waste, and they are not going to recycle if they lose money. The service fee they add on enables them to cover their costs and overhead. The recyclables that are collected create an income. The opportunity to operate profitably is easier for larger refuse companies and recyclers because the more of a commodity one has the more income received for it with lower processing costs. Refuse services offer an excellent alternative for many communities.

DEPOSIT PROGRAMS

Deposit programs are another way in which the private and public sectors have joined together to accomplish recycling objectives.

Many states today are considering beverage container deposit laws. In 1990 ten states had such a law in effect (Oregon, Vermont, California, Iowa, Maine, New York, Massachusetts, Delaware, Connecticut, and Michigan).[1] Many feel that this is a very successful method for getting the public to recycle aluminum, glass, and plastic. The law places a 5¢ to 10¢ deposit (tax) on each bottle or can.

---

[1] California is a special case. There is no specific deposit on a can, but there is a refund of up to 3¢ when the can is returned to a redemption center.

The money is then refundable at any beverage retailer or designated recycling center. This gives the public a convenient way to recycle and a real incentive, too. The consumer is refunded the 5¢ to 10¢ per can upon return. And sometimes recyclers will also pay the going price for the recyclable material as a bonus. For those containers not returned by the public, the 5¢ to 10¢ per beverage container which is collected and not refunded goes directly to the state. This excess of collection over refund is then used to support general recycling programs. Certain states use some of the excess to finance solid waste management programs and remit the rest to the retailers and wholesalers to help cover the cost of handling the containers.

Unfortunately, there are a lot of problems with a deposit law. The first is that recyclers, who have already been recycling for years, do not have the resources to switch directions. Many recycling programs are supported, as I said before, by the value of the beverage containers as a commodity.

Aluminum Cans For Burned Children, for example, is a recycling program maintained by donations alone. All of the proceeds go to help children who are victims of fire. This type of program is eliminated when states mandate a deposit law.

Still, the biggest argument against a deposit law is that it is not designed to achieve 100 percent recycling. It is true that there is an incentive for the public to recycle because they each want their 10¢ back. But not for the retailer or wholesaler. The retailer and wholesaler incur a great expense when they handle returned beverage containers. (An estimated $30,000 per year per supermarket!) Some will not or cannot afford the cost. The state helps by sharing unclaimed deposits. This works as a reverse incentive to recycle, however, because the less the retailers and wholesalers pay out to redeem cans, the more money the state has to share with them. If the state achieves 100 percent recycling, in other words, there will be no funds left to distribute to the retailers or wholesalers.

THE NEED TO COOPERATE!

As we can see, there is much more to recycling than just reusing products and materials over and over. For a recycling effort to be successful, recyclers must take advantage of the resources that are close and accessible. Both profit and nonprofit operations can take advantage of incentives to create the excitement needed to collect large volumes of materials. Every recycling district needs to form a recycling network which bands together for maximum results. As recyclers, we need to watch what the other guy is doing, so we can keep on growing. We need to study what is going on in other areas and communities.

Until we reach 100 percent recycling there is room for all profit and nonprofit efforts. For this reason, because we all have the same final goal, it is hard to understand the resistance we often find to helping each other.

For example, here are some of the things that happen to thwart our efforts at recycling, even when we all have the same final interests. (These are all personal experiences.)

1. The owner of a major supermarket asked us to set up a recycling operation in the parking lot. The zoning board approved it. The landowner ordered us out.

2. The park manager for a city contracted with my firm to collect cans in the park and pay the proceeds to charity. His superior at city hall overruled him because he said he would provide the services directly through the city. It never was done. Not one can was recycled!

3. We signed a contract with a major shopping area to provide recycling to the shoppers. The city councilman said it violated ordinances and closed the operation, even though we and the owners had gotten a ruling by the zoning chief permitting it.

4. But to *show that most people do cooperate,* we set up an operation in Springfield Township, and learned (when the police stopped by) that we might be violating a local ordinance. The zoning manager and mayor helped us by introducing a variance bill. Our first meeting was on Friday. The zoning manager called the legal notice of the variance request to the daily paper that day (which met the legal requirement). On Tuesday, at its regular meeting the township approved the variance. We never lost a day of recycling, and this is now one of the most active collection centers in the state.

To accomplish any significant goal there is a need to be cooperative, to create convenient recycling for the public and businesses. There will always be new approaches to the solid waste problem, which will not always agree with a particular point of view. Therefore, we need to be flexible and open-minded. A mature approach is needed, which recognizes opportunities at each shift in recycling. To work together is hard but not impossible.

There will always be an influx of strange, new materials into the recycling stream. Manufacturers or producers will expect you to recycle their new product, so they can declare it environmentally friendly. The community also wants you to recycle it. The best results almost always involve cooperative effort at all levels.

I know that working together is an ideological way of looking at the solid waste recycling business. This view is certainly true to most of those who are in the business. But I have not said to give up your ship or reveal all your secrets. There are people in the private, public, profit, and nonprofit sectors who are not honorable. As I have said, some feel that everyone is doing it wrong, and there is no room for the wrong doers in their community. All I have said is to share with each other, and help each other.

Even though there are adversaries, I have found that most people can be encouraged to work together to meet their goals. Often, all they need is someone who takes the lead. Profit, nonprofit, private, or public recyclers are all trying to reach the same goal. And, *they all keep unwanted waste out of our landfills.*

8

Planning for Convenience

Planning for public convenience is one of the most important parts of any recycling program. To reach a goal of 100 percent recycling, everyone must participate. Every home, business, and school has to make recycling a part of their everyday way of life. This means making recycling so convenient that even the laziest of us will participate. The source of recycling materials comes from the residents of the targeted community, and the easier it is for them to recycle, the more materials the recycler will receive.

CONVENIENCE IN THE HOME

Recycling begins in the home. The more convenient something is the more readily people will accept it. In the home there must be a container big enough to hold recyclables, but not something which will be in the way. Some companies or communities provide containers for curb-side pick-up programs. For homes not in a community with such a program, an extra trash can well marked for recyclables may be satisfactory. All food containers which are designated to be recycled should be washed out to prevent bugs and eliminate contamination.

Homes with curb-side pick-up will have to take the recyclables to the road on the scheduled day to be picked up. For most residents of a community, curb-side pick-up is currently the most convenient way to recycle. Some programs charge for this service, but recycling in the home will hopefully reduce the regular trash pick-up cost. Residents who do not have such programs can look in their phone books for the most convenient recycling centers.

For a home without curb-side service, aluminum cans are the easiest household waste to recycle. In most communities there is an abundance of aluminum-can recyclers. Some are located in parking lots of stores, so one can recycle and shop in one stop. Other recyclables will have to be taken to a recycler who handles more than one material. One advantage to dropping off the recyclables in person is the higher price that is usually paid.

Apartment houses, dorms, barracks, and other housing with large numbers of people also need a convenient open location to take recyclables—such as a separate trash container, well marked to keep it separate from the regular garbage. Either the residents of the housing, the janitors, or maids should place all recyclables in the marked container at least once a day. All recyclables should be taken to a central point located outside to avoid bug infestation. Having a central point to take the recyclables makes it easier for the recycler also. This should be one of the goals of any recycling system—not only to make recycling easy for the residents, but for the handler too.

CONVENIENCE FOR BUSINESSES AND GOVERNMENT OFFICES

Businesses are the perfect sources for recyclables. Because of the large number of employees, there is a constant volume of waste, such as aluminum, glass, and plastic containers. These are easily recycled by placing convenient recycling receptacles in strategic points, such as cafeterias and beside vending machines. The receptacles should be emptied into a central point for pick-up.

Many businesses create a lot of recyclable waste. Stores, for example, create a lot of packaging waste, such as plastic, paper, and corrugated. Manufacturers create metal waste from machining. Offices create a large volume of high-grade paper waste. All of these present opportunities for a recycler. As with the beverage containers, there is a need for receptacles at strategic locations. The two main differences is that there is no bug problem as there is with the food containers, and the weight of the recyclables is much more. This means that the containers in each office must be small enough to be easily carried to a central point. Large offices with central collection points in the halls for paper can use larger containers, if they are on wheels. Managers can take advantage of the collected paper, and use the quantity of waste to show employees actual examples of waste in their business. The best step to take when a business is serious about reducing solid waste is by talking to a professional.

Pick-ups at businesses are much more efficient than those at homes because a recycler can collect more in less time. The one thing to remember when dealing with businesses is to not limit yourself to how much you can haul. In other words, plan your operation to be able to handle large volume. The more you can get into a truckload, the fewer trips you will need to collect everything. Even then you may have to return at frequent intervals. Paper, corrugated, and metal shavings tend to compact in a bin, but glass, cans, and plastic take a lot of space. If your pick-up vehicle or auxiliary equipment does not reduce the size of the material, you end up hauling a lot of air.

DROP-OFF RECYCLERS

Many recyclers are located in one location and do not offer pick-up service. They rely on the local residents to bring the materials for recycling to the recycling center. Here again, the best operations are those at central locations such as scrap yards. Scrap yards are able to create enough volume just by being in a central location. The key to their operations is that they buy the steel, aluminum, copper, and so on, from their customers. As described earlier, these are another form of buy-back centers. (Some would not admit that a scrap yard is a buy-back center, let alone a recycler! Yet, scrap yards have been around much longer than recycling has been in vogue, and we can learn a lot from them.) But to reach a goal of 100 percent recycling requires that we make recycling convenient for the people who do not care or will not go out of their way, even if paid. Most of the time people do not have the time, and to reach our goal we must get everyone to participate.

CONVENIENCE IN OPERATING THE SYSTEM

Operating convenience is a matter of safety and efficiency. It is an essential for optimum recycling. One of the most convenient systems I have seen is a transfer station of the type discussed earlier.

After pick-up, the trash is dumped into a concrete pit at the transfer station. Pickers at the station then go through the solid waste to pick out the recyclables. The transfer station manager, acting as a dispatcher, directs the various types of materials which come in to increase efficiency. For example, loads coming from offices which have a large quantity of paper go to a certain spot at the station to help the pickers. In this process there may be no extra boxes or preseparation because all separation is done after it is picked up.

Unfortunately, most of what could be recycled at the transfer station is not. Because of the cost of pickers and the limited amount of time they have to go through the waste, this system often fails in achieving its real goal. Yet, I feel, the basic concept is sound. It provides recycling without depending on each resident. With this system, everyone becomes a recycler without necessarily being aware of it.

Incineration is another convenient way for a community to recycle. The recyclables are lost per se and do not complete a conventional recycling cycle, but they are turned into energy by burning. This process does not involve the individual directly either except for taking the trash to the curb for pick-up.

The problem with the incineration process is that pollution is created by burning the waste. Also some products, like aluminum, cannot be burned in the incinerator because of the danger of explosions. The strongest argument against incineration is that recyclables are lost. To create a true recycling cycle, products must be reused over and over. This not only saves our landfills, but our natural resources as well.

CONVENIENCE FOR THE RECYCLER

Convenience goes beyond helping the customer. The recycler, too, must be considered; for to do a good job, he or she also needs to operate in a convenient, efficient manner.

At businesses, apartments, and stores, recycling receptacles should be placed in convenient places for the recycler to pick up, just as it is for the people using it. (Because of unsightly appearances, the trash bins are not always set up in convenient spots and the driver has trouble getting to them. Some buildings now include the trash bin in their landscape scheme to make it more appealing.) If the trash bin or dumpster is conveniently located the driver can be in and out and on to another pick-up. (Residents will learn quickly if a pick-up is inconvenient for the recycler by the build-up of materials not being regularly hauled away.)

Convenience is also important at curb-side pick-ups. Some communities ask their residents to separate the recyclables, such as paper in one container, glass in one, and cans in another. If the recycler has to pick up different containers and place the recyclables in several different places on the truck, it is going to take longer than if the items are commingled. The commingled material is then taken back to the recycling facility and processed over a separation system.

Most separation-type vehicles limit the size of loads of any one item that can be put into them. This increases the number of times the truck has to go back to the recycling facility and creates a waste of valuable time and increases handling costs. As we have mentioned before about pick-ups at businesses, the more a vehicle can carry the more efficient the operation will be. (See Figure 8–1.)

The less a recyclable material is moved or handled, the more convenient and efficient an operation will be. The biggest cost in recycling is handling. Handling fees involve picking the recyclables up at the home or business, storing, separation, processing, storing after processing, and hauling them to a buyer. Each handling adds cost.

After separation of the recyclables into different categories, the handling should be kept to a minimum. It is best to crush, smash, or shred the recyclables right into the trailer or vehicle in a single step. This can be done with a blower, forklift, conveyor, or by placing the processing equipment over the trailer and letting gravity fill it. By reducing handling, this provides the most convenient way to handle recyclables because when the vehicle is full it is sent to the buyer. Otherwise, if the recyclables are stored in a warehouse after each phase of processing, they will need to be handled several times. I would rather use a

Figure 8–1 This truck is large enough to handle a milk run of commingled pickups at homes and businesses.

smaller building and several tractor-trailers than a big building and only one tractor-trailer. The trailers can be easily set aside for delivery to the buyer, and it keeps the operation from becoming cluttered.

The convenience for the residents providing the recyclables is very important, but the convenience for the recycler cannot be overlooked.

Overall, the recycling system from home to end user must be designed and operated in a convenient and efficient manner. To recycle effectively there must be a goal of 100 percent reduction of our solid waste in an individual community, business, or home. To have a 100 percent recycling rate, everyone must become involved.

9

Legal and Practical Aspects of Recycling for the Smaller Community

As a part-time law director for a village of 3,000 for the last ten years, and as President of Universal Recycling Corporation, I have had many years to observe the dilemma facing the small political subdivisions as they try to deal with the problems of recycling. Most communities are relatively small in population. In Ohio, for example, there are over 900 political subdivisions. Of those, only seven exceed 100,000 in population. Less than 30 have a population in excess of 50,000. That leaves over 850 political subdivisions in the state which we can define as a smaller community. This same analysis can be applied to nearly every state in the United States. Thus, the perspective of the author is one that applies to the greater majority of communities in the United States.

These small communities have a very limited staff of employees. Unlike their larger counterparts, they do not have a large service department, law department, city engineers, and facilities to deal with the problems of recycling. A typical village or small city may have a part-time mayor, a part-time law director, a clerk treasurer, and a few people working in the service department.

The mayor and law director probably spend only a few hours a week working for the community, and have a full-time job elsewhere. The engineer is probably on a consulting contract and provides services only when needed. The service department is no doubt understaffed and overworked. It is responsible for maintaining the streets, sewers, water system, the community buildings and vehicles, cutting grass, plowing snow, reading water meters, and so on.

These communities are not equipped to handle the problems that the mandatory recycling movement is laying at their doorstep. Many states are now adopting legislation which requires a reduction of solid waste being dumped at the local landfills. California and Ohio are typical. They both require a 25 percent mandatory reduction by municipalities of solid waste within a short period (two to three years). Other states are taking an even more stringent approach, either in the time line allowed, or in specific prohibitions of particular solid waste items being dumped in the landfill. For instance, in Ohio tires are currently prohibited, and yard waste will also be entirely prohibited from being dumped in a landfill after the effective date of the legislation. The yard waste will be required to be delivered to composting facilities, and thus recycled. However, there are only a very few composting facilities in the whole state. Furthermore, the state EPA has not yet finalized the regulations for permits and operating standards for the composting facilities.

These smaller communities simply do not have the expertise or the labor force to deal with establishing and maintaining a viable recycling program which will meet the many requirements of the state legislatures. While the legislative goals are laudatory and in many cases necessary in light of the dwindling number of landfills, the majority of communities will most likely not be in compliance when the mandatory features become effective if they have to do it themselves. The economics of running a recycling program means that most small communities cannot afford the price tag, even if they can formulate the necessary legislation, and have the labor force to implement it.

The most logical solution is to allow the private sector to fulfill this task. Generally, the private sector performs more efficiently than government when both perform the same function. The private sector can combine a number of small political subdivisions on a regional basis and provide an affordable recycling facility. This is where a company like Universal Recycling Corporation can provide a service to the smaller communities. It can apply the expertise of its employees and consultants to the particular needs of that community and provide a system which is regional in scope. This can be done on a consulting basis so the community does not have to employ the personnel themselves. Furthermore, the community can share the capital costs with the surrounding communities.

The first step in the recycling process is collection. In many small communities the council (or legislative body) enfranchises one or more private garbage collectors to pick up the garbage. The community sets the rate structure and the standards for service, and licenses the private collectors to operate within the territorial limits of the political subdivision. The service department may inspect the vehicles, check the EPA permits, set certain standards for collection, and the like, but it does not collect the garbage.

Simply put, this proposal is to have the communities set up a legislative scheme that allows the private sector to add recycling to its garbage collection system. The private sector already has equipment, employees, and the expertise to collect the solid waste being generated by the consumer (both residential and commercial). While the industry is becoming more concentrated, there are still a large number of local, independent garbage collectors. From their perspective, the small independent collector is facing precarious financial prospects. They face increases in tipping fees at the landfill, labor costs, worker's compensation costs, and liability insurance, all compounded by the inability to obtain rate increases in a timely fashion.

Add to this the increased competition from the larger companies and the independent collectors are wondering if they will still be in business when recycling becomes mandatory. Again, these small companies do not have the personnel or expertise to deal with the problem individually. They need a source for information or guidance from people experienced in the field—firms and individuals, for example, who can provide the consulting services to the collectors as well as the communities to formulate a regional solution which would otherwise be unaffordable.

The local legislative response should be to allow all the garbage collectors an even chance to maintain their existing customers for recycling and garbage collection. The communities should try to develop a system which encourages competition and fosters the continuation of the small businesses which provide the citizenry with service. Rather than the political subdivision or a huge conglomerate being forced upon them, the customer should have a choice for this service.

The system should not be one of radical change, if it can be designed to use the existing infrastructure. Whatever the design of the recycling system, it has to be user friendly so the populace as well as the collectors will participate. While many people want to recycle, they will only do so if it is not a major hassle to them. Many communities are utilizing a central drop-off system. Participation rates approximate 10 percent. Curb-side programs, on the other hand, achieve participation rates as high as 85 percent. The methodology of the curb-side program must be such that the populace and the collectors can easily transfer the postconsumer waste from the house, to the curb, to the recycling center. The community should bear the initial expense of the containers or recycle carts to maintain uniformity, and to make it affordable for the homeowner to become a participant. This expense can be recouped by the community through a rental fee added to the customer's bill.

While the focus so far has been on single-family residential homeowners, the small communities also have to differentiate between single-family and multi-family residential collection, as well as the entirely different problems of commercial solid waste. The legislative response must allow different approaches for each of these categories. The whole burden should not be laid upon the backs of the single-family residential homeowner simply because that sector makes up the largest number of participants of the various categories.

There have been successful apartment recycling programs instituted in several states. *Resource Recycling* (June 1990) reports on an apartment recycling project. The community's council must allow for the differences that apartment dwellers face, and the increased difficulty in communicating with them, compared with the single-family homeowner.

This point emphasizes the need for an educational component to the legislation that is drafted by the community. The community must realize that a major educational campaign will be necessary to demonstrate the need for recycling as well as the how-to type of classes for both adults, and children. Simply passing an ordinance mandating the citizenry to recycle does not make an effective solution to the problem. While "recycling" may be the buzzword for the "90s," actually convincing most people to do it and do it properly will require giving them the information to accomplish it in a form that will be effective. The best place to start is in the school, where there is a captive audience which is already being educated. However, the adult population will need a more creative approach. Whatever form of educational program works in the community, it will require many hours of paid or volunteer staff time to reach the potential recyclers.

Although the primary focus of this and earlier chapters is on residential postconsumer solid waste, we need to address the large amount of materials that are generated from nonresidential sources. Every day businesses generate a large proportion of the solid waste now being transported to the landfill. Office buildings generate huge amounts of paper, much of which is recyclable. Computer paper prices rank among the highest items per ton of the solid waste stream. Another example is construction site waste. Scrap cardboard and lumber can be reprocessed into recycled paper pulp and medium-density pressed wood. While examples are endless, the point is that the community must include these items in the legislative response to the recycling problem. The collection of these items will need a different approach than residential postconsumer waste. But that should not deter the community from establishing the standards, even if they are implemented in stages.

After the solid waste is collected, the next step is to sort and process the materials so that they can be delivered to the buyer. This step is the one that involves very high capital and operating costs. A single small community cannot afford to purchase land, a building, and equipment worth hundreds of thousands of dollars. Again, the solution is to develop a regional recycling center, which in the industry vernacular is known as a *materials recovery facility,* or as the case may be a *small materials recovery facility.* The acronym then becomes SMRF, and everyone can envision lots of little blue beings ("smurfs") busily processing the recyclables at the SMRF. While this is a humorous vision, it does not really accurately portray the operation of the SMRF.

Unfortunately, many of the items which are recyclable today are not justified economically. In many areas, as we have seen, the price received for newsprint, colored or mixed glass, and metal cans (except aluminum) does not pay for the cost of collection, sorting and processing, and transportation. In order for the recycling system to work, these items will have to be subsidized somehow if they are to be collected. This means that the communities and the private sector will have to work as a partnership to make the system work. The regional SMRF probably will be placed on land funded by the community in which it is located. That community can then receive a reduced rate on the fees charged its populace (compared to the other communities using the facility) for a period of time to recover its capital costs.

Another area that is perhaps the most controversial with business is the attempts to have business incorporate a certain percentage of recyclable materials in their products. We have already discussed this problem. As we saw, many states have or are contemplating legislation mandating minimum recycled contents in purchased items. These types of approaches may work in some instances. However, in many cases, the infrastructure may not yet be on line to accomplish the legislative goal. Furthermore, there are so many industries and so many local variations that a national or even state policy may not be effective for some industries.

A suggestion is to set standards at the state level, but to allow the communities to receive a portion of the "recycling tax" from the companies based on a percentage of their compliance. Thus, a state might set a 25 percent content requirement for a particular industry. If the local company fully complied it would receive a credit and not owe any tax. If the company partially complied, it would receive a partial credit. The company would pay the difference in a "recycling tax" to the local community where it is located, which would be used by that community to fund the community's recycling effort. The funds could be used to purchase containers, fund the purchase of land, or the cost of building the SMRF. In any event, the community must begin now, to plan for the day mandatory recycling becomes effective. The legislative process of the community can help the community set the stage for implementation. This time of committee meetings can be used to receive input from the citizenry, the collectors, and private companies affected by the legislation. If the mayor and council properly inform their constituencies, the local recycling effort should be able to be put in place without tremendous resistance, and should have a good chance for success.

A simple outline is set forth following this chapter which may provide guidance in the formulation of the ordinance for a community about to establish a recycling program. Naturally, each community must adjust the provisions of the ordinance to deal with variables such as the size of the community, markets for recyclables, the number of private collectors, the availability of other communities to share costs of a SMRF, and the state mandates which apply to the community. The outline is meant to be a starting point from which the law director and the legislators may diverge to accommodate the special needs of the community. A workable ordinance will depend on involvement from the various segments of the community impacted by the legislation. The best advice is get them involved early in the process.

UNIVERSAL RECYCLING CORPORATION
ORDINANCE OUTLINE

  I. Preamble
 II. Enabling Paragraph and Rule-making Authority
III. Definitions

IV. Residential
   A. Single Family
   B. Multifamily
V. Business
   A. Permanent Sites
      1. Commercial
      2. Industrial
   B. Construction Sites
VI. Preparation of Recyclables
VII. Notice and Public Education
VIII. Existing Operations and Licensing Haulers
IX. Rates and Annual Review
X. Inspections, Compliance, and Antiscavenging
XI. "User-Friendly Recycle Cart"
XII. Yard Waste and Composting Center
XIII. Time Deadlines and Effective Dates
XIV. Fines

10

Building Support for a Community Recycling Program

Developing an effective waste-reduction and recycling program may at first seem like an overwhelming task. The impediments to getting the program up and running are often obvious, while identifying the necessary resources requires research and planning.

There is often considerable pressure to begin recycling programs immediately. Shrinking disposal capacity and rising disposal costs, public interest in environmental preservation, and increasingly directive state waste management and recycling laws are pushing local officials to action. But if long-term effectiveness and efficiency are your goals, avoid the temptation to throw together a program prematurely.

Capitalize on the public interest by setting up a planning process which includes interested and affected parties and is open to public participation. There are no "quick fixes," no "perfect" model programs that can be transplanted without careful evaluation of the host community. There is one rule of thumb: The output will reflect the input. Recycling planning needs to be done thoroughly and thoughtfully. Most successful recycling programs reflect unique characteristics of their home communities. What works in one can easily fail in another.

A thorough and open planning process is the key to building public support and to obtaining the resources to implement a recycling program which will meet or exceed your goals and expectations.

KNOW THE GROUND RULES: STATE AND FEDERAL
POLICIES AND REGULATIONS

There are few areas of public policy which have changed as rapidly as solid waste management. The scrap industry has been a very important source of materials for U.S. manufacturers and has been a mainstay of U.S. exports for decades. During World War II recycling was an integral part of the war effort. More recently community organizations promoted recycling drives as a way to involve citizens in conserving resources and to raise funds for worthy causes. The realization that recycling can play a vital role in managing municipal solid waste is in most parts of the country a recent development.

In 1988 the United States Environmental Protection Agency published *The Solid Waste Dilemma: An Agenda for Action.* The U.S. EPA acknowledged, "Although solid waste management is primarily a local responsibility, the problem is national in scope, and we need a national strategy to solve it." EPA asserted that

> to the extent practical, source reduction and then recycling are the preferred options for closing the gap and reducing the amount and toxicity of waste that must be landfilled or incinerated. To foster implementation of this preference for source reduction and recycling, EPA set a national goal in January 1988 of 25 percent source reduction and recycling (up from the current 10 percent) by 1992.[1]

As we saw earlier, a number of states have set goals for waste reduction and recycling ranging from 15 percent to 50 percent of the solid waste stream within the next three to ten years. Some states have made the recycling of certain materials mandatory or have banned designated materials from being landfilled or incinerated. Other states require local governments to set up recycling programs. Some states require local governments to set up an "opportunity to recycle." These requirements can be met by a variety of programs and a number of options are available to local planners. A rapidly increasing number of states require curb-side collection of designated materials. Some require commercial and industrial enterprises to set up recycling programs.

Since state solid waste management and recycling laws are changing so rapidly, it is impossible to include a list of state requirements. It is essential that planners thoroughly understand both the federal and state regulations and policies which will influence the programs they develop. Information on federal laws and policies can be obtained from the Office of Solid Waste, U.S.EPA. Inquiries may be directed to the Washington, DC office or to the U.S.EPA regional office nearest you. The U.S.EPA maintains a toll-free Solid Waste Information Hotline. See listings in the appendix.

Each state has one or more agencies which regulate solid waste programs and which provide technical and financial assistance for solid waste management and recycling. The names and responsibilities of these agencies differ

---

[1] United States Environmental Protection Agency, *The Solid Waste Dilemma: An Agenda for Action* (February 1989), Washington DC, p. 22.

from state to state. A list is provided in the appendix. However, often responsibilities and resources are split among several agencies so you may find additional sources of assistance. If you have difficulty finding your state recycling program call the U.S.EPA, the state legislator who represents your area, or the office of the governor of your state and ask for their assistance in obtaining information.

LOOK FOR HELP: SOURCES OF INFORMATION, TECHNICAL ASSISTANCE, AND FINANCIAL AID

The U.S. EPA provides a number of publications which can be useful in planning and promoting local recycling programs. Most are free. A current list can be obtained by calling or writing the U.S. EPA.

Most state recycling agencies provide free or low-cost publications. Many states hold recycling workshops and seminars and/or provide speakers for local programs. Utilize these resources. Contact with state agencies not only provides information for planning your program but builds relationships and communication channels to help you keep up with changing requirements and conditions.

National professional and trade associations are excellent sources of information. Many provide planning publications, fact sheets, and brochures which can be used for public education. Some have national staff available to speak at seminars or provide hands-on technical assistance. Most can identify state or local chapters or members who can provide local information. A few trade associations provide grants or seed money for pilot or demonstration recycling programs. These opportunities are usually limited to projects which are on the "cutting edge" of recycling services or technology. A list of national trade and professional associations and of state recycling associations is provided in the appendix.

A number of states provide grants or loans to local governments, nonprofit community organizations, or to private business and industry to assist in starting or expanding community recycling programs. The amount of money available, the eligibility requirements, and the application procedures vary from state to state and are constantly changing. There are, however, basic considerations to keep in mind when deciding whether to apply for a grant or loan and for preparing a successful application:

1. Thoroughly understand the eligibility and application requirements. Most state agencies will meet with you to discuss the grant or loan program and to explain the requirements. Even if the process seems self-explanatory, a face-to-face meeting often provides important insights about the evaluation criteria. You may be able to review successful applications or submit a preapplication draft. Take advantage of these opportunities, if they are available.

2. Carefully assess your needs. Grants can be very useful to fund the costs of program planning, the initial capital costs of starting or expanding a

recycling program, and/or the costs of public education and program promotion. However, long-term subsidies for waste management or recycling are usually not available. Be sure you identify local funding sources for long-term program operation.

3. It may seem obvious, but read the application carefully, follow the instructions, and provide all of the required information. Grant reviewers will appreciate a straightforward presentation. Avoid jargon, and keep the presentation as concise as possible. In general the basic information will answer the following questions:

- Who will implement the program?
- Why is the program needed? What are the expected results?
- How will it be implemented? Give a step-by-step description with a time line.
- What is the total cost? How will the grant or loan money be used? How will the other costs be paid?
- How will the program success be evaluated and reported?

BEGIN THE PLANNING PROCESS: INCLUDE AFFECTED AND INTERESTED PARTIES

Involving the right people from the start is crucial. Create a Planning Advisory Committee. Include representatives of all parties who are interested in, affected by, or responsible for solid waste management in the community such as government officials, public and private waste management associations, recyclers, and environmental and civic groups. Many will possess valuable experience and expertise. Their support and assistance will be needed to establish a successful recycling program.

In large communities the Planning Advisory Committee may prove to be too large to accomplish detailed planning. If this proves to be the case, select a representative core group, but be sure to tap into the larger group often. Participation can be accomplished through committees and/or by opportunities to review and comment upon drafts of the plan as crucial phases in the planning.

The Recycling Advisory Council can be helpful in selling the recycling plan to the community. Do not be afraid to include those who oppose the recycling program or are skeptical in the planning process. Part of the purpose of an open and comprehensive planning process is education. Understanding and acknowledging the reasons for opposition are the first steps to solving problems and answering objections. Lively debate and discussion usually results in a better plan which will win broad support.

Place the person or persons responsible for the actual planning work within the local government agency which has responsibility for solid waste policy or for the collection and disposal of waste.

Consultants can be useful or necessary for gathering initial data for the plan, or to develop parts of the plan, but the local staff and the Planning Advisory Committee should maintain the primary responsibility for completion and evaluation of the overall plan. Local ownership of the plan is essential to public acceptance and to effective implementation.

UNDERSTAND THE WASTE MANAGEMENT SYSTEM

Accurate information is essential. Develop a complete factual picture of the community's current waste management system and the waste stream itself. What is in the waste stream and in what proportion? Who generates the waste and how much? How is waste handled and what are the present costs?

You can use recently published U.S.EPA national waste composition figures as a starting point, but verify national figures locally. Survey local residential, business, and industry waste generators or conduct local waste composition studies by sorting incoming wastes at the transfer or disposal facility.

Develop a step-by-step model of the present waste management system. Who collects waste from individual households, apartments, commercial and industrial enterprises, and public buildings? What are major components of each of these waste streams? Are some materials already segregated from other waste? What materials are already recycled in your community?

Develop disposal cost figures and projections if they are not already available or reevaluate existing cost information if it does not reflect all of the costs of collection and disposal. Compare present costs with projected future costs. In most localities disposal costs are rising. If new disposal facilities are required, future disposal costs may be much higher in order to recover the higher construction and maintenance costs of new facilities with more stringent environmental controls.

Even the information-gathering process can be implemented in ways which will help build support for the recycling plan. Involve both public and private sector waste managers and recyclers. Be sure they know what information you need and why. Ask them to help you design information-gathering mechanisms which are compatible with the way they keep and report information. Respect proprietary information and set up mechanisms to insure that such information is kept confidential.

EVALUATE THE OPTIONS

Once the current waste management system is understood, the community is ready to decide which recycling program or combination of programs will be the most effective. Start big—look at all the options and then narrow the possibilities. Start with the attitude of diverting 100 percent of the recyclable waste stream and then eliminate only those materials which cannot be feasibly collected or marketed in your area.

Look for parts of the community's waste stream that contain a high percentage of already segregated, relatively "clean" recyclable waste. Start with the commercial and industrial waste streams. Then look for sources of segregated household waste. For instance, in many communities leaves are collected separately in the fall and can easily be composted.

In choosing collection methods, look first at those methods which are likely to divert the most materials. In general weekly curb-side collection is the most effective. Less frequent curb-side collection, buy-back centers (mobile or permanent locations where recyclable materials are purchased from the public), drop-off centers, or recycling drives tend to be less effective. Move to a less effective method only if the more effective method is logistically impossible or prohibitively expensive. Note that in many communities a combination of approaches will be necessary to address different portions of the recyclable waste stream or to attract the participation of varying socioeconomic groups.

Be realistic about the factors that limit the choice of the recycling program or collection method. For example, limiting factors for curb-side programs may be the lack of municipal collection systems, low population density, a transient population, or economically depressed conditions in urban areas.

Recognize that new recycling efforts do not necessarily conflict with existing ones. Establishing a curb-side program, for example, need not hurt buy-back or collection drives. Include present successful efforts of recycling businesses and recycling drives whenever possible.

VOLUNTARY OR MANDATORY RECYCLING? _____

A number of state and local governments have enacted mandatory recycling laws. These could more accurately be described as laws which exclude certain materials from the disposable system. Mandatory curb-side recycling generally means that residents are prohibited from mixing materials which are designated for recycling in with the waste put out for disposal. Residents are encouraged to put the materials out for the curb-side recycling collection. However, the materials may be taken to a buy-back center or may be donated to a charity collection drive.

State and local governments may ban certain materials from designated disposal facilities. A number of communities no longer allow leaves or yard waste to be deposited in landfills. Bulky or toxic materials like tires, lead acid batteries, or appliances are often excluded. A few communities have banned more common recyclable materials from the landfills such as aluminum cans, glass bottles, or corrugated cardboard. The burden usually falls upon the waste haulers who deposit materials in the facility to be sure that banned materials are not included in the waste they collect.

There is no clear information that mandatory programs necessarily generate higher recycling rates than voluntary programs. Obviously the community must be prepared to enforce mandatory recycling requirements if the program is designated as mandatory. Well-managed and promoted voluntary programs often have high participation rates.

PUBLIC OPINION SURVEYS

When local staff and the Recycling Advisory Committee become immersed in gathering recycling information and developing the recycling plan, they can easily lose touch with the general public. A public opinion survey can provide valuable information for the design of the recycling program and the public education campaign. Questions can be designed to evaluate knowledge about recycling, willingness to participate, preferences as to type of collection program, and the degree of commitment to recycling. For instance, a survey could help planners decide whether the program should be mandatory or voluntary and whether residents will be willing to pay for convenient recycling services.

The survey can be implemented by a consultant or can be done by the local planners. It is usually a good idea to get professional assistance in designing the survey questions and in selecting the sample of residents to be surveyed. Poorly phrased questions can inadvertently illicit unreliable information. You need honest answers.

Questions also should be included to associate the answers with the various age, economic, and social groups within the community so that the recycling and public education programs can be tailored to the appropriate audience.

Focus groups may be used in place of or in addition to public opinion surveys. A focus group is a small gathering of individuals selected at random or to represent specific segments of the community. The group is convened in order to gather specific information or test a hypothesis about knowledge or attitudes of the group members on a particular topic. Focus groups can often provide information or insights not easily gathered through surveys. Focus group discussions must be skillfully managed and carefully analyzed to produce the desired insights.

FINANCING THE RECYCLING PROGRAM

Developing capital cost estimates and accounting for the recycling program are discussed in succeeding chapters. Sales income from recycled materials and avoided disposal costs are two major parts of the financial equation for recycling programs, but there are a number of other resources that should be considered in financing the establishment or expansion of your program.

Utilize the existing capital investment and technical expertise of waste management and recycling businesses. The business expertise of experienced recyclers is a valuable resource. Evaluate the private capacity to collect, process, and market recyclable materials and consider the possibility of contracts for these services before committing community resources to duplicating recycling collection and processing equipment and processing facilities.

Consider increasing disposal charges to help pay for the recycling program or establishing recycling as a fee-paid service. Waste generators pay for the expense of solid waste collection and/or disposal at the landfill or an incinerator. It is appropriate that they pay for the collection and processing of recyclable materials which would otherwise have to be collected and hauled.

If the community will be developing a financing package for other solid waste projects, capital costs for recycling equipment and facilities can be included in the same package. Recycling facilities are usually far less expensive than disposal facilities. The recycling program will probably decrease the amount of the waste stream directed to disposal to a greater degree than the recycling program will add to the financial package.

COOPERATE FOR ECONOMIES OF SCALE

It is important to remember that the materials collected by recycling programs are only of value if they can be utilized in the manufacture of new products. Industry requires large volumes of material processed to exacting specifications. Recycling is essentially a volume business. Recognize and take advantage of the economies of scale offered by cooperative collection and processing programs. Neighboring towns and cities, counties, regions of states, or several states may find that they can collectively market materials or command prices which would otherwise be out of reach.

Public recycling programs may work with or through private processors or brokers to market materials. Some state agencies, state recycling associations, or waste management and recycling trade associations have programs to assist local governments in locating opportunities for cooperative processing and marketing of materials.

EDUCATE, EDUCATE, EDUCATE

Thorough and clear communication with the community is vital to a successful recycling program. If the planning process encourages public participation, the community will probably know something about the proposed recycling program long before it actually begins. The Recycling Advisory Committee can help disseminate information and can serve as the core public education team. Public education and recycling promotion requires a detailed plan and a significant financial investment. Planning and funding education and promotion should be considered every bit as important as the collection and processing system.

There are many reasons why people recycle. Some do it for economic reasons; others are strongly motivated to clean up the environment; others feel it is their civic responsibility.

Those who are motivated most strongly by money will usually save or collect high-value materials such as aluminum cans and scrap metals which are purchased by buy-back recycling centers. Although these recyclers will usually not be the primary audience of a community recycling promotion effort, opportunities for buy-back recycling should not be ignored. In economically depressed areas the money received for recycling is an important motivator.

Most community recycling programs will appeal to citizen interest in a clean environment and the individual's desire to contribute to the betterment of his or her community. Most recyclers will admit that they build a stronger self-image by recycling. They are actively doing something to save energy and natural resources and to reduce waste.

Many children become involved in recycling through programs in their schools or by participating in recycling projects sponsored by youth organizations like 4-H and Scouts. Like their elders, children are motivated to care for the environment and to be good citizens, but children also respond to recycling promotion efforts because they are fun. The recycling message can be carried through colorful posters, comic and coloring books, costumed characters and puppets. Many communities hold special recycling contests and events aimed at gaining publicity for the recycling program while involving and educating children.

RECYCLING PROMOTION

Most people believe that recycling is a good idea. However, not everyone willingly recycles—the throw-away habit is hard to break. People have to be given good reasons to recycle. They must thoroughly understand the recycling program. The program must be convenient. They must be motivated to overcome their objections or inertia until recycling becomes a habit. Some of the messages you need to convey follow.

Recycling saves energy

It takes less energy to make products from recycled materials than from virgin materials. The energy saved by recycling just one aluminum can could light a 100-watt bulb for about three and one-half hours.

Recycling conserves natural resources

By reusing resources we can conserve nonrenewable resources, and reduce America's dependence on imported minerals and energy. Recycling one ton of newspaper saves 17 small trees, and paper manufactured from secondary fibers uses 60 percent less water and energy than comparable virgin paper.

Recycling protects the environment

By reducing the amount of waste needing disposal, recycling saves land and reduces the potential for air and water pollution. Recycling one ton of material saves three cubic yards of landfill space.

Recycling has economic benefits

Recycling reclaims valuable materials and returns them to commerce. Jobs are created and money is returned to the economy for materials which would otherwise end up at a disposal facility. The cost of collecting and processing recyclable materials is often less than the cost of waste collection and disposal.

The community must understand the recycling program and why it deserves their support. Demonstrate support and action from the top down. It is extremely important that community political, civic, and business leaders visibly and actively support recycling. Government should lead by example by starting recycling programs in government buildings.

If organizations are involved in the recycling programs which naturally attract support such as sheltered workshops, utilize the public's willingness to support their programs.

Utilize the planning process to build support. If your planning process has been public and thorough, the members of the community will feel that they have a stake in the program and will be anxious to see it succeed.

Start the publicity campaign early and allocate resources to make it an ongoing part of the program operations. Initially, education efforts inform people about the recycling program and how to participate. Ongoing education can reinforce positive messages about recycling, update the community on the success of the program, and remind people to participate.

If the planned program is mandatory, have an enforcement plan, publicize it, and stick to it.

The Public Relations and Promotion Plan

As stated before, the recycling promotion effort should have a plan and a budget. Without promotion, citizens will not understand the recycling program or how to participate. Without a long-term promotion plan your activities will be hit and miss, your message will be inconsistent, and participants will be confused. A plan helps you set standards for your promotion efforts and stick to them.

It is generally a good idea to develop a promotional plan for an entire year. Some promotional activities take several months of advance preparation. Your plan should clearly address the following issues.

See Figures 10–1 through 10–7 for an example of a successful start-up program. These figures show both direct contact with the public in question and answer sessions at a local high school gym, plus a direct mail company advising

Figure 10-1 Successful recycling begins with an informed public. In this photo, the town turns out in a local high school gym to learn about recycling: how to prepare for pick-up, which items to place at the curb, what it will cost, and when to put items out for pick-up. This session was put on *before* the actual recycling program began in order to instruct the residents in their part in the program. (*Used by permission of Steven Flight, Recycling Coordinator, Copley Township.*)

each resident of the details of the program, thus providing follow-up and reinforcement for the program.

Set the objectives for the promotion campaign

In general your objective is to encourage people to recycle. However, your campaign will be more effective if you set reasonable and measurable goals. For instance, your initial goals might include speaking to 20 civic organizations, making educational presentations to all third grades in the school district, and getting participation of 70 percent of households in the curb-side recycling program.

Define the audience and appropriate messages

Most community recycling programs will have a theme or "catch phrase" as a way to create a lasting impression. Using that phrase in everything you do gives a consistent image and develops a local identity for the program. If your recycling

Figure 10-2 Here, the instructor, Ms. Patricia J. Smith, is answering questions from residents about the recycling program. Ms. Smith is president of Waste Options. She is a consultant to communities on writing grant proposals, and she is also a lecturer at the Institute for Global Action recycling seminars. (*Used by permission of Steven Flight, Recycling Coordinator, Copley Township.*)

program has a number of segments like curb-side collection in residential areas, office paper programs, and commercial recycling, the theme can be used as an umbrella for messages tailored to each program and audience.

Give clear, basic information

It is very important to give clear, basic information on the recycling program. Residents must know exactly what can and cannot be recycled, and how materials must be prepared. For curb-side programs they must know how and when to set out materials. If special containers must be used, they need to know how and when they will get their container. Locations and times of operation for buy-back, drop-off, and collection drives should be available in a form which can be saved for later reference.

Repeat important points frequently

In addition to the basic information, develop a few points that you want to get across to the public such as the reasons for them to recycle and an incentive for

COPLEY TOWNSHIP RECYCLING DEPARTMENT

STEVE FLIGHT
Recycling Coordinator

1540 S. Cleveland-Massillon Road
Copley, Ohio 44321

Business: (216) 666-1853
Fax: (216) 666-2245

AMAZING AND FUN FACTS

- A ton of paper made from 100 percent recycled, rather that from virgin fiber, saves 17 trees, 4100 kwh energy (enough to power the average home for six months), 7,000 gallons of water, 60 pounds of air-polluting effluents, three cubic yards of landfill space and taxpayer dollars that would have been used for waste-disposal costs. In many municipalities, waste disposal costs in landfills and incinerators total nearly $100.00 per ton.

- Americans throw away almost 700 million bottles each week. In two weeks, we throw away enough glass bottles to fill up both the twin towers of New York's World Trade Center. Each are 1,350 feet high!

- If every person in Ohio said "just one pop bottle won't hurt anything . . " and dropped one bottle this year, there would be 4,398,709.5 pounds of empty bottles (16 oz. size) - the equivalent weight of 675 full grown elephants!

- If every person in Ohio dropped one gum wrapper on the ground this year, the wrappers, put end-to-end, would be 447 miles long. That's enough to go from Cleveland to Cincinnati and back!

- Collecting and disposing of waste in America costs $4.5 billion each year, the third largest tax burden on local communities after roads and highways!

- Americans comprise only 5% of the world's population but produce 20-30% of its trash!

- For every $1,000.00 worth of sales in fast food establishments, 200 pounds of trash is created!

- Each four foot stack of newspapers recycled saves the equivalent of a 40 foot pine tree!

- Americans go through 2.5 million plastic bottles every hour, only a small percentage of which are now being recycled!

- Americans throw away enough aluminum to rebuild the entire U.S. commercial airfleet every three months!

- The average American discards an amount of waste equal in weight to the Statue of Liberty every five years!

- Recycling one ton of paper saves one acre of trees!

- Recycling one glass jar saves enough energy to light a 100-watt bulb for four hours!

- Making new aluminum cans from recycled cans takes 95% less energy than producing aluminum from bauxite ore virgin material!

- Annually the U.S. produces enough solid waste to completely fill five million large truck trailers - a fleet that would stretch two times around the world if placed end-to-end!

Figure 10-3   *Used by permission of Steven Flight, Recycling Coordinator, Copley Township.*

What Can You Recycle ?

Plastic Bottles

Plastic one and two liter soft drink bottles, plastic water, milk and juice jugs in gallon size and smaller juice bottles. Also windex and automotive windshied washer fluid bottles.

Glass Bottles And Jars

All varieties of glass bottles and jars of any color. Include: Beverage, wine, beer, whiskey and all food product jars and bottles. Also glass medicine and condiment bottles. Remove lids and caps. No need to rinse unless solid food residue, such as mayonnaise, mustard and ketchup remains.

Cans

Aluminum and steel "tin" cans. Beverage and food products. Include coffee, soup, sauce, vegetable and pet food cans. Also include metal lids from glass bottles and jars with cans.

Foil

Aluminum foil and foil type food packaging, such as T.V. dinner trays and pie tins. Clean off remaining food residue.

Newspaper

Separate from other recyclables. Place in paper grocery bags or a box. **DO NOT** tie with string.

Motor Oil

Place your used oil in separate plastic jugs, leave in open view. **DO NOT BAG OR OTHERWISE CONCEAL OIL**. Keep lids on tight. Do not mix motor oil with other fluids. Label - USED MOTOR OIL.

Batteries

Auto, truck or motorcycle batteries are acceptable. If batteries are leaking, **PLACE IN DOUBLE PLASTIC BAGS AND LABEL**.

Computer Paper

Those who use abundant amounts of computer paper, please save in a box or bundle.

It makes no difference how many or few recyclable items you can save. If you generate very limited amounts of the listed recyclable items, it is still important to save them. Even an occasional container of materials when multiplied by hundreds of homes will represent a significant refuse reduction. This is the reason for the entire effort.

The most important issue is simply getting involved. Participate as you are able, with as great a variety of items that you are able to contribute.

NOTE: If you feel you only need to place the recycle container on the curb every other week instead of weekly because of the size of your household, please do so.

We prefer a full or almost full container.

Figure 10-4 *Used by permission of Steven Flight, Recycling Coordinator, Copley Township.*

COPLEY TOWNSHIP RECYCLING DEPARTMENT

STEVE FLIGHT   1540 S. Cleveland-Massillon Road   Business: (216) 666-1853
Recycling Coordinator   Copley, Ohio 44321   Fax: (216) 666-2245

WELCOME TO THE COPLEY TOWNSHIP RECYCLING PROGRAM!

Dear Copley Resident,

We are pleased to offer you a recycling program through a grant we received from the Ohio Department of Natural Resources, along with matching funds from the Township. We are proud to be one of only two Townships in the State of Ohio to receive a recycling grant. With your help, Copley Township will be one of the first Townships in Summit County to have a curbside recycling program offered to all of our residents.

Your current trash hauler will also play a very important part in this program. After several meetings between Township personnel and the haulers who are serving the residents of Copley Township, we were able to work together to offer you the most comprehensive and efficient program for a minimal cost compared to most programs in the area. We will be delivering to each household an 18.2 gallon container to put all of your recyclables in that will be collected once per week at your curbside, but not necessarily the same day your trash is collected. You will be able to place glass, plastic and cans in the container with newspaper placed along side of the container in a brown paper bag (see additional information on what and how to recycle in this packet). We will also collect waste oil and old batteries that you may wish to dispose of. We will also have a collection site in the Township where you may dispose of any metal products such as old swing sets, washers, dryers, old steel sheds, etc. The hauler's part in this program will be to help us fund the program in two ways: 1) For each residence the hauler serves, the hauler will contribute fifty cents to the Township to help us operate the program; and, 2) The haulers will bill the households of the Township an additional one dollar per month on your regular trash bill. This will save the Township a billing expense which helps minimize the total overall cost of the program.

You may ask why am I charged one dollar per month if we received a grant? The grant and the Township's matching funds will enable us to purchase the 18.2 gallon container for you, the resident, at no cost. It will also allow us to purchase a recycling truck and other safety equipment for operations. It will help us in educational programs and informational packets about the program such as the one this letter was contained in. But when we address the daily operations of the recycling program, there is little money left from the grant or the Township match to help us with manpower, processing and shipping fees of recyclables collected and increasing fuel cost.

Remember, there is no market for most recyclables collected at this time! We look to see this change in the near future with new laws on mandatory use of recycled materials. Together we can make this a successful recycling program and show that Copley Township and it's residents are willing to work together for the betterment of our environment. Additional information on why and how to recycle is enclosed for your use.

LET'S MAKE COPLEY A RECYCLING COMMUNITY! !

Steve Flight
Recycling Coordinator

Printed on Recycled Paper

DIVISION OF

**LITTER PREVENTION
AND RECYCLING**

Funded by the
Division of Litter
Prevention & Recycling

Ohio Department of
Natural Resources

George Voinovich
Governor

Figure 10-5 *Used by permission of Steven Flight, Recycling Coordinator, Copley Township.*

COPLEY TOWNSHIP RECYCLING DEPARTMENT

STEVE FLIGHT
Recycling Coordinator

1540 S. Cleveland-Massillon Road
Copley, Ohio 44321

Business: (216) 666-1853
Fax: (216) 666-2245

COPLEY TOWNSHIP RECYCLING PROGRAM BEGINS APRIL 1, 1991

You are in Zone Number _____ **2** _____ .

Your pick-up day is _____ **Tuesday** _____ . *

* EXCEPTION: Recyclables will not be picked up on the below listed holidays.
If your pick-up day falls on one of these holidays, please save them until
your next regularly scheduled day, in which they will be picked up.

- Memorial Day (Monday, May 27, 1991)
- Independence Day (Thursday, July 4, 1991)
- Labor Day (Monday, September 2, 1991)
- Thanksgiving Day (Thursday, November 28, 1991)
- Christmas Day (Wednesday, December 25, 1991)
- New Years Day (Wednesday, January 1, 1992)

If you have any questions on this issue, please call 666-1853.

DIVISION OF

Funded by the
Division of Litter
Prevention & Recycling

Ohio Department of
Natural Resources

George Voinovich
Governor

**LITTER PREVENTION
AND RECYCLING**

Printed on Recycled Paper

Figure 10-6   *Used by permission of Steven Flight, Recycling Coordinator, Copley Township.*

Figure 10-7   Total recycling involves total community support. Here, the local druggist joins in the team effort to get everyone involved and informed. (*Used by permission of Steven Flight, Recycling Coordinator, Copley Township.*)

them to recycle. Repeat these points over and over again. Don't present an idea once and let it go. It usually takes repeated exposure to new ideas before the message really gets through.

Develop messages to weaken the objections that recycling takes too much time, it's inconvenient, and what I throw away doesn't make any difference. Create a sense of urgency. Make recycling an attractive activity: Recycling is good; recycling is the "in" thing to do.

Select promotional tools

There are a multitude of ways to get a message across to an audience. Getting it to the right audience means selecting the right tools and media to reach them. These promotional strategies fit into five major categories:

- Paid advertising
- Public service announcements
- Press activities
- Public participation activities
- Printed materials

Here is a sample of ways to reach an audience:

- Newsletters
- Broadcast or print public service announcements
- News kits/press releases
- Consumer brochures and pamphlets
- Bumper stickers, decals, litter bags, refrigerator magnets
- Posters, signs, truck and bus signs, billboards
- Education/curriculum programs
- Buttons, patches, T-shirts
- Paid radio, television, or print advertising
- Audiovisual aids and talks at civic meetings
- Displays and exhibits
- Point-of-sale materials (like shelf signs at grocery stores which point out recycled packaging)
- Newspaper supplements
- Inserts in utility bills
- Door hangers

Set your timetable

Once you have decided on your message and promotional tools, set dates for events and campaigns and develop due dates leading up to the events. For instance, if you want to have a poster contest to select student artwork to use on community billboards, you will need six months' lead time. School contacts must be made, information packets distributed, posters collected and judged, winners selected and announced. Artwork must be completed, and the billboard printed and posted. At several points in this process there are opportunities to get publicity for your program. Local media may announce the contest and then announce the winners. Local stores may display all of the posters which are entered. Information about the recycling program will go home to parents with contest packets. Media may cover the billboard posting.

Develop a promotional budget

Your budget should be set in advance so that you have time to develop sources of funding. Most communities will try to make maximum use of free publicity. Sponsors may be found for many promotional activities. Free or low-cost educational materials or brochures may be available from the state, from trade organizations, or from recycling-oriented businesses. However, you will probably need to pay for some materials. It is particularly important to be sure that you have enough to cover basic information materials such as a recycling brochure or a door hanger.

Recruit volunteers

Volunteers can be extremely helpful in getting the message out about your recycling program. In many cases the Recycling Advisory Council can serve as a core for volunteer recruitment. Volunteers can help prepare materials, can staff events, can speak to school and civic groups, and can go door to door to explain the recycling program to their neighbors. Remember that any message is strengthened by being delivered by someone known and respected in the community.

Buy Recycled Campaigns

Marketing materials is a constant challenge for most recycling programs. Prices of materials fluctuate, and occasionally the market for a particular material will entirely disappear for a time. The public should constantly be reminded that merely segregating materials for special collection is not recycling. Materials are not recycled until they are used to make products for which there is a market.

Individual consumers, businesses, and local governments can all help by making a conscious and consistent effort to buy recycled-content products. Newsprint, printing and copying paper, paper towel and tissue products, glass containers, and aluminum cans all can be purchased with significant recycled content. Plastic containers are recycled and the recovered plastic can be found in a wide array of products: carpet, fiberfill, geotextiles, janitorial products, and curb-side recycling collection bins.

In 1989, American Recycling Market, Inc. published the first *Official Recycled Products Guide*, which lists recycled products suppliers and vendors. If your local government or business plans to buy significant quantities of recycled products or if you will sponsor a "buy recycled" campaign, a subscription may be an excellent investment. The U.S.EPA maintains a Procurement Guideline Hotline which provides information about recycled products that meet the EPA standards for recycled content in paper, oil, retread tires, and insulation products. Many state recycling agencies will assist you in locating sources of recycled products or provide materials to use in educating the public and businesses.

Dealing with Problems

No planning effort is without snags and setbacks, but certain problems can be anticipated. Common problems in recycling follow.

Apathy

Although in many parts of the country solid waste disposal is an immediate and costly problem, in other areas waste disposal costs are still low. Many communities may question the need for recycling if there is not an immediate waste crisis. However, planning is most effective when there is not an immediate crisis.

Realistically, disposal costs and the problems related to disposal are likely to increase. A good recycling planning process will look at both the immediate situation and the future. If present conditions do not warrant major investments in a new recycling program, additional public education and support for existing recycling opportunities may be indicated.

Competing interests

Many parties in the community may already be involved in recycling or interested in becoming involved. Their interests may conflict with each other or with the new recycling plan. Look for ways to include as many as possible in the new program. But be realistic—you may not be able to satisfy everyone. Attempting to do so may result in a poor plan or an ineffective program.

Market problems

Markets for some recycled materials fluctuate. Prices rise and fall. The market for a particular material may disappear. All recycling programs are impacted by markets. The recycling plan must be flexible enough to manage change without crippling the whole operation. If a material which you normally collect cannot be marketed, be honest about this with the public. If you cannot stockpile the material, stop collecting it and try to be clear about the reason.

Siting problems

Public resistance may develop to the siting of recycling facilities. Although the public generally thinks that recycling is preferable to disposal, they may be very concerned about a recycling center in their neighborhood. Many members of the public are not familiar with modern recycling operations. They may picture a junk yard or dump. The recycling plan must thoroughly address concerns about the environmental and economic impact surrounding the location of recycling facilities. The facility must be designed to be clean, safe, and attractive. Landscaping and buffer zones should be included. It may help to take citizens on tours of other recycling plants that meet your community standards.

SUMMARY

The keys to developing a successful community recycling program are careful planning and good public education. The U.S.EPA, a number of state solid waste and recycling agencies, trade associations, and professional organizations can provide information, technical and, in some cases, financial assistance.

Involving all of the interested and affected parties within the community in the recycling planning process will not only help build a good recycling plan, but will help build community support.

Public education and an aggressive recycling promotion effort will be needed to gain public support and participation. The promotion effort should be planned as carefully as the collection and processing components of the recycling program. Promotion activities should include clear information about the recycling program, reasons for recycling, and information about buying recycled-content products.

No program will run perfectly, but careful planning and promotion will build a program the community will point to with pride.

11

Economics, Productivity, Opportunity

Although there has been much discussion of the need to recycle and of what to recycle in the press, no one has given serious thought to the need to operate efficiently.

In fact, two main streams of thought have surfaced in recent years, both of which virtually ignore the question of economics. The first of these has to do with the option of curb-side separation versus comingling. The question discussed in the literature revolves around the problem of which system gets a higher percentage of materials recycled. In other words, if we separate at the curb, do we get more recyclables per ton of waste than if we separate at the transfer station? Obviously, the cost of achieving either is not the central question in this debate.

This is also the case in the second argument, where we are asked if total recycling of everything is possible. This is called *intensive recycling*. It is being tested by New York City in a pilot program to determine its feasibility. Although everyone recognizes that there will be high costs involved, the decisive element in the program is feasibility of the objective rather than the cost. Presumably, if the city can afford it and if it can be done, it will be done.

Now, this approach is not contrary to good business, but nevertheless, at some point efficiency and cost must be considered—*if it is to be good business!* Stated another way: It is feasible and realistic to set goals to achieve both a high rate of recycling and cost effectiveness.

The auto industry offers a good example. Over many years, American automobile quality became increasingly poor because industry had gradually accepted the philosophy that quality and cost efficiency were incompatible: that is, to have high quality would increase the cost of the car. Therefore, to compete with cheaper imports, we loosened our standards. Now we have learned that the cost of rework, maintenance, and customer resentment really made the final car more expensive. *Poor quality costs money.* And that statement is true of all human endeavors. This is the meaning and purpose behind these chapters on management. In its broadest definition, we are saying that sound management principles using defined objectives will achieve optimum goals more fully and efficiently than any other approach. This is the thesis of the book, and it will be explained and illustrated as we proceed.

PRODUCTIVITY TRENDS IN THE UNITED STATES

By the year 2000, according to the Bureau of Labor Statistics, services will constitute over 76 percent of all employment. (See Table 11-1.) And yet, of all human endeavors, services are the least efficient. Because of its magnitude, this inefficiency places an enormous burden upon the economy. By comparison, manufacturing, farming, transportation, and mining, as the other major employers in the economy, are still highly competitive with other industrialized nations, despite much of what we read.

As an example, using Japan for comparison the United States in 1986 had 19.78 million persons employed in manufacturing versus 19.87 million in Japan.

TABLE 11-1   GOODS AND SERVICES—PRODUCING EMPLOYMENT, 1972-2000.

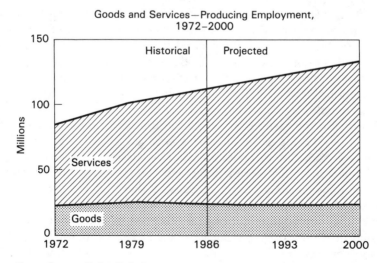

Source: Bureau of Labor Statistics

This is a difference of less than 100,000 workers. But the U.S. population was 241.80 million versus 122.00 million in Japan. Thus, with the same size manufacturing base, the United States is carrying twice the load. Not surprisingly, the per capita income in the United States is $17,528.00 and Japan is $21,820.00.[1]

In plant-by-plant comparisons, in which verification can be made, two of our major manufacturing plants in America, Lincoln Electric and Nucor Steel, are a third again as productive per employee as the same industries in Japan! This doesn't prove that the United States is ahead of Japan in all respects, but it does suggest that much of the difference in per capita income between the two countries can be attributed to other factors—such as services—rather than manufacturing efficiency.

Of all the services, recycling is most like manufacturing because it deals with a defined product, with measurable quantities of production. Some services, like lawyers and doctors, produce intangibles which are less clearly measurable in terms of output. But recycling has the qualities we associate with manufacturing, and it lends itself to the same types of thinking, and therefore, management.

Furthermore, its growth is like that of manufacturing in the magnitude of its impact upon the economy. (See Table 11–2.) Thus, in modern America, at the community level, waste handling has become our third largest expense, falling just behind education and road maintenance. Actually, it may be the largest expense, if we accept an editorial in *The Wall Street Journal* (December 17, 1990). This editorial pointed out that New York City (based on a recently completed cost study) had revised its cost of disposing of waste from $63 per ton to $273! As the editors pointed out, "Recycling is always more expensive than expected."[2]

In fact, almost everything we do has gotten more expensive. Take a look at the facts:

1. Of the 18,000,000 jobs created between 1987 to 1988, 80 percent were not a contribution of high-tech (as we fondly wish to believe) but low-tech services. (Quite contrary to popular beliefs, America is no longer the center for creative leadership. On patent applications, for example, the Japanese are catching up so rapidly—on patents filed *within* America—that they could surpass us by the year 2000!) (See Table 11–3.)

2. Where once productivity meant increased output per hour of labor, today it means more total people employed to produce an increase. Hence, the United States registered annual increases in gross national product in the 1980s because *18,000,000 more workers* were employed to boost output a mere 2.5 percent per year. (The inflation-adjusted figure is 0.7 percent according to the BLS.) (These new workers are really women joining the work force, who are employed almost entirely in services!)

---

[1] Data from: *U.S. Statistical Abstract 1987*, CIA World Fact Book 1988, Japanese Embassy sources. Most figures are for 1986.

[2] *Wall Street Journal*, December 17, 1990, editorial page.

TABLE 11-2 CHANGES IN EMPLOYMENT, 1800-2000.

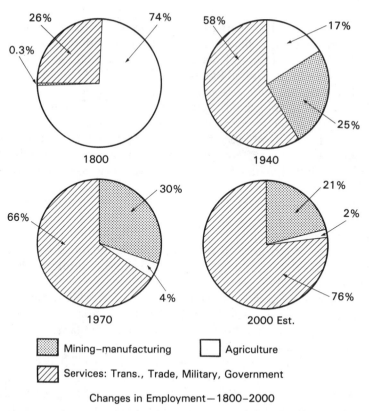

Mining–manufacturing   Agriculture

Services: Trans., Trade, Military, Government

Changes in Employment—1800–2000

TABLE 11-3 THIS GRAPH INDICATES THE TOTAL NUMBER OF PATENTS ISSUED FROM 1930–2000.

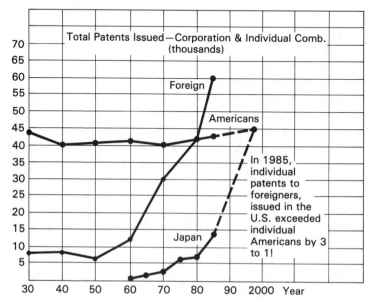

3. Even the number of hours worked is a problem. Americans work 1,904 hours per year (1988), compared to 2,101 for the Japanese. (That's a loss of 10 percent in output, right there!)

4. Both at home and in government, we have become spenders! Thus, in one short seven-year period during the 1980s, we have transformed America from the *world's largest creditor* nation to the *world's largest debtor*! We have literally lost control of the spending process because we have failed to appreciate the need to maintain the pace of productive output. During that decade, total worker output increased about $100 billion *per year*, while personal consumption and federal expenditures increased almost $300 billion!

5. We have taken to living off the future, instead of insisting on balancing our needs by controlling costs. Every dollar of tax increase since 1947, according to Senator William Roth of Delaware, has *triggered $1.58 in new spending*. In 1982, to reduce the deficit, "we got a $100 billion tax hike called the Tax Equity and Fiscal Responsibility Act." According to Stephen Moore writing in the October 1990 issue of *Reason*, the people were promised that these new taxes would be matched with three dollars per dollar in spending cuts. But, in truth, "spending skyrocketed by $200 billion over the next three years."[3]

This drift into freer and freer spending is most severe in the service sector. This need not be the case. To deal with this we can, for example, adopt the lessons learned by other productive sectors.

The farming sector in America has been faced with the same economic and competitive problems as other activities. Despite these deterrents, farm productivity is soaring. Take a look at the figures. From 1800 to 1900, farm employment dropped nearly 50 percent. In this century it has plunged almost 90 percent. Furthermore, this plunge occurred at a time when the total U.S. population was increasing from 5.3 million in 1800 to 220,000,000 in 1980. Farm population in total numbers peaked at 32 million persons (men, women, and children) between the years 1910 and 1935. Then it plunged rapidly, dropping 70 percent in the next 35 years. Since the dawn of the Industrial Revolution in America, farm employment as a percentage of population has declined steadily. The decrease in farm employment and the corresponding release of people to the cities provided the workers needed for the mills and factories.

While a farm worker in 1800 could feed perhaps as few as 1.25 persons, by the 1930s, he or she was feeding 10 people. Forty-five years later one farm worker was feeding a small army of nearly 100, if we include those being fed overseas.

Productivity on the farm increased almost tenfold in a span of 45 years. At the same time, wives and children of farmers have been contributing less of their time to farm chores, and many persons listed as farmers earn a substantial

---

[3] Stephen Moore, *Reason*, October 1990.

portion of their incomes in the city. Furthermore, the trend has been consistent, and farm *productivity has grown steadily each decade.* In fact, farm productivity has progressed more rapidly in our modern day than in the post-revolutionary period. The productive revolution began as a series of discrete and well-documented inventions in the early nineteenth century. It picked up speed in the 1850s with the introduction of imported fertilizers, and since the introduction of the tractor after World War I, it has moved forward rapidly.

The revolution in farming has paralleled and is closely related to the Industrial Revolution that took place in the country. The farms supplied the workers to the plants and industry mechanized the farm so that it could release more workers. Farm growth, however, has been faster. Between 1955 and 1978 alone, farm output increased 520 percent compared to 322 percent for industry.

The U.S. Statistical Abstract for 1979 shows farm output to be doubling approximately every ten years, while industrial output doubles roughly every 24 years. These differences in output-growth can be traced to human creative initiative. Industry and farming are vastly different forms of enterprise. A farm is largely a small operation, with only a handful of employees. It is entrepreneurial by nature. It appeals to people who are annual risk takers and fiercely independent. When they invest money, they have to live with their decisions, affecting entire families and their futures. Those who make wild, unsound decisions go broke. The wise ones succeed and prosper. Hence, the process winnows out the inept and rewards the shrewd and daring. Industry, on the other hand, tends to become bureaucratic. It is dominated by large, stable corporations, employing thousands of employees. It encourages professionalism and conservatism. It lacks the factors that encourage innovation. Boat rockers are discouraged or shunted out of the system, while those who play the game remain. Bad decisions are absorbed by the system.

It is no surprise to find that our top 1,000 companies have shown no growth at all, over the past 15 years. And yet, growth is closely tied to sudden breakthroughs in productivity. These increases in productivity bring lower costs, which result in increased sales and increased employment.

In a bureaucratic organization, there are many social restrictions against progress. There is no death penalty for innovating in America, as there was in Rome, although labor-saving machines are sometimes bombed by unionists. Courts frequently are called on to interfere with and restrict the pace of change within crafts. Firemen on the railroads were employed as required by law for 50 years after the position was eliminated (by replacing the coal-fired locomotive with the diesel). Nuclear energy plant construction and operation is fought in the courts, the press, and the legislatures, creating massive cost overruns. Today, the United States is behind many countries in Europe, such as France, in the use of nuclear power. We are like England which once led the world in the use of water power and steam, to drive its industrial plants. Both Germany and America skipped ahead by adopting more efficient systems of power, such as direct-drive electric motors, and they neatly by-passed England in productivity by World War II. The English bureaucracy clung to belt-driven machines 40 years after America had discarded them.

Despite these obstacles, which all societies face, innovation and entrepreneurship in America today is still the single most powerful driving force for progress that we have. No rules, no government incentives, no political speeches could produce the results that the country is witnessing decade after decade. The facts speak for themselves: America is literally being supported on the backs of a few entrepreneurs. There are enough incentives left in the tired, old, free-enterprise system to attract the ambitious, who would rather set out on their own than pay homage to the "golden handcuffs" of modern society. (In Jefferson's day, even the government had no pensions or benefits.)[4]

Thus, despite the small percentage, the actual number of freewheeling innovators in America (and the world) is still enough to keep priming the pump, and their accomplishments are breathtaking. For example, just since World War II, these entrepreneurs have founded businesses that have achieved net values of more than $500 billion, totaling over six times the net worth of all the giant corporations combined.

In the past decade and a half, as we saw, the Fortune top 1,000 firms have had virtually no growth in employment. The value of ownership has declined 25 percent. By contrast, small, newly organized firms have created over 10,000,000 new jobs during this period, and have provided more than 80 percent of the job openings for minorities. Eighty percent of the minority workers are on the payroll of small firms. The Small Business Administration estimates that between November 1982 and July 1984, 70 percent of all new jobs were created by businesses with less than 500 employees.

Of importance to us in recycling is the point made by Burton Klein in the book *Dynamic Economics.* He shows that new developments seldom emerge from large firms. Even when an idea originates within a large corporation, the new invention is seldom launched there but is launched by either a small business or a breakaway engineer. His examples include the transistor and photovoltaic cells (developed by Bell Labs). Klein based his conclusions on a study of 50 major breakthroughs in the past 80 years.

Farm Journal magazine stated once that as much as 80 percent of new farm machinery originated on the farm. The invention is then either manufactured by the inventor (Hesston farm machinery, for example) or sold to a large farm machinery manufacturer (such as the floating hay rake, invented by a farmer in the Midwest). These breakthroughs continue to occur in the field even when firms like John Deere build $50,000,000 development centers (in Moline in the 1960s), and General Motors has its own research and development center and internationally-known training schools.

---

[4] If we include all persons subject to special pensions, bonuses, insurance, and medical and dental programs—security provided from the cradle to the grave, a la feudal manor—close to 80 percent of all of society is under the umbrella.

Thus, we see that the fields dominated by the great corporations are the old markets and routine products. These are areas where efficiency is achieved through repetitive mass production, in which incremental improvements alone are made.

Because real opportunity lies in the untapped and developing areas, recycling and waste management may be one of the greatest opportunities for the coming generations. It also means enormous opportunities for creative talent and leadership. And creative genius *is not limited* to race, creed, or elitism. Opportunity goes to the inspired and ambitious!

For the truth is that for the best, most original minds, there are no limits. Hard work and initiative are the real human resources. These are, and always have been, the sources of wealth in any country.

The extent of these opportunities shows up in our own economic mobility. Sociological studies show, for example, that in the 1980s, only one third of the rich males in America had inherited their wealth. Two thirds of the rich became wealthy on their own!

Wealth in this country is highly mobile. Every generation, two thirds of those in the bottom strata move up, and a like percentage move down. The poor pass the wealthy as they go by. It cannot be said often enough that *the real wealth in a country is its people.* Those countries with the richest minerals often have the poorest people. Because of its lack of natural resources and land, Japan should be poor, but it is one of the richest nations today.

Modern studies indicate that the creative fire never dies out, provided that it is continually fed by the promise of success and the eternal need to be recognized or appreciated.

Furthermore, in studies made of a wide range of geniuses, it has been found that education does not necessarily increase creativity. Naturally, creative leaders have to have enough understanding of their fields to master the areas in which they are operating, but many driven men or women are self-taught and become intolerant of the pace and restrictions imposed at the college level. This impatience to get going may explain why the third year of college is the typical grade completed by a wide range of outstanding scientists and entrepreneurs who have become quite wealthy. Einstein and Edison were both school dropouts.

A similar finding applies to the field of management itself. In *Myth of the Well-Educated Manager,* J. Sterling Livingston, writing in the *Harvard Business Review* (J/F1971) discusses studies made of Harvard Business School graduates fifteen years or more after graduation. He made the following observations:

> How effectively a manager will perform on the job cannot be predicted by the number of degrees he holds, the grades he receives in school, or the formal management education programs he attends. Academic achievement is not a valid yardstick to use on measuring managerial potential. Indeed, if academic achievement is equated with success in business, the well-educated manager is a myth.

> Managers are not taught in formal education programs what they need to know to build successful careers in management. Unless they acquire through their own

experiences the knowledge and skills that are vital to their effectiveness, they are not likely to advance far up the organizational ladder.

. . . much management education is, in fact, misdirection because it arrests or distorts the ability of managerial aspirants to grow as they gain experience.[5]

Most revealing "is the finding that men who attend Harvard's Advanced Management Program (AMP) after having had approximately 15 years of business experience, but who for the most part have had no formal education in management, earn almost a third more, on the average, than men who hold MBA degrees from Harvard and other leading business schools."[6]

None of these studies denies the value of education. Rather, at least to me, they emphasize the fact that ability to use the mind is an innate talent, waiting to be cultivated. As soon as the mind reaches the point that it understands how to proceed, the innovators and go-getters break out of the mold, drop out of the education process, and scramble to get going.

In my own observations and direct operating experiences in recycling, I have felt that the field is wide open—that we haven't even begun to tap the potential that this subject offers.

Because there are nearly 65,000 communities each getting into recycling in its own way, we have all the incubating characteristics of the small farm, with its unlimited potential for innovation and creativity. And on the other hand, we have the standardized flow characteristics of a production shop, without all the restrictions and hidebound attitudes which have come to engross so much of manufacturing.

Seen in still another light, what I am saying is that no other area of American economic activity offers so much challenge and so much opportunity for accomplishment. Here we have a virgin, untested situation that has no hidebound rules, other than the fact that the country is groping for solutions.

Thus, it is absolutely true that waste is our fastest growing resource. It is also our fastest growing opportunity!

---

[5] J. Sterling Livingston, "Myth of the Well-Educated Manager," *Harvard Business Review,* Cambridge, MA, Jan./Feb. 1971, pp. 67 ff.

[6] Ibid., p. 69.

12

Methods Engineering: How the Work Should Be Done!

As we have seen, we will soon have 65,000 communities grappling with the problem of recycling. Unfortunately, most of them will be so preoccupied with just getting the job done that little attention will be given to the most important need of all: doing it economically. (If it is not economical, it will be difficult to maintain over time.) Hence, this chapter is concerned with the processes of designing economical systems.

Because these principles first surfaced in manufacturing, we can see how effective they are by citing a few examples. It is surprising to note how certain basic ideas of management repeat themselves, showing that certain principles remain valid and unchanged. But still, they have to be relearned with each generation.

THE EVOLUTION OF THE CONCEPT OF PRODUCTIVITY

Both the Egyptians and the Sumerians as early as 5,000 years ago were using what we proudly call "modern management techniques," probably because they were as logical then as we are now.

Both as a percentage of the gross national product (GNP) and in terms of actual numbers of people employed, the Pyramid of Cheops built at the dawn of civilization completely dwarfs the projects of modern man. The huge blocks of limestone or granite used in the pyramid weighed up to 350 tons. They were quarried at Tura, on the east bank of the Nile, and then were floated downstream to Gizah above Cairo, where they were then dragged up a ramp to the plateau 100 feet above the river. The Greek historian Herodotus tells us that 100,000 men were employed continuously for ten years just in the quarrying operation. The architects and overseers who planned and supervised the project had to learn to control and coordinate this vast army of workers and to solve the mechanical problems of lifting the heavy blocks into position. The only tools available were wood, stone, and manpower, since the use of metal in Egypt trailed that of Sumeria by a thousand years and then was limited to dagger points and ornamentation.

The accuracy of the Egyptian calendar is well known, rivaling that of our modern system for recording the passage of the years; but the accuracy of the pyramids themselves is an even greater marvel of human accomplishment. The base of the Great Pyramid measures approximately 775.75 feet on each side, with a deviation of less than one inch on each of the sides. The monument was planned to scale in advance, and extant mathematical texts confirm the calculations and planning that preceded the construction of the pyramids.

At the same time that the Egyptians were developing rudimentary tools of management, the Sumerians in the Fertile Crescent were establishing independent systems of their own. The early Sumerian texts are better preserved than those of the Egyptians because they were impressed on clay tablets (cuneiform), as compared to the less durable papyrus of the Egyptians.

In Sumeria, standardized weights and measures evolved early to facilitate commerce. One of the oldest-known legal texts, the Code of Hammurabi (ca. 1800 B.C.), is largely devoted to commercial regulations. Without a standard system of weights and measures which could be applied throughout the Fertile Crescent, large-scale manufacturing and trade would have been impossible.

The earliest record we have of writing is found in the first Ziggurat of Erech, in Sumeria, built about 3000 B.C. There can be no doubt that many of the essential needs of modern production techniques were being described by these tablets.

Combined with the techniques for handling large masses of labor and its concomitant logistics, the total Sumerian system presented a fairly respectable body of knowledge. In fact, it was to be another 5,000 years before humankind advanced its control over production again.

This advance came in the field of accounting.

Very little advance occurred in accounting until about 1340, when the concept of double-entry bookkeeping was introduced, first into banking and later into the records of the arsenal of Venice. The arsenal, which covered 60 acres of territory, produced the ships that made Venice the most powerful maritime city-state in the Mediterranean.

The bookkeeping system developed at the arsenal recognized the familiar types of expenses: namely, fixed, variable, and extraordinary. By the middle of the fifteenth century, separate bookkeepers were hired to maintain the records, and separate journals and ledgers were posted. An early form of cost accounting was used.

The arsenal also practiced the policy of numbering and warehousing finished parts; it operated assembly lines, had personnel procedures, and practiced standardization of parts and inventory control. To accomplish a flow-type production, the various parts used in the ships' rigging and in artillery were stored in warehouses along both sides of a channel. All parts were numbered and stocked in designated bins. As the hulls of the galleys were towed past the open warehouse windows, the various parts were handed out, in proper sequence, to fill the needs of the assemblers. Through such methods, it was possible to complete "ten galleys, fully armed, between the hours of three and nine," according to one visitor from Spain. Detailed cost studies were common, and one report showed that it cost three times as much to find a log as the log was worth. The study resulted in setting up a separate lumberyard, in which the material could be stored in an orderly manner, to avoid searching through a random pile. The degree to which standardization was used and appreciated is shown by a directive that required that all sternposts be built to a single design in such a manner that they could all use a common rudder, which was to be built and stocked in advance. Design changes had to be approved by the general manager. Depending on the job, workers were paid either by piecework or on a day rate.

Throughout history, there has been a recognized relationship between time and output. Scheduling and planning of work require some means of measurement. Maintaining human productivity has meant using a whip or establishing hourly quotas on output. The Egyptians and the Sumerians recognized this in project planning and in running the early textile factories in Babylonia. The length of the day offered a crude method of measurement, but the day varied in length and provided less control than an hourly record. Hence, once the clock was invented, the means for evaluating effort was vastly improved. The invention of the time-study watch further improved the ability to measure because activity could now be measured in fractions of a minute. It is no accident that the modern pioneers of scientific management were interested in both time study and scheduling. They learned it from the past.

THE MODERN MANAGEMENT PIONEERS

Advances came rapidly with the close of the Middle Ages. Large factories began to evolve. The gun factories of France and Sweden were the first large industries of Europe. In preparation for its defenses against the Ottomans, Austria in 1404 built the first giant cannon on record. It had a barrel nearly 12 feet long. Forty-nine years later, Mehmet II, for the siege of Constantinople, had a cannon built that measured 26 feet in length. Its trajectory was more than a mile, and the missile buried itself six feet in the ground upon impact. The Sultan was delighted and ordered another cannon twice as large.

Factories and public demand expanded rapidly in the next four centuries and brought about the need for better management and higher productivity, giving rise by the end of the nineteenth century to a group of consultants, preaching the principles of "scientific management." The techniques devised by these pioneers have become as commonplace to industry everywhere as the bikini is to the beach. The three best-known names in this group are Frederick W. Taylor, Henry L. Gantt, and Frank B. Gilbreth. All of them have much to say that applies to recycling.

Frederick Taylor (1856–1915)

Taylor's background included work as a production manager, an executive, and a consultant. He was one of the first to make use of time study in measuring output and to replace trial and error in decision making with more formal approaches. At the time, his thoughts were considered radical and in 1911 Congress appointed a committee to study them and other systems of management. He presented a number of papers and arguments on behalf of the use of time study.

Taylor's emphasis was on the use of improved methods as a way to increase production, although he also added the spur to speed up the individual. In one comment, he mentioned that only a few could maintain the pace he set for steel handlers at Bethlehem Steel, and that most that tried fell by the wayside and took other jobs. In time study, we must distinguish between increased productivity due to a "speed-up" as opposed to increased output due to the use of better methods. The speed-up comes about through inept or ruthless management practices. It begins by paying labor an incentive for each piece produced. As the workers learn to produce more and gain increases in pay, management reduces the amount of the bonuses so that the workers have to work harder and harder to make the same pay. This practice used widely in Taylor's day produced so much bitterness in the labor movement that for many years time-study engineers were not allowed in some companies or the government.

A related problem for Taylor was that his studies resulted in people losing their jobs because of increased productivity. This is a continuing problem for industry, one that goes with the introduction of automation. Walter P. Reuther, head of the C.I.O. in the 1950s, was given a tour of the Ford plant and was shown new automatic machinery. His guide asked him, "How will you get these machines to join your union?" The answer by Reuther was, "How will you sell them Fords [if you have no workers to buy them]?" Fortunately, for the workers, increased productivity ultimately means lower costs and increased sales, so that efficient industries tend to expand. We saw this earlier in the last chapter when we showed that efficient businesses are the real source of new jobs.

Unfortunately, the limits of human capability are still misunderstood or misinterpreted by those in charge. Some firms still overload the worker, in the belief that it is the foreman's job to get out more work.

Henry Gantt (1861–1919)

Henry Gantt was for many years a close associate of Taylor, and later, he too, went into consulting. Gantt's approach differed from Taylor's somewhat insensitive attitude by placing greater stress on the person doing the job. He felt that the attitude of the individuals and their motivation were as important to productivity as skills and knowledge of the job. (Modern studies show that any typical worker can add 30 percent to his or her output by increased effort over a short interval, but methods improvements can multiply output by 20 or more times.)

Gantt also emphasized the common interests of employer and employee, a view that is widespread today. In a paper presented to the American Society of Mechanical Engineers in 1908, he developed the philosophy that "to teach and to lead" would eventually replace the current trend toward "driving" the worker, as a way of management.

The first chapter of his book *Organizing for Work*, published in 1919, emphasized the responsibility of industry to the community. The community needs service first, he said, regardless of who gets the profits. The business system had its beginnings in the service it rendered, and its sole reason for existence, as far as the community is concerned, is for the service it renders. Profits must therefore only be in relation to the quality of its service. Any reward that business takes in excess of the services rendered is therefore an "exercise of autocratic power." He emphasized that disputes on the division of profits between labor and management should not be permitted to work against the community. He seemed to fear the nationalization of industry, for he emphasized the need for social responsibility. Failure to accept these responsibilities, he suggested, would lead the community to attempt to take over.

Gantt's de-emphasis on profits, with its corresponding shift toward service as the raison d'être of industry, heralded a trend that has become one of the mainstays of modern management theory taught today.

Despite Gantt's strong humanitarian tendencies, he is best remembered for his work in production control. Gantt developed a graphic method for portraying production schedules, which today bears his name, the Gantt chart. A typical use for the Gantt chart is to schedule jobs and people. Time is portrayed across the top. Individual jobs are depicted graphically. People assigned are on the left. The time required (see Table 12–1) to do the job is indicated by a bar.

Frank B. Gilbreth (1868–1924)

Frank Gilbreth is the third important pioneer to contribute to management thought. Like Gantt, Gilbreth placed heavy emphasis on the human element in productivity. Gilbreth had an enormous capacity for detail, as demonstrated in the novel *Cheaper by the Dozen*, written by members of his family. The result of his interests in productivity was the development of motion study as a basic management technique.

Gilbreth was no longer concerned solely with macromeasurements of the time needed to complete a task, but rather he emphasized the importance of detailed measurements, such as the movement of a finger. His work was the forerunner of the motion-study systems such as Methods-Time-Measurement (MTM) and others which could set time standards from a book of tables without

TABLE 12-1 GANTT CHART WORK SCHEDULE FOR THE WEEK

Shift day	Monday	Tuesday	Wednesday	Thursday	Friday
Line bins			Holiday		
Glass 1 Brown 2 Green	Mary	John		Mary	John
3 Clear Paper 4 News	John	Mary		John	Mary
5 Corrugated 6 Office	Bill	Helen		Bill	Helen
Plastic 7 2 Liter 8 Cartons	Helen	(Bill off today) Mark		Helen	Bill
Open 9 10		No operation			
11 Waste		No operator needed			

the use of a stopwatch. Because to do so meant that the method employed by the worker had to be clearly in the mind of the time-setter, Gilbreth came to recognize and emphasize what he called the "one best way." He pointed out that from the standpoint of motion study, fatigue, and skill, the cavemen did a better job of designing tools than we do today because, he said, "The tool designers of today have not actually had these tools in their hands and examined them from the standpoint of the laws of motion study, fatigue study, and standardization."[1] (Compare this to earlier remarks made in the last chapter on the dangers of overeducating creative people.)

In his pamphlet *Science in Management for the One Best Way to Do Work,* presented in Milan in 1923, he pointed out that progress in management has been largely by the "drifting process." He said this process never has produced the best results. What is needed is a program of measurement, one that will preserve and evaluate each step along the way, so that improvement can be planned. We are in an "age of measurement."

His concern for humanity is revealed in a comment he made regarding the early drawings on the Assyrian, Babylonian, and Egyptian monuments. He said these drawings show the division of labor and a recognition of the importance of rhythm as a means of efficiency. They also show the ancient concept of the gang boss and his method for achieving output. The boss is depicted with a large club and two long daggers. "The large club is poised in the air in the right hand, and one long dagger in the left, and the second dagger is always so

---

[1] p. 9

located and positioned that it can be grasped with the shortest and quickest motions."[2]

Gilbreth strongly objected to the "secret time study," which was resented by the worker. He regarded it as valueless unless the worker was willing to cooperate. Gilbreth was far more interested in motion study than time study. How long it takes to do a job is less important than how the job is done. A man can only work so fast, but he can always work "smarter."

Finally, he emphasized that the "science of management" is an underlying principle, that it applies equally to all activities, from sports to management, and that there is always a "best way" of doing anything.

Many of Gilbreth's ideas can be applied to any form of production.

As we saw, as early as the Sumerians and Egyptians, people had begun to associate time with output. If we knew a man could produce 100 bricks an hour, and we needed 800 bricks, we needed a worker for eight hours. This was known and used by the Egyptians. What Taylor, Gantt, and Gilbreth did was to bring these ideas into the modern perspective, using more accurate times and actual clock measurements of production. But they also went a step further. They picked up on a point that the ancients may have overlooked or never sensed: namely—and this is very important because it is the key to breakthroughs in production!—*that changing the method you use to do a job can greatly change the time it takes to do it!*

We will now see how this *revolutionary* new idea made so much difference to the modern world. Again, we will show that some of the most obvious ideas in the world, such as the "one best way" of Gilbreth, passed right in front of people's eyes for 5,000 years before they spotted it. As we proceed, keep in mind the arsenal of Venice.

ORIGIN AND FULFILLMENT OF THE IDEA
OF MASS PRODUCTION

Frederick Taylor and Henry Ford were contemporaries. Both men were interested in the concept that productivity could be increased by making certain changes in the way work was done. (This process, when formalized, is called *methods engineering, work simplification,* or *methods improvement.*)

Ford made use of the term *mass production* in the title of an article ghost-written for him for the thirteenth edition of the *Encyclopaedia Britannica* in 1926. Mass production meant not only producing items en masse, but also producing them for the masses. Ford did both by lowering the price of his car so that all might buy, and producing enough to supply many buyers. This sense of productivity is a concept that directly concerns us here.

Along with cutting prices by almost 60 percent between 1908 and 1916 (and despite wartime inflation), Ford introduced the $5.00 eight-hour day in

---

[2] p. 5

1914. Before long, you could buy his car or a "Big Wheel" bicycle from Pope Manufacturing in England for about the same price.

Ford achieved productivity increases in two ways: First, he applied the principle that parts produced in large, repetitive quantities can be produced at great savings; and second, that assembly-line production, using belts and chains to move the pieces to the assembler, would also produce dramatic savings. In other words, the first step was to produce large quantities of identical parts, and the second was to move them automatically to the assemblers.

The first assembly lines began appearing at Ford in the spring of 1913. At that time, the use of individual workbenches, in which each worker assembled a complete magneto-flywheel, was replaced by a moving line of parts, in which each laborer carried out a single function of the assembly. The experiment produced savings which were so dramatic that within a year, virtually every assembly operation in the company had been switched over to a moving line. Power-driven belts and chains soon replaced manual slides to further speed up the operation and to establish a fixed pace of performance. The effect on production was even more dramatic than before. The effect on observers was also dramatic or, more precisely, traumatic. The lines were condemned publicly by the press. The outcry caught the attention of Charlie Chaplin, who made a movie in 1936 ("Modern Times") condemning mass assembly lines as the road to insanity.

The assembly line at Ford is of specific interest because it represents a continuation and extension of the idea of volume part production. Ford himself emphasized that assembly-line production depended on and could only be accomplished by the ability to produce parts with such exactitude that rework and refinishing were eliminated in the assembly department. To take time to fit parts manually at assembly would have precluded any form of mass assembly. Assembly operation would have been reduced to the domain of the skilled practitioner and would have been quite time consuming. Assembly would have been a continuation of parts manufacturing. And this, of course, was the very thing that had to be avoided for the Ford system to succeed.

Accordingly, Ford put great emphasis on precision manufacturing, specialized machine tools, and highly precise gauging systems, so that parts would be complete and totally interchangeable before they reached assembly. At the same time, manufacturing of such parts had to be economical—more economical, in fact, than noninterchangeable parts. We will come back to this point because it represents an important breakthrough.

When Ford first set up operations he was convinced that mass part production meant less cost. He indoctrinated his people with this belief, and he was so dedicated to this ideology that he soon had collected together the greatest cadre of cost-reduction engineers in the world. Compared to his competitors, Ford's costs plummeted, and he soon had more than 50 percent of the market. He made enormous profits as well.

His approach, however, was not strictly along the lines of the teachings of Frederick W. Taylor. Although Ford had a time-study department, the bulk of his gains did not come from getting more effort out of the worker (although the pace of the assembly line had this effect), but from technological innovation. Time study at Ford was used primarily for planning and scheduling. By and large, Ford relied on innovation, such as replacing castings which required extensive machining with stampings, or by building machines with multiple spindles to do several operations at once. His work was really closer to that of Frank B. Gilbreth, another contemporary, who stressed that time study could, at best, accomplish only limited increases in output. Gilbreth, as we saw earlier, pointed out that a person could work only so fast, and maintain a certain pace; further increases in output could come only from a change in the method of manufacture or redesign of the part. The latter approach, he argued, could accomplish unlimited increases in output. This proposition is exactly what Ford found to be true. After experimentation, Ford found that in some cases, he had to slow down the assembly-line conveyors because the pace was too much for the workers to maintain. Workers had limits. He could redesign the part or the assembly procedure, however, and easily double or triple production. His actual increases, in some cases, were tenfold.

Inherent in the idea of mass production is the old concept, dating back to the classical Greeks, of the benefits from the division of labor. But the Greek philosophers' appreciation of these benefits resulted from a recognition that crafts had to be learned, and craftsmanship provided benefits in both quality and economy of output. In no case did the classicists advocate reducing the skill of the craft to such simplicity and standardization that the need for craftsmen was totally eliminated, so that they could be replaced by unskilled labor. This is exactly what Ford accomplished. Ford used his highly creative technicians to replace the journeyman with the untrained worker. He broke the job down into simple steps that anyone could do.

Several principles can be derived from these illustrations taken from history.

1. The first principle is the association of production with time.
2. The second principle is that these production figures can be used to establish norms by which we can set output levels for workers. In the same way, these figures can be used to relate work load to manpower levels. Given the workload, for example, we can determine how many people we need, if we have time standards. These standards play another role. When Ford set up his assembly lines, he broke the magneto-flywheel assembly into several steps, assigning one step to each worker on the line. But, in assembly work, the amount of work per person is seldom equal. Ford found this to be true. Some persons worked so hard they couldn't keep up. Others had very little to do. To correct this problem, therefore, Ford had to do what we now call *assembly-line balancing,* to even out the workload. This is done by rearranging the specific jobs.

   This type of problem also exists in recycling. At the transfer station, the workload for each bin is a function of the mix of waste dumped on the conveyor. If one of your employees cannot handle the workload, you will have to slow down the conveyor to fit this worker's pace, and everyone else will be loafing. If you can figure out a way to balance the load, you can speed up the conveyor, and everyone works at a reasonable, acceptable pace. Speeding up the conveyor is not intended to speed up the people, but to arrive at a fair pace for everyone.

Balancing the system may mean redesigning the width of the bunkers, adding some handier drops at the bunkers, or rearranging the sequence in which the bunkers are used. Instead of three glass bunkers in a row, for example, the best solution may be to split them up, handling cans and glass at one station, and paper and glass at another.

This process of analysis is what we mean by *methods engineering*.

3. A third principle is that quality is higher and productivity better when the task is kept simple and the operator is able to establish a routine. A boring routine can be broken up by shifting the employee to different tasks at regular intervals, but this must be done carefully. If you've ever driven in England, where they drive on the other (wrong?) side of the road from us, you are aware of the dangers this poses when you may be called upon to react in an emergency. You tend to revert to the American way, which can cause a catastrophe!

4. The most important principle of all is that the productivity breakthrough began as an idea. Ford tested his conveyor in one simple example first. It was so unexpectedly successful that he installed the system everywhere it could be used. But the steps leading up to his conveyor system took a great deal of planning and study.

METHODS ENGINEERING

There are a number of excellent books on both methods engineering and time study. The best approach is to take a concentrated course on the subject, such as those offered by the H. B. Maynard Co. in Pittsburgh. The Maynard books on the subject are considered to be classics. (He knew the Gilbreths and most of the pioneers we mentioned.)

A good methods engineer was expected to save a company $100,000 a year 20 years ago! In recycling, methods engineers should be able to earn their salary many times over every year. From my experience in being around methods engineers, a good one can probably cut the costs of recycling in half within a decade, making the same type of improvements in efficiency that Ford did. If we have 65,000 recycling communities by the end of this decade, we should have at least quite a few trained methods engineers on hand by 2000 A.D. to tackle the problem. Then we will see some real improvements. Then recycling will no longer be an obligation, but it will become an asset. Instead of shying away from an onerous, unprofitable task, it will be a competitive, sought after plum. This assumption is not ungrounded. Even today, Japan *buys* our wastepaper, converts it into boxes, and sells it back to us!

To help you get started, I will outline a few of the key concepts or principles taught in a methods engineering course. Like the self-taught physician, however, you should be aware of the limitations this approach imposes. Reading a book on open-heart surgery, no matter how clearly written and explicit, is not quite equal to working with trained surgeons.

Key Concepts of Methods Engineering

1. **Work with both hands.** Do not use one hand as a holding fixture, while the other performs work. This fundamental concept is often overlooked. Too often we see workers holding a part in the left hand, while assembling with the right. A simple holding fixture often permits assembling with both the left and right hands. This way we finish two assemblies in the time it took to do one!

2. **Keep everything handy and organized.** Keep the reach distances short. Have drop chutes in convenient locations to avoid awkward reaching and fatigue. Workplace layout is a fundamental area for great improvements in productivity. Some hospitals today use methods engineers to train people who have had heart attacks to lay out their kitchens to reduce the number of unnecessary steps they take. Most people are unaware of the inefficiency of their kitchens. They are unaware of the extra work they do every day because of poor planning.

Take a look at Figure 12–1, for example. This is an actual sketch of my kitchen at home. Before you read further, study the figure and see if you can rearrange the utensils and items for greater efficiency. *This is methods engineering.*

Here are some clues (you probably spotted many other possibilities for improvement).

1. Why are the light bulbs next to the table? We don't eat them or use them at the table! Even switching them with the placemats would reduce the steps taken to set the table!

2. Why is the radio closer to the table than the toaster?

3. Why are the cookbooks stored next to the table? When we're eating we don't use the cookbooks. They are used mostly in the vicinity of the stove, refrigerator, or food bins.

4. If the coffeemaker is near the table, why is the coffee can stored at the other end of the cupboard?

5. And so on, and so on. Get the idea?

There is an almost unlimited opportunity in this simple example for enormous reductions in wasted movement. These improvements don't amount to much, when only three meals are eaten each day, but when they involve the handling of the same items thousands of times, a second saved per item can be significant.

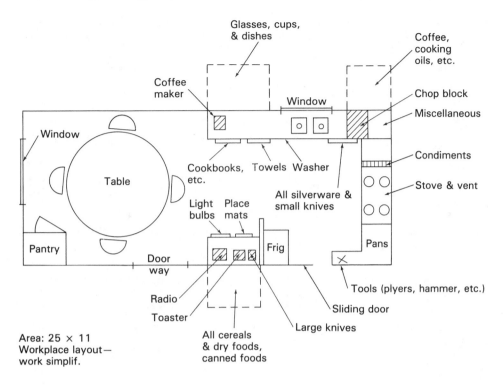

Figure 12-1 Layout of a typical kitchen.

Think of the curb-side pick-up truck that picks up trash at 480 stops each day. The city or contractor may have ten of these trucks out at one time, making up to 5,000 pick-ups a day!

Think of five to six sorters working the conveyor line at a transfer station, and the number of repeat motions each makes *every* minute![3]

Think of how time saved at the curb may increase time at the transfer station, or vice versa.

---

[3] For a community with 100,000 residents, 100,000 plastic bottles are generated each day. These then pass down the SMURF (such as at Turtle Plastics). When the operator removes the bottle, he or she raises it above the rail along the side of the conveyor and moves it to the drop chute fourteen inches away. He does this 100,000 times per day! If we study this motion, and move the chute closer to the conveyor, and reduce the height of the rail, we can save $1/10$ of a second every time. Thus, we are saving 10,000 seconds, or three hours, of time each day per operator. At five operators, we can reduce our staff needs by 40%.

Even the conveyor's width is important: Most MRFs are three to four feet wide. Each operator has to extend himself to reach bottles all over the belt. A two-foot wide belt would save hours of time each day, as well as much *backache!* This is Methods Engineering: Working not harder, but *smarter.*

The opportunities are unlimited. The problem is engrossing and challenging. Indeed, we can cut our costs and improve our operation. All we need is to understand the challenge.

This leads to another important point: In either setting time standards, or making a methods engineering study, it is a fundamental requirement that the engineers be *completely* versed with the operation. They should preferably do the job for a few days so they can function with authority.

Time Study

A proper time study requires detailed knowledge of the job. The first step is to list all of the major elements of the job. Then these are timed over several cycles, perhaps for an hour or longer, so as to achieve a meaningful average.

Since each person works at his or her own pace, the time-study engineer has to evaluate the person under study to determine whether the operator was fairly representative. A fast worker, for example, would be an unfair example to use in establishing a standard for all workers. Hence, times have to be adjusted to fit a norm. This leveling or evaluating of a worker's speed requires a concept known as pace-rating. Pace-rating is an art and it requires proper training to be fair and accurate. There are films available for this purpose, which provide a basis for comparing workers against an accepted norm.

Work Sampling

Perhaps no method used by methods engineers is of more value to the study of recycling than work sampling. Time study is a limited approach in that it consists in studying a single individual or a single type of work. But in recycling the variety of duties is enormous, and a more comprehensive method is often needed. For example, a method that can look at the broad picture and come up with a quick evaluation of the operation is required.

This we can do with work sampling. In fact, the friend who offered to rearrange my kitchen was the first person I knew to actually apply industrial engineering techniques to waste-collection operations. The method he used was *work sampling.* The work was done 20 years ago for a garbage-collection system in the Quad Cities.

Work sampling has been around since the 1950s. Until that time, an accurate picture of worker utilization required an all-day time study with a stopwatch. In addition, a realistic picture meant that the study had to be extended over days or months to get true variation in jobs. Otherwise, the observer might watch the operation during a period in which the worker spent a whole week on one activity. The observer was also limited in the number of people or pieces of equipment that could be observed and recorded accurately. The sum total of these conditions meant that good utilization figures were expensive and few companies had them.

The method of work sampling permits an observer to determine utilization figures at a fraction of the cost, and with any degree of accuracy desired. Work sampling (once called *ratio delay*) operates by the same rules as quality control for sampling inspection.

In watching a person (or piece of equipment) at work, it seems reasonable that one observation each minute during the day would produce about the same answer as an all-day study with a stopwatch. If one-minute intervals will work, why not five-minute intervals, or why not hourly? This is essentially the concept of sampling. Through the use of statistics, it is possible to determine the relationship of the interval to accuracy.

Statistics state the interval-accuracy relationship in three ways. To achieve accuracy, we must make a stipulated number of observations (determined by formula). These observations must be made at random intervals, rather than periodic, and the observations must be instantaneous. Suppose we know (from the formula) how many observations we are going to make. Observations should be made at random because people are creatures of habit: We take our coffee breaks at the same time each day; we take personal time at the same time, and so on. Hence, without care in selecting the observation times we may find the worker on personal time (or the equipment idle) every time we look. Even arbitrarily making the observations at different times during the day introduces a bias in the answer. Unconsciously, if we suspect Joe of being idle from 8:30 to 9:30, we may, without knowing it, concentrate our observations on this period of the day. In addition, the observation must be instantaneous. The observation is made for the purpose of seeing what activity is in progress at the time it is made. If observed too long, the activity may change. Hence, the observation should be made as if a photograph were taken. We are interested in what happened in the photograph, not what happened before or after it was taken.

Steps in a Work-Sampling Study

1. Determine what you are going to study. You may be interested only in employee utilization; you may want to study individual people, or you may want to get a broad picture of the whole operation. (The beauty of work sampling is that a single engineer can study the whole recycling operation for a city the size of Emporia, Kansas.)

2. Break the study into elements like you do for a time study. If you decide to study handling equipment or pick-up crews, you may be interested only in the ratio of nonproductive time to productive time, or you may want a detailed breakdown on nonproductive time. (For an example, see Table 12–2.) If you study the people in your office, you may want to know what percent of Joe's time is spent on paperwork; on the telephone; in the shop; talking to supervisors, subordinates, peers; on personal time; and so on. C. L. Brisley once made such a study of top executives in business. His study pinpointed a number of weaknesses in a person's daily routine. Some spent too much time reading. Some spent too much time with subordinates, suggesting a failure to delegate duties and responsibility. Others worked long hours overtime, and so on.

TABLE 12-2 WORK SAMPLING OBSERVATION SHEET

Crew	On Pick-up	Delay No Mat'l.	Return to Yard	Unloading at Yard	Going to Location	On Break	Personal Time	No. Oper.	Total
#1	𝟋𝟋 𝟋𝟋 ////	///	/					//	20
#2	𝟋𝟋 𝟋𝟋 //	////	/	/		/		/	20
#3	𝟋𝟋 𝟋𝟋 𝟋𝟋 /	//	/			/			20
Average	70%	15%	5%	1.3%	1.3%	1.3%	0	5%	100%

Note: The working element is 70%

3. Determine the number of observations that must be made. To do this requires that you must state the accuracy you want in your study, and you must estimate the percentage of the element closest to 50 percent.

   The accuracy requirement (or precision interval) is a function of the number of observations. Hence, the greater the accuracy required, the more observations to be made. To match the accuracy of a time study, for example, you will want an error of no more than 5 percent. Hence, if time-study accuracy is desired, the precision interval is 5 percent. For our example, we will use 5 percent. We will match a time study.

   In the second step, we broke the study into several elements. One of these elements will be closer to 50 percent (above or below still counts) than the others. If we are acquainted with what we plan to study, we can probably guess the percent of this element. Let us say, for illustration, that we guess it to be 70 percent; then we have a basis for calculating the number of observations. (This is close to the average percent that most people work.) Actually, this figure of 70 percent is only an approximation. It need not be accurate. An alternative method is to begin the study. Then when you are part way through, you can use the findings to estimate this element percentage. (Refer to Table 12-2.)

   Having determined an acceptable accuracy and the main element percentage (70 percent), we can read the required number of observations from the nomogram, Figure 12-2. The number is 350 (illustrated by the line).

4. The next step is to set up random times for making these observations. To do this, we need to determine the span of time over which the study is to be made. If we are studying the pick-up crews, we will probably want to include time spent on special projects. Hence, our study should last at least a month. This gets an accurate picture of the way in which equipment (or people) are utilized for that month.

   The study then covers 20 working days. We divide 350 by 20 to get the number of observations to be made each day (in this case, 18). These 18 observations must be made at random *each* of the 20 days. To do this we use a random number table (Table 12-3) and relate it to time (Figure 12-3).

Sample Size, Precision Interval and Control Limit Nomogram

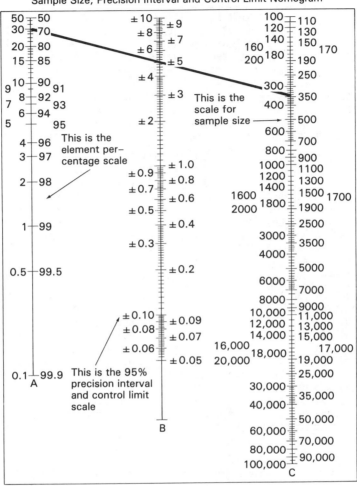

Courtesy of the National Institute of Management.

Figure 12-2 Sample size, precision interval, and control limit nomogram. (*Courtesy of the National Institute of Management, Bath, Ohio.*)

The random number table is necessary, as we said, to keep bias out of the study. Here is how to use the table: Note that every minute of the day from 6:00 to 6:00 is numbered, in Figure 12–3. (These numbers correspond to the numbers in Table 12–3.)

Since the figure covers 12 hours, the table can be used for any shift, day or night. For our example, we start when they start, say 8:00 A.M. and quit at 5:00 P.M., when they quit. Therefore, the numbers will be between 120 and 659. Referring to the random digit table (Table 12–3), we now read off *18* numbers that fall inclusively between 120 and 659. The easiest way is to

TABLE 12-3 3-DIGIT RANDOM NUMBERS

718	057	239	870	389	578	030	103	365	128	319	953	515	098	604	260	721	144	869	911	600	
781	735	590	475	360	202	881	584	564	271	481	070	880	509	466	420	865	766	270	668	680	
295	895	329	460	878	218	441	772	171	237	466	624	274	985	754	916	042	442	117	577	243	
399	191	067	485	016	326	826	189	487	285	663	611	192	674	821	352	164	437	747	438	168	
452	499	819	513	305	196	925	816	115	304	034	599	782	986	410	415	472	656	189	483	196	
250	390	096	914	061	377	507	586	092	276	945	922	184	642	279	367	424	335	457	530	696	
398	721	245	840	900	950	898	607	555	418	308	986	176	610	714	893	594	344	778	766	482	
655	064	336	617	508	050	744	986	351	339	809	046	243	729	742	779	939	393	315	318	878	
762	190	326	620	230	078	242	081	773	546	476	083	432	096	238	759	890	707	528	556	374	
129	986	917	445	813	989	636	403	172	767	924	359	710	795	793	314	885	549	781	172	702	
959	368	260	117	846	266	108	786	758	506	270	693	534	751	485	160	776	956	323	814	812	
290	427	897	612	881	277	622	682	548	790	687	931	829	971	223	655	217	486	112	000	262	
247	318	808	604	436	867	991	932	657	562	077	707	939	080	094	471	309	122	709	052	903	
518	372	956	993	748	289	145	661	504	698	775	937	065	462	153	533	840	943	178	861	543	
267	112	758	656	417	909	282	318	659	669	315	890	420	624	211	161	941	426	042	317	613	
101	652	665	596	818	713	561	009	978	947	238	873	896	505	915	564	621	660	292	756	727	
755	526	579	626	536	676	309	428	443	139	436	359	197	857	774	495	454	074	200	559	719	
438	470	404	670	439	758	250	849	174	713	637	642	626	405	381	831	329	331	949	910	054	
917	838	764	389	391	802	876	197	378	535	892	925	618	154	779	328	488	765	096	920	976	
455	276	491	685	311	966	693	465	761	087	075	788	858	340	318	939	193	332	554	359	483	
699	212	709	908	930	909	750	615	172	627	799	311	066	891	211	568	934	074	909	825	547	
030	459	184	688	164	163	203	138	871	511	110	106	155	758	952	657	943	032	741	873	837	
396	136	227	786	301	209	216	173	295	215	426	965	967	845	954	244	610	187	671	925	209	
408	337	673	941	234	093	469	374	036	036	428	912	217	000	274	803	305	348	409	591	270	
726	475	777	330	235	223	863	579	685	834	216	366	130	483	684	301	151	881	043	684	755	
709	173	719	795	738	087	883	735	359	618	562	906	020	090	277	384	424	256	048	884	423	
520	619	825	460	297	739	140	866	063	083	053	611	527	286	739	487	223	481	422	275	483	
512	631	228	540	199	372	056	189	492	772	684	195	647	890	179	858	157	798	529	624	286	
509	481	685	303	784	379	360	269	313	023	406	353	164	346	159	713	562	447	813	758	723	
413	657	518	298	293	950	729	057	453	710	600	179	761	401	027	172	685	733	074	212	005	

start reading left to right and keep going until we get the number of observations needed.

The selection of 18 numbers should be made each day and should start where we left off the day before. Because of the structure of the random number chart, we can read the numbers as they are, or any other way, so long as we get all our times the same way.

To illustrate, reading from left to right, the first number is 718. That represents a time of 5.58. That's no good, so we throw it out and go to the next number, 057. That's no good either, so we go to the next number, which is 239. Bingo! 239 is at 9:59. We need 17 more, and we get them the same way. After we get them, we put them in sequence by order of time.

5. The next step is to make the study. At the first predetermined time, the observer reaches the first pick-up crew. Glancing out of the car window, the observer checks to see what the crew is doing. *They are working!* So the observer marks a stroke in the "On Pick-Up" column of Table 12–2. Driving

WORK SAMPLE ACCUMULATOR AND DEMONSTRATION FORM

Time	No.	Time	No.	Time	No.	Time	No.	Time	No.	Time	No.	Time	No.	Time	No.
	001		091		181		271		361		451		541		631
	002		092		182		272		362		452		542		632
	003		093		183		273		363		453		543		633
	004		094		184		274		364		454		544		634
6:05	005	7:35	095	9:05	185	10:35	275	12:05	365	1:35	455	3:05	545	4:35	635
	006		096		186		276		366		456		546		636
	007		097		187		277		367		457		547		637
	008		098		188		278		368		458		548		638
	009		099		189		279		369		459		549		639
6:10	010	7:40	100	9:10	190	10:40	280	12:10	370	1:40	460	3:10	550	4:40	640
	011		101		191		281		371		461		551		641
	012		102		192		282		372		462		552		642
	013		103		193		283		373		463		553		643
	014		104		194		284		374		464		554		644
6:15	015	7:45	105	9:15	195	10:45	285	12:15	375	1:45	465	3:15	555	4:45	645
	016		106		196		286		376		466		556		646
	017		107		197		287		377		467		557		647
	018		108		198		288		378		468		558		648
	019		109		199		289		379		469		559		649
6:20	020	7:50	110	9:20	200	10:50	290	12:20	380	1:50	470	3:20	560	4:50	650
	021		111		201		291		381		471		561		651
	022		112		202		292		382		472		562		652
	023		113		203		293		383		473		563		653
	024		114		204		294		384		474		564		654
6:25	025	7:55	115	9:25	205	10:55	295	12:25	385	1:55	475	3:25	565	4:55	655
	026		116		206		296		386		476		566		656
	027		117		207		297		387		477		567		657
	028		118		208		298		388		478		568		658
	029		119		209		299		389		479		569		659
6:30	030	8:00	120	9:30	210	11:00	300	12:30	390	2:00	480	3:30	570	5:00	660
	031		121		211		301		391		481		571		661
	032		122		212		302		392		482		572		662
	033		123		213		303		393		483		573		663
	034		124		214		304		394		484		574		664
6:35	035	8:05	125	9:35	215	11:05	305	12:35	395	2:05	485	3:35	575	5:05	665
	036		126		216		306		396		486		576		666
	037		127		217		307		397		487		577		667
	038		128		218		308		398		488		578		668
	039		129		219		309		399		489		579		669
6:40	040	8:10	130	9:40	220	11:10	310	12:40	400	2:10	490	3:40	580	5:10	670
	041		131		221		311		401		491		581		671
	042		132		222		312		402		492		582		672
	043		133		223		313		403		493		583		673
	044		134		224		314		404		494		584		674
6:45	045	8:15	135	9:45	225	11:15	315	12:45	405	2:15	495	3:45	585	5:15	675
	046		136		226		316		406		496		586		676
	047		137		227		317		407		497		587		677
	048		138		228		318		408		498		588		678
	049		139		229		319		409		499		589		679
6:50	050	8:20	140	9:50	230	11:20	320	12:50	410	2:20	500	3:50	590	5:20	680
	051		141		231		321		411		501		591		681
	052		142		232		322		412		502		592		682
	053		143		233		323		413		503		593		683
	054		144		234		324		414		504		594		684
6:55	055	8:25	145	9:55	235	11:25	325	12:55	415	2:25	505	3:55	595	5:25	685
	056		146		236		326		416		506		596		686
	057		147		237		327		417		507		597		687
	058		148		238		328		418		508		598		688
	059		149		239		329		419		509		599		689
7:00	060	8:30	150	10:00	240	11:30	330	1:00	420	2:30	510	4:00	600	5:30	690
	061		151		241		331		421		511		601		691
	062		152		242		332		422		512		602		692
	063		153		243		333		423		513		603		693
	064		154		244		334		424		514		604		694

Figure 12–3 Work sampling procedure sheet. (*Courtesy of the National Institute of Management, Bath, Ohio.*)

Time	No.	Time	No.	Time	No.	Time	No.	Time	No.	Time	No.	Time	No.	Time	No.
7:05	065	8:35	155	10:05	245	11:35	335	1:05	425	2:35	515	4:05	605	5:35	695
	066		156		246		336		426		516		606		696
	067		157		247		337		427		517		607		697
	068		158		248		338		428		518		608		698
	069		159		249		339		429		519		609		699
7:10	070	8:40	160	10:10	250	11:40	340	1:10	430	2:40	520	4:10	610	5:40	700
	071		161		251		341		431		521		611		701
	072		162		252		342		432		522		612		702
	073		163		253		343		433		523		613		703
	074		164		254		344		434		524		614		704
7:15	075	8:45	165	10:15	255	11:45	345	1:15	435	2:45	525	4:15	615	5:45	705
	076		166		256		346		436		526		616		706
	077		167		257		347		437		527		617		707
	078		168		258		348		438		528		618		708
	079		169		259		349		439		529		619		709
7:20	080	8:50	170	10:20	260	11:50	350	1:20	440	2:50	530	4:20	620	5:50	710
	081		171		261		351		441		531		621		711
	082		172		262		352		442		532		622		712
	083		173		263		353		443		533		623		713
	084		174		264		354		444		534		624		714
7:25	085	8:55	175	10:25	265	11:55	355	1:25	445	2:55	535	4:25	625	5:55	715
	086		176		266		356		446		536		626		716
	087		177		267		357		447		537		627		717
	088		178		268		358		448		538		628		718
	089		179		269		359		449		539		629		719
7:30	090	9:00	180	10:30	270	12:00	360	1:30	450	3:00	540	4:30	630	6:00	720

Figure 12-3   *(Continued)*

to the next crew at the appointed time, the observer checks what they are doing and continues marking strokes at the appointed times and in the proper column until the day is done. Twenty working days later, when 350 observations of the crews have been made, the observer adds the strokes in each column and computes the percent of each element. (If there are 175 strokes for "On Pick-Up," the crews are working at pick-ups 50 percent of the time.)

These data show how all the crews are working. It is the average for them. If the observer wants to compare crews, he or she must set up one Table (12–2) for each crew, and make 350 observations of each crew. If the observer also wants to know how each individual is doing, a separate chart is needed for each person.

In fact, if the observer is satisfied with the average for the crews as a whole and there are ten crews, the observer only need make 35 observations during the month. In this case, it would not be necessary to make 350 trips to the field, but only 35, because each trip counts for ten observations. In this case, 35 trips in a month reduces to at most two a day, for one month, to get an accurate breakdown of a ten-crew operation. If you have 100 people on your staff, and check all 100 just four times (at random), you have an accurate estimate of the utilization of your people! It is important to note here that productivity between crews will vary widely, and that a crew average is no measure of where supervision is necessary. For this, you will need the average of each crew. Once you have these figures, you can also plan your future work schedules.

If one of the times in our sample occurs at 12:12, and this is the lunch hour, it should be discarded and another figure selected (as discussed). The value of these figures which highlight unproductive time may not be appreciated until such a study is made. For example, a "downtime" percentage of 12 percent means you are losing the capacity of one crew out of eight for this reason. Hence, better methods for controlling work flow should be studied. (See Panel 12–1.)

Work sampling entails more than we have discussed here. For one thing, it has been used to set time standards, by pace-rating the operator at the time the observation is made. But the material covered here is completely adequate for making a good study of crew, equipment, and labor utilization. And it can be learned by a few simple trial runs.

PANEL 12–1 REASONS FOR IDLE TIME BY EMPLOYEES

1. POOR SUPERVISION

2. LACK OF WORK DUE TO:

   NO MATERIAL TO WORK ON

   BREAKDOWN OF EQUIPMENT

   POOR WORK PLANNING (POOR SCHEDULING)

3. _____

4. _____

5. _____

6. _____

WORK SAMPLING FOR:

   PICK-UP CREWS

   TRANSFER STATIONS

   OFFICE HELP

   SUPERVISORS

From *Community Recycling Seminars*, by Institute for Global Action. Used by permission.

13

The Professional Manager: Some General Principles

The problems of management are quite broad and require much ingenuity. In the recycling business we are not just concerned with materials collected at the curb. We are concerned also with separation, quality of the final product, efficient handling, proper preparation for delivery to the buyer, labor relations, utilization of labor, equipment maintenance, preventive maintenance, a wide-flung operation with people working in an extended geographic area, accidents and injuries, sickness, operating costs and cash flow, and others too numerous to mention. All of these have to be dealt with effectively by the manager.

In addition, the manager must work to build an efficient operation. The question for management is how to come to grips with the running of the whole operation. Obviously there is no way in which managers can concentrate and concern themselves with everything that goes on. If a manager has several crews in the field, crew chiefs and supervisors will handle incidental decisions. The manager delegates these to people who can be trusted. Besides delegating to others, however, the manager must learn to concentrate on those areas which will produce the most telling results. Subordinates must be guided to do the same.

MANAGEMENT BY EXCEPTION

When you arrive at work each morning, a single sheet of paper should be on your desk. This is a list of perhaps no more than six items that need immediate attention.

Let's say your conveyor on the sorting line breaks down. If you have five people on that line, those people are out of a job. *Right now* you have to act. You check with the other group leaders. One tells you he can use an extra hand baling paper. Another can put two to work at resorting the glass and plastics that won't meet specs. Two find work in the mixed waste bunker, sorting out items that do not get into assigned bunkers. Hence, fifteen minutes after coming to work, you have your full crew working productively and have dealt with the problem. Because you responded quickly, five employees had productive jobs to do rather than being sent home, or wasting time in the cafeteria while the equipment is being repaired. In fact, if you had gotten to work half an hour early, like you should, no time would have been lost at all.

This is what we mean by *management by exception.* Too often today, we get voluminous reports, with great detail about the previous day's activities. These may run on for pages, with trivial detail dominating, and emergencies buried in the trivia. (Daily production reports in large businesses may be an inch thick!)

Naturally, you want to know this information. It is important, for example, to know how much was produced by each worker, the amount shipped, the dollar value, and so on. But this should be a report for reading at your leisure. The Exception Report should demand attention by capturing your eye as soon as you arrive for work. It is a list of urgent problems that have accumulated during your absence. More than that, it is a notification of all *critical* problems in a timely fashion that occur all day long!

Another effective device is to have a red light at each operator's station which can be switched on when a problem develops. The light should go on at the same time in the manager's office. The purpose, again, is to learn of problems at once, and to solve them without delay.

The best managers are those who want to be told bad news at once during the day. Good news tells us what we want to hear, but it may not help us do our job. The manager's job is to anticipate and solve problems.

Good managers do not like surprises. If a problem develops, they want to be told about it. If possible, they want to be told in advance. They want to prepare for it and deal with it routinely. Emergencies are seldom handled efficiently.

Management by exception is, therefore, the means by which good managers concentrate their attention on maintaining an effective, well-run operation.

MANAGEMENT BY OBJECTIVES

Management by objectives (MBO) is goal oriented. Through established goals and objectives, it attempts to bring all levels of the organization into harmony, so that everyone has the same perspective of the purpose of his or her job.

Very few recycling operations are profitable, but that should be the long-term objective. This goal, in turn, spawns numerous subgoals which are concerned with getting the job done.

For example, typical subgoals in recycling are labor cost per ton of shippable (good!) material; minimum losses due to rejections by the processing mills; minimum standards for tonnage of recyclables per 1,000 residents in the area, dollars shipped per labor hour, sales dollars (income) per labor hour, and so on.

The objectives which are measurable in precise figures provide the means for establishing bonuses and other incentives to everyone in the group. At Lincoln Electric, the bonus system is so effective that not only does the company produce its welders cheaper than the Japanese, but for the last few years its employee bonuses have been equal to their regular annual paychecks! If administered accurately, therefore, bonuses are effective in cutting costs. The Lincoln employees provide a major source of creative ideas for cutting costs. It is they who have proven that America can outperform any competition it encounters, given the right incentives.

There is a problem in establishing accurate goals or standards throughout the organization, and the fact that different people can arrive at different goals to accomplish the same final objective suggests that the objectives need careful attention and development in first setting them up. The formulation must start with the top management and be coordinated at the top. If objectives are developed for the pick-up crews, for example, that later prove to be at cross purposes with the final goals, then they must be redefined.

Furthermore, each set of objectives must be formulated in such a way that improvement can be measured, planned, and tracked on a regular (probably monthly) basis. Many of the standards are identical to those contained in the budgets for a department. Examples of these are given in the next chapter.

The standards that are established and used to measure accomplishment are arrived at by study and consultation with each group leader or supervisor. In a similar way, those which will be used to evaluate the managers must be derived by joint consultation with them before they can become committed to these standards. Throughout the operation, formulation of the yardsticks relative to the ultimate goal are not significantly different from the process used in setting up budgets. The problems and the mistakes commonly committed are the same. Just as some managers sometimes use arbitrary figures handed down from the top to set budgets, so some firms pass down the objectives from the top without allowing for interplay between people—without checking with those ultimately involved to see if the goals are realistic, attainable, and acceptable. Being frustrated by such practices, the operators at the lower level who had no hand in developing the figures have no incentive to make them work; furthermore, they have an excuse if the objectives fail because they never agreed to them. Incentives and initiative start from the bottom and work upwards. Guidance starts from the top. Supervisors provide the catalyst that makes things work. They see that the objectives are realistic and usable. They see that they represent improvement and are not "padded," but the supervisors do not ram them down the throat of their people. They secure enthusiasm by fairness.

In summary, the manager's role is to oversee the establishment of the goals, to make sure they are workable and possible and that they are sufficiently challenging so as to assure benefits for the community and enthusiasm from the person being measured. The manager must also ensure that once the goals are established, every effort is made to meet them. The goals should be high but attainable. They should challenge and inspire confidence and initiative. These objectives should foster high morale and employee enthusiasm, and they should promote team effort by getting everyone working toward a common goal. In the end, the manager is a teacher and a planner.

PARETO'S LAW

This is an economic law that directs people's efforts in the most efficient manner. More specifically, it is a method that gets the "cream" and discards the "whey."

Pareto's law is named after a venerable Italian economist, who probably never suspected his name and ideas would be used in such a cavalier way as we do today. Vilfredo Pareto, who wrote on economics in the 1500s, discovered a truth, which everyone already knew but was afraid to ask. What was this startling discovery? Pareto said that sooner or later 20 percent of the people end up with 80 percent of the wealth. Actually he was wrong. He was too generous to the poor. The figures are more like 10 percent and 90 percent. In the United States, by last count, 283 families had 79 percent of the wealth. But the socialists and Marxists, who thought they were smarter than the founders of our republic, declared the system unfair. "Pareto is dead!" they said. "With our system," they declared, "we can have a richer poor and a poorer rich." But they were wrong, too, and Pareto survived. After years of communism in Russia, the system has proven no match for Pareto. The difference between the highest and lowest salaries paid in Russia at its very proudest moments has been of the same order of magnitude as the United States—about 50 to 1. This we learned from Max Eastman in 1937 and two years later from Leon Trotsky, one of the founders of the Russian system. Trotsky, who fled for his life and was assassinated in Mexico estimated that the upper 11 percent or 12 percent of his people received 50 percent of the nation's income. Thus, we are more equal than the socialists because our upper 10 percent in 1939, at least, received about 35 percent of the national income.

Pareto's law shows up nicely as a curve, and some people even call it *Pareto's curve*. (See Figure 13–1.) In the curve shown here, 12.5 percent of the people have over 50 percent of the wealth (as in the United States and Russia), and 12.5 percent of the people have about 3 percent of the wealth. Now these people hang on to this 3 percent so tenaciously that not even the most efficient system of taxation ever conceived, nor coercion, welfare, nor lotteries have ever been able to budge it loose.

Thank heaven we live in America with a per capita income of $20,903 versus Russia with $1,780 (1990 figures, International Monetary Fund).

Pareto's law was first introduced into the field of management in the 1950s by H. Ford Dickie at General Electric as a procedure for controlling inventories.

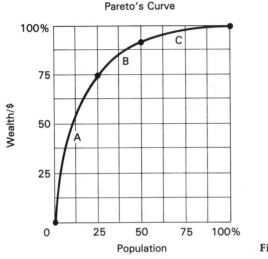

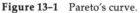

Figure 13-1 Pareto's curve.

Hence, it is of direct interest to us because in recycling we deal in enormous volumes of inventories.

The inventory application derives from the fact that inventory items and dollar volume create a curve exactly like Pareto's population curve. Here's an example.

At Capewell Manufacturing a study of their hole-saw catalog, made up of 66 sizes of hole-saws, showed the following pattern:

A. 15 saw sizes did 64 percent of all sales (20 percent of the items).
B. 26 saw sizes did 27 percent of all sales (40 percent of the items).
C. 25 saw sizes did 9 percent of sales (40 percent of the items).

Note the parallel of the last group (C group) and the poor people in Pareto's curve. The C group is large but has very little dollar volume. The very rich, on the other hand, in A group get 64 percent of the dollar volume.

We describe first how the preceding data are developed, and then how to use them.

Developing the Information

An inventory breakdown like the preceding one, which can be applied to recycling, is done as follows: First, we need the total annual sales for each hole-saw size in *dollars*. This is available from the accounting department. The total list has 66 items.

Second, these sales dollars are listed in descending order, with the best seller at the top. That is it. Now, count down the first 15 items on the list, add up their sales and you get the figure just given for the group A items. Count the last

25 items on the list, and you find out their total sales for the year were only 9 percent of the company's sales of all hole-saws.

In recycling, we are dealing with 18 recyclables, if we accept the breakdown in Figure 13–2. (Figure 3–1 is reprinted here for convenient reference.)

Actually, there are batteries, paints, pesticides, oils, and thousands of items in the community pick-up which do not appear in this figure but could be included in the discussion. Although these items are considered inventory when they are assets, for our use here we are concerned only with total expenditures by categories. Our first step is to arrange all expenditures in annual dollars. For simplicity, these should be our cost per ton to process a given recyclable (or waste) *times the annual tonnage we handle!* This gives us the total annual cost for handling each recyclable. Then, we put these annual costs into a column of descending order.

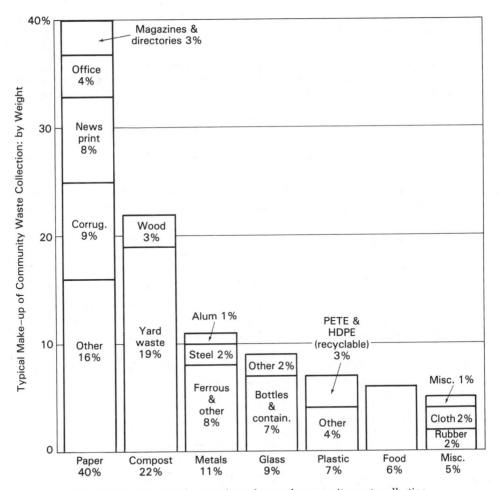

Figure 13-2   Graph indicating the make-up of community waste collection.

Let's work up some figures based on typical data for a community of 100,000 residents. (See Figure 13–3 for representative community figures.) Many of these figures are lower than those in many communities. Tipping charges in New Jersey, for example, may exceed $80.00.

Monthly cost for collection is, say, $15.00; landfill tipping charges are $40.00 a ton; composting and burning costs are $45.00 per ton.

The average waste per person per day in America is about 4 pounds. Hence, the community produces 73,000 tons of waste per year. An average family of four produces 16×30 pounds of waste per month, or 480 pounds, at a cost for pick-up of $15.00 or $0.03125 per pound, or $62.50 per ton. Therefore, it costs $62.50 \times 73,000$ tons, or $4,562,500.00 for the pick-up operation each year. We will come back to this figure.

Now, at the transfer station, yard waste and food are the only items that do not get dumped on the conveyor-sorter. (See Figure 3–2 for percentages.) At 19 percent + 6 percent this represents 25 percent of our annual tonnage, or 18,250 tons, which costs $45 per ton to compost/burn, or $8,212,500.00 per year (assuming we do not landfill it).

Continuing with data from the typical community, it will normally sort out office paper, corrugated, aluminum, steel, bottles, and PETE. Here, I assume 100 percent recycling just to simplify the details. I have left out newsprint because so much of this today goes into landfill. It can be included in Table 13–1, when it applies.

This community has a conveyorized sorting system, balers, densifier, and forklifts plus trucks for hauling. The transfer station hires a total of 20 persons, including supervision. Its annual payroll including benefits is $400,000. Hence, handling the waste at the transfer station of 54,750 tons (yard waste and food omitted) comes to $7.31 a ton. Combined with Figure 13–2, we get the resultant information as shown in Table 13–2.

We can now put all of these dollar volume figures in descending order, as shown in Table 13–3. In this dollar volume table, the top 12.5 percent of the list accounts for 86.6 percent of the dollars. The bottom 12.5 percent accounts for 1.37 percent of the dollars. The results are clearly a Pareto curve, and not too different from the distribution of income among the rich and poor.

Before going on, refer again to Table 13–2. These figures also form a Pareto curve. Yard waste and other paper, for example, are 11 percent of the items but represent 35 percent of the total tonnage. Aluminum cans and miscellaneous items are also 11 percent of the items but only 2 percent of the tonnage.

We are now ready to go on to the analysis and application of this information.

Principles of the Concept

Again, let me give a general, broad perspective of the concept, and then we will narrow it down to the typical community example. There are advantages to this approach, because you will see things I have overlooked in the example, and can use.

Council may approve a smaller trash fee hike

By Marilyn Miller Roane
Beacon Journal staff writer

Akron City Council members apparently think the city's proposal to raise garbage collection rates $2.25 a month is too much.

Council President Dave Bryant, D-7, said he thinks the council will not approve the entire increase, but will opt for some middle ground.

The figure bouncing around the council is $1.75.

The council is to review the proposal tonight.

The administration's plan would raise the fee from the current $7 a month to $9.25 beginning Jan. 1.

Those who qualify for the Ohio homestead exemption would see their bills go from $5.10 to $6 a month. The homestead exemption gives a lower rate to the disabled or residents 65 or older whose income is less than $16,500 a year.

Finance Director Linda Sowa said the increase is needed because it costs more money to operate the garbage program than the city is collecting from its fee.

The city trash program will be $1.3 million in the red by the end of 1990 and again by the end of 1991 if the fees remain the same.

She said the increase is needed to keep up with the rising costs.

For example, the charge for trucks to dump garbage at the city's landfill has increased from $20 to $24 a ton, and the charge to dump at the recycle energy plant has increased from $42 to $47 a ton. The city is charged for dumping at either facility, even though it owns both.

The increase also is blamed on new regulations by the Ohio Environmental Protection Agency.

Council members say the EPA keeps coming up with more stringent regulations, forcing the city to find new ways to dispose of garbage.

For example, by the end of 1992, all Ohio cities must come up with a way to reduce the amount of garbage they send to landfills by 25 percent.

Akron's current $7 fee falls at the lower end of the rates charged in the area.

The rate is higher in Canton ($9.25 a month), Cuyahoga Falls ($13.43) and Medina and Wadsworth (both $10), but lower in North Canton ($6.70) and Rittman ($6.75).

Private haulers in the area charge $9 to $20 a month.

The last increase in curbside rates for Akron residents was Feb. 1, when trash bills rose from $6.50 to $7.

TRASH COLLECTION COSTS

Area monthly trash collection rates

Cuyahoga Falls	$13.43*
Medina (city)	10.00
Wadsworth	10.00
Canton	9.25
Akron	7.00
Rittman	6.70
North Canton	6.75

*Will increase Jan. 1

Akron curb service costs

Akron curb service revenues and expenditures

Beacon Journal

Figure 13-3 Article detailing representative community figures.

TABLE 13-1   INCOME TABLE

Item	%	Tons/year	Market value/ton	Annual value (income)
Office	4	2,920	150	$438,000
Corrugated	9	6,570	60	394,200
Aluminum cans	1	730	1,000	730,000
Steel cans	2	1,460	150	219,000
Bottles/containers	7	5,110	25	127,750
PETE/HDPE	3	2,190	50	109,500
	26	18,980		

First, notice how virtually universal the curve is for many types of applications:

1. The inventory breakdown for a small division of Minneapolis-Honeywell is shown in Table 13–4.
2. Many inventories are of this type: James Young at Automatic Sprinkler Corporation reported that their A group, with 10 percent of the items represents 75 percent of the dollars, and the C items included 80 percent of the items but only 13 percent of the dollars. At a boat company, out of 330

TABLE 13-2   ANNUAL TONNAGE HANDLED AT THE TRANSFER STATION

Item	Percent	Tons/year	Transfer station processing cost/yr. @ $7.31/ton
Yard waste	19	[13,870]	NA
Other paper	16	11,680	$85,381
Corrugated	9	6,570	48,027
Newsprint	8	5,840	42,690
Ferrons/other	8	5,840	42,690
Bottles/containers	7	5,110	37,354
Food	6	[4,380]	NA
Office paper	4	2,920	20,460
Plastics/other	4	2,920	20,460
Magazines, etc.	3	2,190	16,009
Wood	3	2,190	16,009
PETE/HDPE	3	2,190	16,009
Steel cans	2	1,460	10,673
Glass/other	2	1,460	10,673
Cloth	2	1,460	10,673
Rubber	2	1,460	10,673
Aluminum	1	730	5,336
Miscellaneous	1	730	5,336
	16 items*	54,750	$398,453

* Excluding yard waste and food (i.e., non-recyclables in the example). It totals 18 items and 73,000 tons with food and yard waste.

TABLE 13-3 DOLLAR VOLUME TABLE (EXPENSES/INCOME)

	Item	$Volume	
1.	Yard/food (expense)	$ 8,212,500.00	
2.	Pick-up (expense)	4,562,500.00	
3.	Aluminum cans (income)	730,000.00	$13,505,000
4.	Office paper (income)	438,000.00	
5.	Payroll and benefits (expense)	400,000.00	
6.	Corrugated (income)	394,000.00	
7.	Steel cans (income)	219,000.00	
8.	Bottles/containers (income)	127,750.00	
9.	PETE/HDPE plastics (income)	109,500.00	
10.	Other paper (handling expense)	85,381.00	
11.	Corrugated (handling expense)	48,027.00	
12.	Newsprint (handling expense)	42,690.00	
13.	Ferrons, other (handling expense)	42,690.00	
14.	Bottles/containers (handling expense)	37,354,00	
15.	Office paper (handling expense)	20,460.00	
16.	Plastics/other (handling expense)	20,460.00	
17.	Magazines, etc. (handling expense)	16,009.00	
18.	Wood (handling expense)	16,009.00	
19.	PETE/HDPE (handling expense)	16,009.00	
20.	Steel cans (handling expense)	10,673.00	
21.	Glass/other (handling expense)	10,673.00	
22.	Cloth (handling expense)	10,673.00	$ 2,065,358
23.	Rubber (handling expense)	10,673.00	
24.	Aluminum cans (handling expense)	5,336.00	
25.	Miscellaneous (handling expense)	5,336.00	
		$15,591,703.00	$ 21,345

sales codes, only 5 or 1.5 percent of these represented 34.7 percent of the company's total sales. The 20 top items represented 67 percent of sales.

At one division of General Electric Company, 75 percent of the cost is made up of A items, comprising in number only 8 percent of all items. The C items amount to 67 percent of the total items but only 5 percent of the value

TABLE 13-4 INVENTORY BREAKDOWN

Inventory class	Percentage of parts	Number of parts	Percentage of annual use	Annual usage ($)
A	4.0	184	46.8	$1,654,796
B	26.0	1,196	42.9	1,520,402
C	70.0	3,182	10.3	368,892
	100.0	4,562	100.0	$3,544,090

of the inventory. At Eastman Kodak, 8 items out of 41,000 constitute 71 percent of the purchases in dollars. Each of these items spends over $5 million per year of the purchase money. In a study made at Shenango, China a few years ago, the inventory consisted of 1,669 items. Of these, 10 percent or 167 items represented 79 percent of the sales. More dramatically, however, 1,100 items did only $700 volume per month (approximately 60 cents each!). Similarly, at Newport News Shipbuilding, the company used to spend $8 million per year on engines and $20 million on pipe. While the engines enjoyed the benefit of 50 engineers, pipe was handled as hardware.

3. An airforce study showed that 20 percent of the purchases spent 80 percent of the money. This discovery gave rise to the terminology *diamonds* and *popcorn*, which applies to high-dollar purchases versus low-dollar purchases. The terminology conveys to military purchasing agents the fact that less detail is needed in purchasing a bag of popcorn than a bag of diamonds.

4. The backlog of a firm, for instance, will be such that 20 percent of the orders represent about 80 percent of the dollar backlog. Similarly, 20 percent of the purchased parts will represent about 80 percent of the dollar volume of the purchasing department. In the methods department, 20 percent of the methods improvements will account for about 80 percent of the dollar savings. It has not been proven empirically, but there is reason to believe that 20 percent of the tools and gauges are used 80 percent of the time, and very likely 20 percent of the employees account for 80 percent of lateness and absenteeism.

5. Studies have shown that 20 percent of the checks written spend 80 percent of the money. Twenty percent of the phone calls constitute 80 percent of the bill (long-distance calls).

6. Vance Packard related a study of heavy drinkers that reported "85 percent of the volume is consumed by 22 percent of the drinkers." He also pointed out, "The female interests merchandisers more than the male breadwinner because it is the female that typically controls about 80 percent of the family's purchasing decisions." (If you come from an intact family with three children, then it seems that 20 percent of the family spends 80 percent of the money.)[1]

7. When Ezra Taft Benson was Secretary of Agriculture under President Eisenhower, he pointed out that 15 percent of the farm crops received 85 percent of the subsidy paid by the government.

8. Often 80 percent of the purchase order dollars go to 20 percent of the vendors. These are the vendors whose capacities, labor contracts, and delivery performance should be known in detail.

9. In purchasing capital equipment, a business will spend 80 percent of its budget on 20 percent of its items.

---

[1] Vance Packard, *Hidden Persuaders* (New York: Pocket Books, 1958), pp. 34, 99.

10. There is, of course, almost no limit to examples. Even when inventories are trimmed to a minimum, the relationship exists. Thus, as one final example, consider restaurant menus. It is not difficult to believe that a restaurant with a three-page menu finds the public buying two or three items (steak, lobster, fish) in larger proportions than the balance of the remaining items, so that 20 percent of the items on the menu constitute 80 percent of the income of the restaurant. Such studies, of course, have been made before and are the basis for quick-food, limited-menu restaurants. But even when the menu is confined to a few items, the relationship holds.

Rules for Applying Pareto's Law to Business/Operations

Referring to the example in Table 13–4, note the following:

1. The C items represent $368,892 and constitute 3,182 codes. That means each C item does about $120 worth of business a year. The problem is that a volume of $10 per month is not likely to be profitable business. In many companies, set-up costs alone exceed that figure.

   Upjohn Company with a similar problem refused to keep supplying them. They reduced the product line from 2,500 items to 509 ($10,000 was the break-point), below which it was unprofitable to build.

   In most cases, product line simplification can be accomplished with little pain and great benefits, and there is often little justification for many products in the line. It has been estimated that Fords can be purchased with so many options that the total choices available are astronomical. Not bad for a car that you could once buy only in black!

2. Since A items represent many dollars and few stock numbers, they need to be controlled, like diamonds. We can wait until the last moment to order them or place them in production. Operating lead times must be cut to a minimum. We can afford the expense of expediting these items.

3. Similarly, the purchasing department should be instructed to concentrate its efforts on A items. Vendors should be contacted for help in finding substitutes and alternative materials. Records and evaluations should be set up on each A item supplier for delivery performance, quality, and price. Because the A item is high-dollar volume, vendors can be controlled so that deliveries are held to established dates. Early deliveries are not usually acceptable because they build up inventory and take up space.

   In one case, at Butler Manufacturing Company, a grommet costing 4 cents did $234,000 volume per year. At the time, there was only one supplier.

4. At the Minneapolis-Honeywell division just mentioned, one man was assigned to the 184 A items. It was assumed that if he did his job effectively, it would be a sound investment. By comparison, only one man was assigned to the 3,182 items in the C group. The standard procedure used by industry

normally is to assign an equal number of items to each inventory clerk! This approach applies equally to any situation in which people are managed.

5. On the C items, controls can be loose. That is to say, they should be designed to minimize personal attention and time. C items should be ordered infrequently, preferably once or twice a year and sometimes even less. It is common practice in any business to apply "equal treatment" to all items. This, however, is not good management. Evert Welch was referring to this practice when he said,

> Intuitive approaches to inventory control tend to lead toward similar emphasis to each item of the inventory. We are inclined to schedule, to make, or buy the low-cost items on the same basis as the high-cost items. . . . We defend the emphasis we place on the low-cost items in terms of the truism that any dollar saved is a dollar earned . . . (The classification procedure shifts our emphasis to dollar usage) . . . with a given amount of effort to spend on a total inventory, it becomes obvious that effort is best spent where dollars are involved.[2]

Despite the basic soundness of these concepts, it does not follow that they will be applied rationally to every situation offering significant savings. Because we tend to repeat past errors and to accept previous practices, it is safer to assume that we will continue to do as we have done.

It can, in fact, be shown that past performance and past decisions by management do not always produce optimum results even under ideal conditions, using trained specialists. There is reason to believe that managers are inclined more toward mediocrity than toward excellence. Even the best of managers seldom make optimum decisions. Given the wide range of choices available in the typical Pareto application, the chance of a manager being correct in his or her approach to a problem is limited. As a result, even the ablest of managers will commit themselves and their staff to projects that are not providing a maximum return. The following examples demonstrate this point.

Example 1

Industrial engineers are trained to relate savings to costs. Therefore, they should instinctively be adept at picking winners. In fact, the record indicates that they are: On average, industrial engineers were expected to save their companies $100,000 a year, 20 years ago! But can they do better? Look at this: The following example is from a cost-reduction study.

> The Chief Industrial Engineer called in his staff and all foremen and gave a print, and set of methods processing of the top manufactured A item to each one with the challenge to reduce cost. Results: The pattern foreman found a way to reduce the casting weight by two pounds; other suggestions brought about a new method.

---

[2] W. Evert Welch, *Scientific Inventory Control* (Greenwich, CT: Management Publishing Co., 1956), p. 19.

Overall saving was a 23 percent reduction in cost of this one item. They are continuing to attack all A items.[3]

Can't we assume that this item, being the biggest seller in the division, had been in the product line for some time, and that it had, therefore, been by-passed in favor of something else in previous cost-reduction efforts?

Example 2

Moldomation produced complex molds for injection molding. These molds were all quoted to the customer before the purchase order was released.

Quoting is a complex process requiring considerable patience and attention to detail. A mold is made up of several layers of steel plates, usually numerous complex cavities, bolts, pins, dowels, screws, and other attachments, sometimes including hydraulic or air cylinders to help activate the mold as it opens up. The cost estimator has to estimate each element in order to arrive at the quote for the customer. During the day, the estimator will have anywhere from ten to twenty molds to quote. Hence, along with other duties, he has about thirty minutes or less per quote.

Almost invariably, an integral part of quoting is to make up sketches of the part and cavity showing the main features of the mold. The easy parts to quote are the parts listed in the catalog. Standard parts like dowels, pins, stripper bolts, certain inserts, and so on are listed in the standard mold supply catalog. The estimator looks these up and posts the quantity needed and dollar value on an estimate sheet.

Steel plate comes from several sources depending on the grade. The estimator computes the weight of each plate, the cost of grinding top, bottom, and sides, and the price per pound for the steel, and posts these to the sheet. The estimator looks up the screws and bolts and costs them out. If a set of cylinders or other attachments are needed, the estimator prices them from a catalog or calls the supplier for an estimate. If the cavity requires a casting, a quote is requested from the supplier. It is the same for texturing and finish.

The estimator then computes the machine time. Since machine time, almost without exception, is the most costly element of a mold, the estimator reaches this element just as time runs out. Since it is an uncertain element, compared to a catalog price, the estimator is glad to get through it and to move ahead to the next quote.

If all elements were listed, as we have suggested, with the most expensive at the top, the estimator would find that 20 percent of the elements in a quote constitute 80 percent of the price. These are the elements that must be accurate. The nuts and bolts at the end may represent 80 percent of the estimate but only 20 percent of the costs. Even if the estimator rushes through these or guesses them, there may be a 30 percent error that would result in an error of only 6

---

[3] Quoted from a letter to me by Howard Hoving at Minneapolis-Honeywell.

percent in the total estimate. But an estimator cannot afford that type of error on the top A item.

Example 3

If we take the inventory in Table 13–4 and the 4,562 items listed there, and if we assign the items equally to each of four persons, then each person has 1,140 items to handle. Each clerk has some A items and each clerk has many C items. Each clerk is responsible for $886,000 in usage. All items are treated equally. At $80,000 for four clerks, we are spending $17.50 to control each item. Hence, we are spending $17.50 to control each A and each C item. We are spending $17.50 to control an A item doing as much as $100,000 per year (the top item) and spending $17.50 to control the lowest C item with as little as $10 per year. This doesn't make sense!

But, if we put one clerk in charge of 184 items and one clerk over the whole C group, we will spend $20,000 to control $1,655,000, and we will spend $20,000 to control $369,000. Parity will be improved. We will be spending $107.50 to control each A item and we will be spending $6.30 to control each C item.

This example should make clear to you how significant this approach is. If you control your costs effectively, and manage your operation scientifically, you will get results like we are going after!

Example 4

With 20 percent of our customers giving us 80 percent of our business, if our salespeople are assigned by territory and they are undiscriminating, then our sales cost per customer is the same for A or C. As we just saw for inventory, parity in terms of dollar volume can be struck by either limiting sales calls, so that a C customer gets one or two calls a year and A gets a call every two weeks, or by assigning A accounts to a select group of salespeople and the C accounts to others on a basis similar to the inventory allocation, so that we spend less on C account calls.

When you seek customers or outlets for your products, concentrate on the A items by calling on A customers. The C items can be sold, too, but do not concentrate heavily on them.

Example 5

Here is another example that fits directly into recycling.

The general pattern for establishing storage bins is to set them up like a warehouse. They are often located by an assigned item number, so that A and C items are randomly situated in the bins. But the A items are active and take up 12 percent of the space, and the C items are comparatively inactive and take up 30 percent of the space. The front-end loader spends 70 percent of its time chasing after C items because the layout doesn't recognize or plan for the true volume of the operations.

Now we get to the crux of many points made in previous chapters.

Example 6

When we set time standards, we do it by operation and by department. Hence, the conveyor line, the forklifts, or the pick-up operation may have standards. These standards are applied to every item in that department. (This may even be a union requirement.)

Thus, we have good coverage for a department but have failed to concentrate on the expensive operations. Hence, because of the cost of setting standards, we omit large areas of the operation from study. We could actually cover all A items for all operations with 50 percent less cost if we skipped the C items completely!

Let's draw this together for our own activity.

Applications to Recycling

We note first that emphasis is directed away from the broad operation, toward a concentrated area. The A items are the diamonds. They attract one's attention while the popcorn is fed to the dogs.

Consider this scenario: An industrial engineer who operates out of the headquarters of the recycling operation has his office window looking out over the conveyor-sorting operation. Each day he walks through the transfer station and observes 20 workers sorting out the cans, bottles, and other materials into bunkers.

His previous experience has taught him two things: People on day work, working without standards and without incentive, work about 65 percent of the time. This is true of office people and executives and the laborer on the floor. But, our engineer knows that if you install standards and an incentive bonus, you can get 80 percent to 85 percent out of them. That's about a 20 percent reduction in cost. He plans to use the four people, who are no longer needed to fill other openings as they develop, or to take on new assignments.

What he has done is tackle the payroll and benefits expense item of Table 13–3. He has saved $80,000 a year. A good showing, but not his best.

He chose this expense item because he saw it everyday, and he could see inefficiencies staring him right in the face.

Suppose he had tackled pick-up expense instead. The same rules apply. If the pick-up crews are on day work, incentives and time standards will produce the same result: 20 percent reduction in work hours. A reduction of $910,000 in costs! And, furthermore, it is easier to set standards for pick-up crews than yard workers because crew work is highly repetitive, whereas yard work is not. Even the conveyor lines have so much variation in materials dumped on them that certain workers are always standing around. For example, if three loads of corrugated are dumped in the conveyor hopper at once, only the corrugated workers have work for a couple of hours, while the rest are idle.

That difference of $910,000 versus $80,000 is a big difference for no additional work. Again, I repeat: The industrial engineer picked the project he saw in need of attention rather than making an analysis to find the big-ticket items.

Let's look at the top item: yard/food expense. Many communities are now moving away from picking up yard waste. Leaves and underbrush can be mulched on site at home, with available attachments for home mowers or special mulchers. What does this do to the ecology problem?

Here are some thoughts discussed in *Michigan Today* (December 1989), an alumni paper of the University of Michigan. In the article, we find that Professor David Gates, a University of Michigan botanist, and "a hand-full of other scientists" had been warning America of the *greenhouse effect* as early as the 1950s. "Stop burning coal, oil and gasoline or swelter under a permanent blanket of carbon dioxide that is gradually turning Earth into a sauna," they argued.[4] Their persuasiveness started a boom that has become the main doctrine of ecologists throughout the world. It was on the United Nations' agenda for December 1990!

One solution that has been suggested is to plant trees. But Gates questions this. They make the world cooler and more humid, he admits, but it is not a long-term solution. For the fact is growing trees do absorb carbon dioxide, but once they die, the carbon dioxide is released in decay, and the process is repeating the cycle. But is this not also true of mulching versus burning? I have read elsewhere that leaves that are mulched merely pass through the decay process and produce much the same result as if they had been burnt. In a 100-year period during which time a forest is burnt or rotted out, the result is the same. We have merely recycled the atmosphere. As a result of this type of thinking, the greenhouse theory is questioned by many scientists.

Even Rachel Carson in her book, *The Sea Around Us,* is clear on the question of major weather cycles. For example, she talks of a period of "benevolent climate" in which snow and ice were little known on the coast of Europe in the seas of Iceland and Greenland. "Then the Vikings sailed freely over the northern

---

[4] "It's Time to Listen to David Gates," by Sally Pobojewski. p. 5. The article credits Dr. Gates with leading the way in convincing the world of the "greenhouse effect." The article states that "Gates cites recent hard physical evidence from a 126-year study of thousands of worldwide weather monitoring stations conducted by the University of East Anglia's Climatic Research Unit. The British study showed global temperatures have climbed an average of nearly one degree Fahrenheit since 1860" (*p. 5*)

Since warming trends and ice-ages extend over thousands of years, the incidence of one degree of variation in a span of 126 years is statistically insignificant. It is no more meaningful, for example, than studying the rings of a 126 year old tree and then trying to predict what the next ten, twenty or hundred years of rings will look like. Nor would the weather over the last 126 days, for example, be helpful in predicting the next 30. It might, but most likely it would not, because, with any statistics, relevance means that the statistics must be randomly chosen over *several cycles* (several ice-ages) to provide meaningful interpretation!

seas."[5] She points out that Eric's route described in the Sagas would have been impossible during recent centuries. But then, *she says,* the ice moved south, choking up the old sea lanes. The Baltic Sea froze over. Horse and sleigh crossed between Norway and Denmark in the 1300s. Then it changed again! *It became warmer.* We now are finding Viking villages under glaciers in Iceland. The Baltic is open again, as it has been for *500 years.* The world is warming up, but it is still not as warm as it was when Eric the Red crossed into Greenland using a route which even today is clogged with icefloes.

A scientist who has greatly influenced our thinking on the weather is Syukuro Manabe, once called the "dean of climate modelers." He reported recently in *Science* magazine that the global warming will be only 2 degrees Celsius, instead of the original prediction of 10 degrees.[6]

Another scientist, Brian McGowran, writing in *American Scientist* says that we are now living in an "icehouse" rather than a "greenhouse."[7] He believes the 2-degree warmth will make the world more habitable. There will be more rain and more food. This viewpoint is also shared by Robert W. Pease, Professor Emeritus, Climatology for the University of California.[8] The editor of *TAIPAN* magazine (April 1990) was even more outspoken. He accused politicians and lobbyists of spending billions of the taxpayers' money to study a crisis that was all hype. "A funny thing happened," he says. "Temperatures *didn't* rise as predicted."

A large measure of the recycling problem can be traced to a natural concern over humankind's effect on nature. But the emergency may not be real, and we have created our largest disposal problem (yard waste) on what may be an unverified reaction to the work of a few scientists. The cost to the United States alone is at least $19 billion each year.[9]

Let's refer again to Table 13–2. You will note that this list of tonnage figures is also a Pareto curve. The top A item is yard/waste. If we wish to reduce the total tons going into landfill, then getting rid of yard waste will cut the total by 19 percent! The next major savings can be gotten by going after "other paper." Hence, Pareto's curve can be applied to dollars (to reduce cost) or tonnage (to reduce landfill).

Let me wind up this section by adding a few more observations.

1. A few items in the recycling stream make up most of the value in the stream. For example, aluminum cans (1 percent), corrugated (9 percent), and glass containers (8 percent) make up a total of 18 percent of the recyclable stream, but they bring in almost 100 percent of the market dollars from the remanufacturing mills. These items require little or no subsidy from the community.

---

[5] Rachel Carson, *The Sea Around Us* (New York: Mentor Books, 1950), p. 138. For more detail, read her chapter "The Global Thermostat."

[6, 7, 8] All quoted in a Letter to the Editor, *Wall Street Journal,* Feb. 16, 1990 by Robert W. Pease.

[9] Communities like Bay Village and Westlake outside of Cleveland have been able to market their compost to both homeowners and nurseries, and are able to sell 100% of everything they make. These facts suggest that composting costs may be offset by their recyclable value.

2. A single pass through the conveyor-sorting operation will achieve perhaps 90 percent of the objective. Some items will be missed and go over the end of the conveyor into the scrap. Our study and discussions of quality control make it clear that this is so. We can slow the machine down and add more people, but we will never get 100 percent of the glass, aluminum, paper, and plastic. Some will still end up in landfill. As our costs go up, our returns diminish.

3. Twenty percent of the people make 80 percent of the mistakes. If you study your quality reports, you'll see that 20 percent of your people account for 80 percent of your absenteeism, or lateness, or discipline problems. Depending on which problem you are trying to solve, this means more training (if you are trying to correct mistakes), or more supervision to deal with the other problems.

4. Twenty percent of the recyclables cause 80 percent of the problems. Glass is expensive to handle. Of all the primary recyclables, it alone has to be dealt with differently. If you have curb-side recycling and all glass is kept in one plastic bag, a single broken bottle contaminates the whole bag. If you throw all your goods into a single container and co-mingle it, a single broken bottle contaminates the whole truck. Newspapers and corrugated may be ruined. Hence, glass needs special handling, no matter what system you use, so that the integrity of the mass is preserved. Glass is an example. There are others such as batteries and poisons. Hence, 20 percent of the recyclables cause 80 percent of the problems.

We can summarize this whole philosophy by repeating one more time: 20 percent of the effort will produce 80 percent of the results. Why work harder than necessary to be a success? As you move from the top A item to the last C item, *it takes just as much effort to reduce one by 20 percent as the other!* This is the law of diminishing returns.

INTENSIVE RECYCLING

It is a fallacy committed by those who advocate *intensive recycling* that they have ignored this important principle defining efficient human effort. A recent study in Illinois, for example, has concluded that for the state to obtain a higher rate of recovery from the waste stream would cost anywhere from $500 to $1,000 per ton.

Studies in New York by the State Energy Resources and Development Authority concluded that careful separation and a controlled process would net 84.4 percent of residential waste recovery (a result similar to the 20–80 law of Pareto).

In an article in *Resource Recycling*, Jerry Powell says: "Proponents of intensive recycling are strong environmentalists . . . [they] are straight shooters about the cost of such a system. They recognize total recycling won't be cheap and they don't shy away from saying so." Powell points out that the proponents of this concept are few in number, but wield a great deal of clout, and "have been effective in presenting their case in community after community."[10]

In their enthusiasm for getting results, environmentalists have often based their arguments on inaccurate assumptions without taking a look at the total problem, as we have mentioned so often before. They often make misleading comparisons by finding exceptional cases of high rates of recycling, and saying, "If they can do it, why can't you?" Such assumptions are not necessarily well founded because the waste stream in two communities may be of a completely different mix.

Many of the systems which have been advertised to the public have failed in practice and are not mentioned again. Hence, I hear about recycling systems on TV or in the press that are hailed as the ultimate system. My office checks many of these directly by talking to the Chamber of Commerce, the city officials, and someone in the field because we are always searching for breakthroughs. One case that was mentioned on national TV as a model system turned out to be a proposed plan. The woman I talked to promised to send me literature on it after it got underway. I am still waiting.

We have repeatedly pointed out that markets need to be developed, and until this happens, we have gotten the cart before the horse.

I summarize this whole discussion on Pareto by emphasizing again that recycling is a business, and it must be treated as one. When it is, it's own successes will push the rate of recycling to the ultimate.

REPORTS YOU SHOULD HAVE

There is an adage that says: Plan your work and work your plan. If you measure people's output either with standards or otherwise, you must also record progress because control over activity is obtained by auditing progress against a plan.

An efficient operation, therefore, keeps progress reports. Typical of these are reports showing *total tonnage produced* each day for each commodity. This is often graphed or charted. The graph is kept for each month.

A similar graph is a *record of shipments* to date for the month. (See Figure 13–4.) These types of records are crucial if we are to maintain our commitment to the reprocessors. They help keep the material flowing, and show us at once if we are falling behind.

Because the incoming supplies are variable, we cannot count on our monthly production to equal one twelfth of our annual volume. Some items, for example, are seasonal.

Hence, production of that item will lag behind at times. Therefore, to keep a steady flow of goods to the buyer, for which we have probably committed ourselves, it is well to maintain some cushion, or inventory, in an established storage area on the premises. Then we can draw upon this when supplies from

---

[10] Jerry Powell, "Intensive Recycling . . . What it is all about," Sept. 1990.

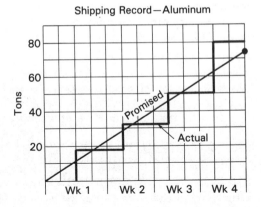

Shipping Record—Aluminum

Figure 13-4 Shipping record for aluminum.

pick-ups fall behind. On the other hand, when supplies exceed our sales, we put the excess back into storage. This way we maintain an even flow to the buyer's plant. We should have records available showing us what these *inventories* are. These can be simple estimates turned in each month by the yard leaders. You also need these figures to compute your monthly financial statements.

Other reports that you will want to see are *tonnage per hour, per employee, by type of material*. These should be a part of your incentive program used to establish bonuses. You also need a report each day of poor materials (nonusable recyclables, in other words). This is called a scrap-loss report. It should be used to correct the production report, and to control the production of scrap. A copy goes to the yard group leaders.

An *efficiency report* should be kept showing production per week on each operation to keep tabs on whether the operation is improving or output is dropping.

Also needed are *comparative reports* showing volumes of certain commodities for previous years during the same month, so changes in the recycling pattern may be noted. Certain commodities go through changes as the price varies. Aluminum beverage cans, versus steel bi-metals, may vary in a community from 50 percent to 96 percent in a single year. The change can greatly affect the cash flow of the operation and your ability to meet your own commitments.

You will need similar reports for the people on pick-up, showing labor efficiency, number of stops per day, number of tons per day per crew, tonnage per labor hour, excessive scrap due to mixed materials, absenteeism, and much of the data reported at the transfer station, including graphs of production against plan.

An actual example of these reports is given in Figures 13–5 and 13–6. The township is the same one training the public at the local gym that we discussed earlier.

RECYCLING REPORT

DAY	DATE	ZONE	TRUCK HOURS	TOTAL MILEAGE	FUEL GALS.	PROCESS FACILITY	ITEMS COLLECTED				
							NEWS-PAPER (LBS.)	CO-MINGLE	OIL (GAL.)	BATTERIES	# OF HOMES SERVED
MON	8-26-91	1	8.0	123	0	I.D.I.	2,879	4,001	9	0	438
TUES	8-27-91	2	7.3	103	30	I.D.I.	1,724	1,996	14	0	391
WED	8-28-91	3	7.5	116	0	I.D.I	3,200	3,920	2	1	326
THUR	8-29-91	4	5.0	80	30	I.D.I.	1,525	2,335	12	0	214
FRI	N/A	N/A	N/A	N/A	N/A	N/A	N/A	N/A	N/A	N/A	N/A
TOTAL	4 DAYS	4 ZONES	27.8	422	60		9,328	12,252	37	1	1,369

WEATHER CONDITIONS

DAY	EXCELLENT	GOOD	FAIR	POOR	VERY POOR	SUNNY/HOT	COLD	SNOW	RAIN	WINDY
MON	X					X				
TUES	X					X				
WED	X					X				
THUR	X					X				
FRI	N/A									

MARKETING DATA				
METAL SCRAP	# OF LBS. 7,960 X .01 PER LB. = $ 79.60			
LEAD ACID BATTERIES	# OF LBS. 822 X .03 PER LB. = $ 24.66			

PROCESSING COST	
CO-MINGLE AT $20.00 PER TON = $122.60	
WASTE OIL AT $25.00 PER 0 GALLONS = $ 0.00	
NEWSPAPER AT $ 0.00 PER TON = $ 0.00	

SUBMITTED BY: _Stan Wright_

DATE: SEPTEMBER 3, 1991

Figure 13-5 Recycling report.

RECYCLING REPORT - AUGUST 1991

WEEK	DATE	ZONES	TRUCK HOURS	TOTAL MILEAGE	FUEL GALS.	METAL SCRAP & OTHER	ITEMS COLLECTED				
							NEWS-PAPER (LBS.)	CO-MINGLE	OIL (GAL)	(LBS) BATTERIES	# OF HOMES SERVED
ONE	05-08	1-4	26.7	431	55.0	0	8,598	9,142	40	0	1,291
TWO	12-15	1-4	24.9	429	60.0	0	7,661	11,559	25	0	1,340
THREE	19-22	1-4	25.4	416	56.0	CFD 126.5	9,368	9,292	29	0	1,254
FOUR	26-29	1-4	27.8	422	60.0	7,960.0	9,328	12,252	37	0	1,369
FIVE	N/A	N/A	N/A	N/A	N/A	N/A	N/A	N/A	N/A	822	N/A
TOTAL	04-29	ALL	104.8	1,698	231.0	8,086.5	34,955	42,245	131	822	5,254

TOTAL WASTE REDUCTION IN POUNDS DIVERTED FROM LANDFILL IN AUGUST = 87,156.50 (TONS - 43.58)   TOTAL TONS APRIL - AUGUST = 278.17

TOWNSHIP BILLING   = $ 112.00
RESIDENTIAL & HAULER SUPPORT = # OF HOMES   2,056   X $1.50 = $3,084.00

MARKETING DATA
METAL SCRAP   # OF LBS.   7,960   X   .01   PER LB. = $ 79.60
LEAD ACID BATTERIES   # OF LBS.   822   X   .03   PER LB. = $ 24.66
TOTAL $3,300.26

PROCESSING COSTS
CO-MINGLE AT $20.00 PER TON   = $422.40
WASTE OIL AT $25.00 PER 275 GALLONS = $ 25.00
NEWSPAPER AT $ 0.00 PER TON   = $ 0.00
PARTS   = $ 0.00
UNIFORMS   = $ 26.28

MISSING CONTAINERS FOR THE MONTH OF AUGUST = 0

OPERATING COSTS
LABOR AT $288.46 PER WEEK = $1,153.84
REPAIRS FOR AUGUST   = $ 0.00

SUBMITTED BY: *[signature]*
DATE: SEPTEMBER 4, 1991

INCOME LESS TOTAL OPERATING COST = $1,672.74 + PREVIOUS ACCOUNT BALANCE = $ 8,449.73 **LESS SOLID WASTE DISTRICT FEES OF $2,942.00 = $5,507.73**

Figure 13-6   Recycling report.

14

Managerial Accounting Methods Used for Recycling Operations

There are two systems for collecting and displaying financial data: One is called *cost of goods sold* (absorption costing). The other is *direct costing*. Of the two systems, direct costing is the most useful for the recycling business because of the volumes involved and the way in which costs are collected. Hence, we explain only the latter.

DIRECT COSTING: THEORY

Under direct costing, *all* costs are divided into two basic categories:

1. *Direct Costs:* Those costs that vary with production, sometimes known as *variable costs*. As production goes up, direct costs increase on a straight-line basis; they decrease as production goes down.
2. *Period Costs:* Those costs that remain the same from month to month, sometimes called *fixed costs*. Period costs are affected only by basic changes, such as expansion of plant facilities or major changes in volume. For most purposes, they are considered to remain the same each month.

The Direct Cost Income Statement

The theory behind direct costing is that the cost of recycling a given volume each month should reflect only those true costs that are used in the production of the product. (These costs apply also to inventory.) Looking at Table 14–1, we see that direct costs are direct material, direct labor, direct expenses (the variable portion in overhead), and commissions or royalties to salespersons.

One advantage of direct costing is that we get a true picture of inventory costs, which is not the case with absorption accounting.

Referring to Table 14–1, after deducting the total direct costs from the net sales, we obtain a figure of profit contribution. This is the number of dollars left after the direct costs are deducted from the sales income. It is what we have left to cover our period expenses, make a profit, and cover our taxes. The ratio of profit contribution to the sales dollar is called the profit variable (PV). This PV

TABLE 14–1 DIRECT COST INCOME STATEMENT
FOR THE FIVE MONTHS ENDED MAY 31, 19XX

	Month of May			Year to date		
	Actual	Planned at actual volume	Planned	Actual	Planned at actual volume	Planned
Net sales	$3,000	$3,000	$2,000	$9,000	$9,000	$10,000
Direct costs:						
Material	500	525	350	1,575	1,575	1,750
Labor	750	600	400	1,675	1,800	2,000
Expense	150	225	150	300	675	750
Commissions	150	150	100	450	450	500
Total	$1,550	$1,500	$1,000	$4,000	$4,500	$ 5,000
Profit contribution	1,450	1,500	1,000	5,000	4,500	5,000
P/V	48.3%	50%	50%	55%	50%	50%
Period expense:						
Supervision	200	200	200	1,000	1,000	1,000
Maintenance	150	150	150	600	600	600
Administrative	150	150	150	900	900	900
Marketing	100	100	100	500	500	500
Total	600	600	600	3,000	3,000	3,000
Operating income	$ 850	$ 900	$ 400	$2,000	$1,500	$ 2,000
Break-even sales	$1,242	$1,200	$1,200	$5,455	$6,000	$ 6,000
Increase (decrease) of fixed overhead inventory	(800)				1,000	
Net income before taxes	$ 50		$3,000			

factor indicates how many dollars are left after deduction of the direct costs. (Thus, we have a measure of product profitability without the distortion of unrelated overhead common to absorption accounting.)

Following the PV is a section of the income statement for period costs. These period costs (or expenses) are broken down into categories such as supervision, maintenance, research, marketing, and so on. They represent *actual expenses incurred in the month of the statement.* In absorption accounting, on the other hand, some expenses (particularly supervision) become buried in inventory; and, the costs presented on an absorption statement are not the true costs for that month. Under direct costing, every dollar spent in that month must be covered (by profit contribution) or else there will be a loss, and there can be no hiding this loss in inventory. Thus, management obtains a more realistic evaluation of the profitability of the operation.

Direct costing provides a simple method for computing the break-even point. The break-even sales point is computed by dividing the PV factor into the total period expenses. This determines the number of sales dollars required to break even or come to a zero profit. Take for example, Table 14–1, May Actual column: 600 divided by 48.3 = $1,242 break-even sales.

Once each reporting period, the direct cost statement must be converted into an absorption accounting statement for tax and audit purposes. Therefore, the next to last item on the income statement adjusts to an absorption-type statement by increasing or decreasing the profit by the amount of the fixed overhead. This figure would have been added to or deducted from the inventory under the absorption method. This adjustment can materially change the income picture, depending on whether the inventory increases or decreases. For this reason, direct costing presents a more realistic picture of income because any increase or decrease in inventory has no relationship to profitability.

Product Profit Contribution Report

The direct cost income statement can be broken down into the product profit contribution report, shown in Table 14–2. This report shows the recyclables that are profitable. It is thus very useful to recycling operations because of the wide fluctuations in sales price for materials. It is more detailed than the income statement in that it shows individual sales of each product, direct costs at standard, and the variance from this standard. It also shows the PV of each individual product. In general, by selling more of the high PV products, we increase the profit of the operation. (These are the items we need to develop markets for!)

Using the direct costing statement, management can thus determine directly the effect of any volume change. For example, under product X, if we added another $5,000 sale within the present capacity of the transfer station, the net profit will go up $2,500. This figure is obtained by multiplying the $5,000 sale by the PV of 50 percent. Since there are no increased period costs, this additional profit contribution of $2,500 is pure profit. Of course, the same

TABLE 14–2 PRODUCT PROFIT CONTRIBUTION REPORT
MONTH OF MAY

	Product X		Product Y		Product Z		
	Actual	Budget	Actual	Budget	Actual	Budget	Total
Sales (shipments)	$5,000		$3,200		$1,000		$9,200
Returns	—		200		—		200
Net sales	$5,000	$5,000	$3,000	$4,000	$1,000	$1,000	$9,000
Direct costs:							
Material	875	875	525	700	175	175	1,575
Labor	1,000	1,000	600	800	200	200	1,800
Expense	375	375	225	300	75	75	675
Commissions	250	250	150	200	50	50	450
Variance:							
Material	25		(25)				—
Labor	—		(200)		75		(125)
Expense	(210)		(126)		(39)		(375)
Reserves	—						
Total direct costs	$2,315	$2,500	$1,149	$2,000	$ 536	$ 500	$4,000
Profit contribution	2,685	2,500	1,851	2,000	464	500	5,000
P/V	54%	50%	62%	50%	46%	50%	55%
Period costs:							
Material period cost	228		127		45		400
Labor period cost	1,552		621		427		2,600
Total period cost	$1,780		$ 748		$ 472		$3,000
Operating profit (loss)	$ 905		$1,103		$ (8)		$2,000

computations work in reverse, if sales decline. In recycling, this increase or decrease in sales could come from quality control, or finding new markets!

The two statements shown in Tables 14–1 and 14–2 provide a wealth of operating information: We can obtain the break-even point directly; we can determine whether to lower or intensify our sort, or the value of gaining additional sales and how much to spend increasing our markets; we can determine which product is most profitable; and finally, we can determine the true overhead or period expenses.

PRICING

Our marketing people need to know how to use pricing to influence sales of commodities and relate them back to actual operations. There is more to this than we see on the surface. Once a community meets the state mandated reduction, for example, it now has a choice of products which are most suitable for building income. One approach is to use the minimum pricing method, illustrated in Table 14–3. This method provides a choice of three prices: (1) the PV price based on the budget, (2) the market price, and (3) the sales price based on marking up material and labor with burden rates. Obviously, each price affects sales volume and operating income.

From the history of past operations, we know what PV to expect at our present operating rate and the profit contribution we will have available to meet our projected budget for next year. To generate more income, we need to increase the PV; in other words, to either get a higher price, reduce material, labor, and direct expenses, or pay less for the materials we buy at our buy-back centers.

Therefore, to obtain the price using a budgeted PV, we divide the total direct cost (for example $3.47) by the budget PV (50 percent). The answer ($6.94) is the budget price. As the target price, this figure will enable us to stay within our recycling budget. As it stands now, if we are to meet current burden factors, material handling, and period cost rates we need to get $8.83. This figure may be high because our overhead is high for this period, or because of other reasons. On the other hand, if the competition is bidding $6.50 on this particular recyclable, and if we need the order (at $6.50), our income will be hurt to the extent of

TABLE 14–3   MINIMUM PRICING METHOD

Customer _____   Quote # _____

Description _____

		Product X material to labor 2-1	Product Y material to labor 1-1	Product Z material to labor 1-2
Material		$ 2.00	$ 1.40	$ 0.88
Labor		1.00	1.40	1.76
Direct expense 47.3%		0.47	0.67	0.83
Total direct cost		$ 3.47	$ 3.47	$ 3.47
Material handling 52.9%		1.05	0.74	0.46
Period cost on D/L 254.2%		2.45	3.56	4.47
Total		$ 7.06	$ 7.77	$ 8.40
Profit 20%		1.77	1.94	2.10
Sales price	(A)	$ 8.83	$ 9.71	$10.50
P/V on burden basis (%)		60.7	64.3	67.0
P/V based on budget by product type (%)		50.0	60.0	65.0
P/V sales price	(B)	$ 6.94[a]	$ 8.67	$ 9.92
Market price		$ 6.50	$ 9.50	$12.00
P/V based on market	(C)	46.6	63.5	71.1

[a] $\dfrac{\text{Total direct cost}}{\text{PV (product)}} = \dfrac{3.47}{.50} = 6.94$

$.44 times the number of units sold. Obviously, this method enables each community to negotiate price effectively on a competitive basis.

Note that although burden rates fluctuate from time to time, the PV does not; it has nothing to do with current burden pools. Neither does the market price have anything to do with the current burden rates. This information enables us to price our products as we add new sorts (new products) to our transfer station. We are not certain of our burden rates for the future and the PV method eliminates this problem. We need only decide what rate of PV the market will support for this new product and compare it against the budget.

It is interesting to note that as the material-to-labor ratio increases, the minimum PV needed to operate profitably drops, due to reduced labor costs going into the product. This relationship encourages higher rates of recycling up to the limits of our sorting capacity and available recyclables.

BUDGETING

Direct costing works well with budgeting. In recycling operations, all budgets start with the tonnage forecast. This forecast estimates the amount of material we will have to sell, how much we can budget for buy-back operations, how much labor to hire, and how much overhead expense will be incurred. If our sales of recyclables do not meet forecasts, then the budgets have to be replanned. This means that shipments must be kept on schedule and conform to the forecast.

Once the forecast is worked up by management, it is costed out by the operating and accounting personnel, who break it into sections. Each section of the budget is prepared by the operating manager in charge of a specific function using the sales plan provided by management.

These smaller budgets are collected together then, and the total budget is submitted by the operating managers to top management. They now have an overview of net income and cash flow. Management and the administration now review the budget in relation to the profit/cost goals of the recycling center. If necessary, adjustments are made. Once all levels of management are satisfied, the budget is published as an operating plan.

Certain controls are instituted. The addition of personnel must be in accordance with the budget and must be approved by the budget director. Purchases of capital additions, even though budgeted, must also be coordinated through and approved by the budget director.

The accounting department is a vital element in the maintenance of the recycling center's profit plan. Accounting has copies of all the departmental budgets, and it is the accounting department's responsibility to ensure that the budgets do not run over on a monthly basis. Variations from the monthly department budgets must obtain the approval of the administration. To assist the department managers in staying within their budgets, they are given monthly reports showing their own progress against the plan.

Table 14–1 contains two columns that provide important guidelines. The first of these ("Planned") is the projected operating plan. The second ("Planned at Actual Volume") allows for the fact that volume will vary from month to month within the plan; therefore, by inserting actual shipping figures, the corresponding planned direct costs can be adjusted to this volume level. Thus, the sales volume was planned at $2,000, and actual sales were $3,000. Actual buy-back (or material) costs were $500, versus a planned figure of $525. The adjusted figures are easily obtainable, since costs vary directly with volume, and are proportional to the sales dollars. In this example, we note that $750 labor was spent versus a planned cost of $600. Armed with this information, the production manager can review job-cost records supplied by the accounting department to determine the cause of this $150 variance. The budgeted period costs are compared directly with actual expenses, as these can be traced back to the detailed budgets of the individual departmental manager.

The budgets for each department are derived directly from the financial records, so that each month-end closing produces departmental breakdowns for that month and for the year to date. It is also possible to run intermediate reports, as needed, on the computer for progress checks during the month. This type of intermediate report would be desirable, for example, for large projects, or sudden shifts in product mix within the community, to keep track of expenditures against a daily schedule, or for contract reporting. Examples are given in Figures 14–1 and 14–2, showing the information in graphic form. These two graphs relate planned or budgeted outlays against actual expenditures and warn of overruns. One graph relates the expenditures against time, and the second relates them against planned costs.

Special projects that extend over several months such as facility expansions, new plant construction, and other long-term programs can be tracked in this way by combining budgeted figures against the periodic computer printouts.

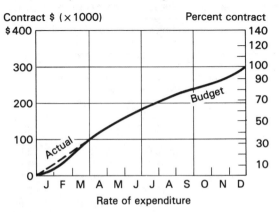

Figure 14-1 Expenditures rated against time.

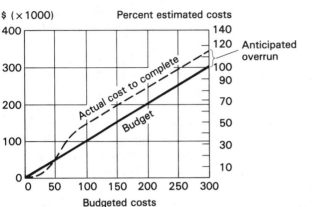

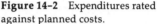

Figure 14-2 Expenditures rated against planned costs.

The monthly printout provides an evaluation of each department and a means for measuring overruns. If a graph is used, these overruns are plotted, as seen. Budgets provide interdepartmental discipline, but they need to be closely followed up with corrective action.

The Detailed Budget

The monthly budgets by department and all subsequent reports are derived directly from the financial data used in the profit and loss statement (P&L). Hence, divisional budget totals relate directly to the figures on the P&L for that division. Table 14–4 is an example of a detailed budget for an accounting department. This is a typical computer printout format. The account numbers in the left-hand column correspond to the chart of account numbers maintained by accounting.

TABLE 14–4 EXAMPLE OF DETAILED BUDGET FOR ACCOUNTING DEPARTMENT

Comparative report no. 811	Budget report—accounting Admin. level #3		December page 1 Dept. #11	
		Current month This month budget vs.		Year to date This year budget vs.
Account no.	Description	Actual	Variation	Actual	Variation
	12 Month projected budget				
Period expenses—controllable					
311910	Salaries and wages 63,603.00	4,911.86	5,060.00 148.14–	59,938.13	63,603.00 3,664.87–
311912	Sick leave .00	19.35	.00 19.35	807.85	.00 807.85
311913	Excused time .00	.00	.00 .00	135.45	.00 135.45

TABLE 14–4 *(Continued)*

Account no.	Description	Current month This month budget vs. Actual	Variation	Year to date This year budget vs. Actual	Variation
311950	Premium time	128.09	19.00	701.68	501.00
		501.00	109.09		200.68
311951	Payroll taxes	461.66	459.00	5,589.49	5,801.00
		5,801.00	2.66		211.51–
311952	Vacation and holiday	436.68	465.00	4,958.56	5,598.00
		5,598.00	28.32–		639.44–
311953	Group ins and workmens comp	142.39	218.00	2,557.08	2,494.00
		2,494.00	75.61–		63.08
311920	Office supplies	8.41	210.00	1,657.42	2,000.00
		2,000.00	201.59–		342.58–
311922	Books and dues	.00	25.00	189.82	200.00
		200.00	25.00–		10.18–
311923	Repairs to office equipment	4.12	9.00	154.75	151.00
		151.00	4.88–		3.75
311924	Postage	132.25	118.00	1,314.23	1,497.00
		1,497.00	14.25		182.77–
311925	Travel	.00	22.00	125.61	199.00
		199.00	22.00–		73.39–
311926	Conference	.00	23.00	185.82	298.00
		298.00	23.00–		112.18–
311928	Professional services	2,165.56–	1,009.00	13,418.23	14,997.00
		14,997.00	3,174.56–		1,578.77–
311930	Telephone	.00	.00	446.47	.00
		.00	.00		446.47
311934	Collection expense	121.16–	4.00	45.98	150.00
		150.00	128.16–		104.02–
311935	Provision for bad debts	630.13	230.00	7,096.72	4,600.00
		4,600.00	400.13		2,496.72
311936	Data processing	3,311.14	2,422.00	38,995.99	36,502.00
		36,502.00	892.14		2,493.99
311946	Copying costs	.00	.00	49.69	.00
		.00	.00		49.69
311947	Miscellaneous	3.86–	62.00	1,594.64	1,003.00
		1,003.00	65.86–		591.64
Total controllable expense		7,895.50	10,355.00	139,963.61	139,594.00
	139,594.00		2,459.50–		369.61

Noncontrollable expenses

Account no.	Description	Actual	Variation	Actual	Variation
311955	Depreciation	.00	.00	.00	.00
		.00	.00		.00
311954	Occupancy expense	1,072.91	.00	15,685.10	.00
		.00	1,072.91		15,685.10
Total noncontrollable expense		1,072.91	.00	15,685.10	.00
			1,072.91		15,685.10
Total period expenses		8,968.41	10,355.00	155,648.71	139,594.00
	139,594.00		1,386.59–		16,054.71

A similar budget is printed for each department. Individual figures within the specific departmental budgets are based on projected operating levels for the coming year. For example, "Salaries and Wages" are derived from present wage levels, anticipated pay increases, and any personnel changes planned. Operating costs, such as "Office Supplies" are usually taken from past records of expenses, adjusted for increases in operating levels. These figures, projected for the year, are shown under the "12 Month Projected Budget" column to the left. Actual expenditures are reported at the end of each month in the column headed "This Month Actual," and year-to-date expenditures are shown in the column headed "This Year Actual."

Variances from the budgeted figures are shown in the columns headed "Budget vs. Variation." The budgeted figure is shown first, and directly under it, the variance is shown. This variance is the difference between the actual expense and the budget for the month, or year to date. The variance is "plus" if the expenditure shows an unfavorable result, and "minus" for a favorable variance (meaning that the department has spent less than its allowance).

Each report is issued monthly, keeping a cumulative record of expenditures versus allowance, so that the managers can gauge their progress to date. In addition, since the yearly total budget figure shows on each report, managers can evaluate the firm's position against future plans. The figures for all columns are totaled at the end of the departmental report so that managers can see how things stand overall. Thus, a manager can be doing badly in one account but be on budget overall. This information enables the manager to take corrective steps in problem areas and allows for adjusting expenditures, while staying within the overall budget.

FINANCIAL STATEMENTS FOR DIRECT COSTING

Table 14–5 is a typical P&L (income) statement for a firm using direct costing. Table 14–6 is the corresponding balance sheet. The period expenses by department are directly related to the total budget figures at the bottom of the "This Month Actual" column in Table 14–4. The two figures would match if the two examples were from the same month and company. Similarly, the P&L format, starting with "Gross Sales" and moving down item by item approximates the chart of accounts.

The most notable feature of a direct-cost P&L is that commissions and other costs varying with volume are grouped with operating costs, while at the same time, fixed costs are all grouped below the "Profit Contribution" line.

Break-Even Charts

The P&L grouping just discussed permits easy computation and display of break-even figures. The break-even point is found by dividing total fixed or period costs by the profit variable (51 percent). This places the break-even point at

TABLE 14-5   INCOME STATEMENT FOR FEBRUARY

	Current period	Year to date
Gross sales	$2,671,762	$5,138,130
Sales returns & allowances	127,357	216,794
Total net sales	$2,544,405	$4,921,336
Direct costs (opns.)	$1,080,138	$2,113,234
Commissions	167,300	344,319
Total direct costs	$1,247,439	$2,457,553
Profit contribution	1,296,965	2,463,782
	51%	50%
Period expenses:		
Engineering	$ 113,020	$ 262,917
Quality control	68,095	142,149
Production	295,303	576,226
Personnel	36,664	79,280
Administration	103,424	193,090
Accounting	102,081	190,410
Marketing	113,116	228,438
Subtotal	$ 831,707	$1,672,513
Occupancy	95,614	193,602
Depreciation	46,150	71,020
Interest expense	54,544	102,366
Amortization of excess cost of acquired business	8,460	16,235
Other income	(63)	(10,313)
Period cost complement	—	—
Total period costs	$1,036,411	$2,045,424
Income before taxes on income	260,554	418,357
Provision for income taxes av. 9%	23,449	37,999
Net income or (loss)	$ 237,104	$ 380,358

about $2,030,000 per month. The profit variable tells us that on every dollar of sales over and above the break-even point (if fixed costs stay fixed), we make $.51 profit.

Figure 14-3 is a break-even chart based on the P&L. To draw the chart, chart paper is marked off with sales (shipments) on the bottom and costs/profit along the left side. Then moving along the bottom, pick the point where $2,540,000 (February sales) would occur and draw a vertical line as shown: It is marked "February" on the chart. The height of this line is equal to "total period costs" plus "income before taxes" taken from the P&L. This adds up to $130,000. A sloping line starting at zero on the graph passed through the top of this vertical line represents the 51 percent profit variable of our P&L. (The graph actually shows a 52 percent profit variable because the graph was constructed from March figures instead of ours, but no other change is required for the graph.)

TABLE 14-6 BALANCE SHEET AS OF FEBRUARY 29

Assets

Current assets:

Cash		$ 725,854
Accounts receivable—net		5,552,875
Inventories:		
Corrugated	$1,820,563	
Aluminum	409,430	
Glass	985,981	
Plastics	201,639	
Period cost complement	1,263,301	
Total inventories	$4,680,916	
Reserve for losses	(428,607)	
Net inventories		4,252,308
Prepaid expenses		$ 588,532
Total current assets		$11,119,569

Noncurrent assets:

Equipment and improvements		5,932,165
Less: Allowance for depreciation amortization		(4,455,477)
Net equipment and improvements		$ 1,476,687
Subs. acquisition cost		543,535
Other assets		411,777
		$13,551,569

Liabilities & stockholders' equity

Current liabilities:

Current portion of long term		$ 393,605
Notes payable—secured		3,596,093
Accounts payable		1,828,434
Accrued liabilities		1,834,401
Total current liabilities		$ 7,652,534
Long-term debt		$ 1,313,597
Total liabilities		8,966,132

Stockholders' equity:

Preferred stock		
Par value $100 per share		
Authorized 50,000 shares		
Issued:		
Class A, 4% 7,480 shares		$ 748,000
Class B, 7% 25,000 shares		2,500,000
Class C, 7% 10,000 shares		1,000,000
Common stock		
Par value $.10 per share		
Authorized 3,000,000 shares		105,820
Additional paid-in capital		245,580
Accumulated deficit beginning of year		(394,321)
Income current year		380,358)
Total accumulated deficit		(13,962)
Total stockholders' equity		$ 4,585,437
Total liabilities and stockholders' equity		$13,551,569

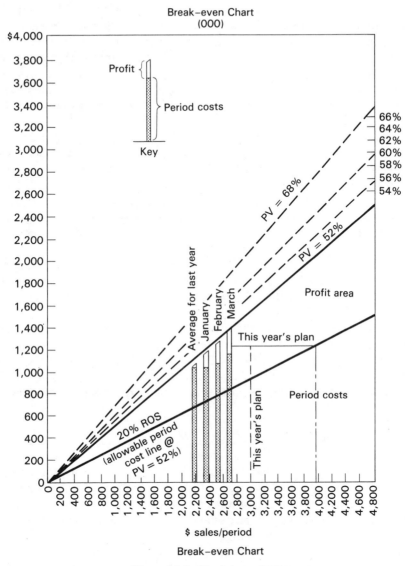

Figure 14-3 Break-even chart.

The shaded area of the vertical lines represents period costs. The open area is profit. The large shaded area represents the amount of period costs that can be absorbed at a given sales figure to get a 20 percent return on sales (ROS) at 52 percent PV. (This is an arbitrary goal set by management.)

The plan for this year calls for average period costs of $1,250,000. If this average can be maintained until sales reach $3,950,000 (indicated by broken vertical line with a bar and dot), then the recycling center will realize 20 percent ROS. The 20 percent ROS line is calculated as follows: The plan for the year calls for average sales of $3 million. Twenty percent of this is $600,000.

Since the recycling center has a goal of 52 percent PV, a vertical line dropped from the 52 percent PV line through the $3 million sales point (coinciding with this year's plan) on the bottom of the chart should show $600,000 of unshaded area (profit area). It doesn't. Instead, our actual period costs exceed this allowable cost figure by the darkened area of the vertical bar. As the PV increases, the increase in profits can be computed directly from the chart. For example, using our February vertical line, a PV of 54 percent would have given us an additional $120,000 profit for the month.

The break-even chart is helpful in controlling creeping expenditures because a copy of the chart can be given to all department managers with a challenge to keep costs stable. A goal can be set to work toward the 20 percent ROS and each manager can see how his or her own costs fit in with that goal. The plan also shows the value of improving the PV. It shows that a $120,000 improvement in profit may be possible by increasing productivity, cutting other costs, or negotiating better prices. These objectives, which may be obtainable at costs less than $120,000, make the effort worth studying. The value of sales increases can also be analyzed. The operation is currently making $220,000 profit (for March) on $2,700,000 in sales. An increase to $2,800,000 in sales will produce another $57,000 profit. Increasing the sales price will also increase the period costs and the profits.

The break-even chart provides another useful service. After the month's final sales have been made, within minutes an estimate can be made of the month's profits. For example, if April's sales total $3,200,000 at the close of the last day of April, then the profits should be approximately $680,000. Practice in developing and reworking the chart will improve these figures over time.

CASH FLOW PLANNING

One of the most important tools for communities getting into recycling is to develop and maintain projections on CASH FLOW. Perhaps no other management tool plays such an important role in survival for small operations than this simple device. An example is given in Panel 14–1. (All figures are projections for the coming months, based on average past volumes and costs.)

In all likelihood, the high failure rate of local recycling operations can be explained by the inexperience of most operators with simple accounting and cash-flow methods. Cash-flow projections, maintained continuously, begun before operations start up, help decide when to act, when to apply for funding, and when to go to the legislature for help.

SUMMARY

Accounting is a method for measuring change in a business. By relating expenses, labor costs, miscellaneous expenses, accounts receivable, and cash

PANEL 14–1   CASH FLOW

Month or Quarter			
Income from sale of recycling	_____	_____	_____
Less commissions	_____	_____	_____
Income from grants, etc.	_____	_____	_____
Income from chgs. (pick-up, etc.)	_____	_____	_____
Other income	_____	_____	_____
(A) Total income	_____	_____	_____
Expenses:			
Labor	_____	_____	_____
Buy-back expenses	_____	_____	_____
Contract costs	_____	_____	_____
Telephone	_____	_____	_____
Utilities	_____	_____	_____
Rent, leases	_____	_____	_____
Interest	_____	_____	_____
Purchase-supplies	_____	_____	_____
Maintenance	_____	_____	_____
Insurance	_____	_____	_____
Freight	_____	_____	_____
Travel, entertainment	_____	_____	_____
Taxes, workers comp., etc.	_____	_____	_____
Miscellaneous	_____	_____	_____
(B) Total expenses	=======	=======	=======
Cash flow (A – B)	_____	_____	_____
Cumulative	_____	_____	_____

From "Community Recycling Seminars," by Institute for Global Action. Used by permission.

receipts, accounting presents a picture of the status of the recycling center in terms of the P&L. It is *static, however, because* the P&L reflects only the current status of the center. Furthermore, it does not highlight problem areas. For specific information on the conveyor and handling levels of activity, it is necessary to set up means for measuring those activities. These measurements are obtained by budgets, cost accounting, and reports. It is by this type of detailed analysis that early corrective action can take place.

Budgets also serve as planning tools that enable management to forecast the next year's income and expenses. The plan must be audited and kept on schedule.

Direct costing and budgeting provide tools for increasing income and reducing costs. Managerial accounting provides guidelines and mileposts to stay on course and avoids crises before they occur. Properly used, a good accounting system is the most essential element of management. It brings together all the training and experience of the recycling managers and presents them with a score card rating their ability.

See Panel 14–2 for a concise summary of the last three chapters.

PANEL 14–2 THREE KEYS TO AN EFFECTIVE RECYCLING OPERATION

1. UTILIZING RESOURCES

   —CASH FLOW

2. UTILIZING PEOPLE

   —WORK SAMPLING

   —QUALITY OF LIFE

   —GOOD MANAGEMENT

3. MAXIMIZING EFFECTIVENESS

   —PARETO'S LAW

   —MANAGEMENT BY EXCEPTION

   —MANAGEMENT BY OBJECTIVES

From "Community Recycling Seminars," by Institute for Global Action. Used by permission.

15

Obtaining Quality of Services: Recycling

EDITOR'S NOTE:

A. C. Rosander quotes the following story in his book Applications of Quality Control in the Service Industries.

The Denver Airport was one of the ten largest in the country. In 1980, the parking lot concession was handled by APCOA, which collected parking fees based on time in the lot. The ticket was time stamped at time of arrival, and on leaving, the elapsed time was computed to determine the precise charge. During the course of the fiscal year, total revenues reported to the city were $5.28 million, of which Denver got 89 percent. The average revenue per ticket came to $1.66 in 1980 (down from $1.86 in 1979, and $2.05 in 1978.)

Professor George Bardwell of the University of Denver "sensed trouble" when he paid a fee of $54 and the cashier rang up $2.00. Bardwell complained to the city, but got no action. He then went to the local press, Rocky Mountain News, which arranged for an audit. The audit was done by sampling techniques (remember work sampling).

In addition to discovering that 100,000 tickets in 1980 were "unaccounted for" the sample showed that the average revenue per ticket was $2.79! (That's a discrepancy in reporting of $1.13 per ticket!)

At $5.28 million reported revenues for the year, at $1.66 per ticket (reported) that's 3,180,000 tickets which were $1.13 short each ($3,593,000!); plus 100,000 at $2.79, for another $279,000!

I add this story to Mr. Rosander's account because I know of no better way to emphasize the importance of what we have been trying to say in these last five chapters.

The methods we have been describing, plus Mr. Rosander's, are the watch dog on the treasury.

Service is people helping people.

The scope of service industries, which includes local, state, and federal governments, is tremendous. Employment in these industries is about 70 percent of total employment in the United States, and over three times as great as employment in manufacturing—about 72 million versus 22 million. As was emphasized earlier, it thus is just as important, if not more important, to emphasize improvement of quality of services as to emphasize the improvement of the quality of products. The latter predominates because quality is defined in terms of dimensions, measurements, and objective factors. Personal and subjective factors, which are common in quality of services, are not so visible in quality of products.

Unique Nature of Services

Services are characterized by several important and unique features:

- People intensive
- Face-to-face relationships
- Large number of transactions: buying, selling, shipping, paying, depositing
- Large volume of paper work: checks, claims, tax returns, policies, tickets, bills
- Numerous chances for making human errors and mistakes
- Time is very important: service time, delay or waiting time, idle time, excessive time, downtime
- Human reliability is very important because of cost and safety
- Some services are monopolies so there is no choice
- Some services are highly regulated by governments: banks, insurance, and so on, so choice is limited or nonexistent
- Services involve a mass market, or numerous markets, not true of most manufacturing
- Services involve very few physical measurements or tests compared with manufacturing.

What Services Are Not

Manufacturing is dominated by engineering but services are not. The exception is certain aspects and functions connected with public utilities, and some aspects of recycling. This no doubt is one of the major reasons why quality of services has progressed so slowly.

Services are not "intangible." Quite the contrary, there is evidence to show that quality of services is as "tangible" as quality of products. The evidence is found in a Gallop study of perceptions of 1,005 persons of quality of products and services.[1] The number reporting poor-quality services was 593 compared with 534 reporting poor-quality products. These persons had no more difficulty identifying services and their quality than they had identifying products and their quality.

The Importance of Products in Services

A vital relation exists between services and products. The product is so closely a part of the service that if the product lacks quality, so does the service. The following examples illustrate the important role products play in services:

- A poor-quality steak means a poor-quality dinner.
- An inaccurate instrument may mean a false diagnosis.
- A faulty bus may mean not only a rough ride but a dangerous one.
- "One size fits all" means no fit at all and the discomfort that goes with it.
- A wrong drug may be ineffective, may make things worse, or may be fatal.
- A defective part means trouble, inconvenience, high repair cost, even danger.
- A faulty anaesthesia machine can result in fatalities.
- A faulty water meter leads to inconvenience, errors, and false billing.

QUALITY OF SERVICES _____

Good-Quality Service

As an example of good-quality service, in the customer waiting room of the service department of an automobile dealer is a placard stating company policy toward customer service:

C stands for courtesy

A stands for accuracy

R stands for reliability

E stands for efficiency

---

[1] *Consumer Perceptions Concerning the Quality of American Products and Services,* conducted for the American Society for Quality Control, The Gallop Organization, Princeton, NJ, September 1985.

The policy calls for courtesy toward the customer, with accuracy, reliability, and efficiency from the mechanics and other personnel. Customers don't often see this placard because they bring in their cars so seldom. This means high reliability, low repair costs, low maintenance costs, long life, and low life-cycle costs. Above all, it means freedom from trouble. No wonder that customers by the millions buy these foreign automobiles.

Here is another example of good-quality service. A supermarket has a flower shop that fills special orders on request. The customer is known very well by the flower girl because he has placed many orders for flowers in the past. He orders a dozen carnations of each of three colors, to be picked up on a certain day. When the flowers are delivered to the store the day before pick-up, the girl finds them small and pale in color—in other words, poor-quality carnations. She rejects them, calls the greenhouse 50 miles away and requests that they deliver three dozen of their best carnations the next day. Result: three dozen excellent carnations, a very pleased customer, and a very pleased person who receives the carnations on her birthday. The flower girl knew what the customer had purchased in the past and took steps to get the quality of flowers that he wanted, without any increase in price. Most sales clerks would not have done this. They would have accepted the first delivery of poor-quality flowers, and then made excuses if the customer wasn't satisfied. This girl knows without being told that a pleased customer is a steady customer. (This is an example of how the quality of the product affects the quality of the service.)

Poor-Quality Service

A customer uses a credit card to buy from a large retail store, which has stores in several neighboring cities. The customer is a long-time customer because this is her favorite store. One month the account statement she receives shows $166 charged to her for goods she never bought. Her records show this. In paying her account for the month, she informs them of the error and asks them to correct it. They refuse to believe her. The central credit department tells her over the telephone that (1) she has forgotten what she purchased, or (2) she let her family or friends use her credit card and has forgotten about it. (The credit department employees are sure she has forgotten what she did.) She persists. The company finally gets the sales slip involved and makes a copy of it:

- The name on the slip is not hers. It is illegible, very hard to make out.
- The goods were sold at Store 6 where she never shopped.
- The goods were sold on a Saturday when she was at home 55 miles away.

The sales slip shows that the credit department has made a serious error, but they still refuse to admit it. All they did was send an affidavit to her to sign stating that someone used her account number without her permission.

There was never any admission by the company that they, and not the customer, had made a mistake. There was never any apology for the insulting manner of the employees in the credit department. There apparently was never any attempt made to determine how the ten-digit account number of the customer got recorded on the sales slip. When this question was answered the whole situation would be cleared up. For all anybody knew, the account number was placed on the sales slip by the credit department to collect a bad debt of $166 from someone else. The other possible answer is that someone got the number from the neighborhood store and used it to buy at Store 6.

Quality of service is defined as meeting the needs and requirements of the user (or resident). Naturally, quality can be perceived from the viewpoint of either the supplier or user of a service.

Quality from the Seller's Viewpoint

Every community recycling operation must meet the needs of its customers and perform in a satisfactory manner. This also means keeping costs under control because, as we saw earlier, building quality into services is an effective way to reduce costs, while at the same time pleasing the customer. The following are examples:

- Reduce errors and mistakes, and hence the amount of rework
- Reduce wasted time: downtime, idle time, job time, service time
- Use better methods, techniques, and processes
- Reduce failures and trouble
- Reduce overhead costs
- Get more and better data at a reduced cost
- Reduce defects in, and inspection of, purchased products
- Reduce customer complaints
- Reduce lost customers.

Quality from the Customer's Viewpoint

The customer is the ultimate buyer of our services. What the customer wants in the form of *good*-quality service can be readily seen by observing what individual customers cite as the reasons for *poor*-quality service.

The predominant reason for poor-quality service is employee attitudes and behavior. Customers want courtesy, consideration and helpfulness, friendliness, and accuracy. They want a trouble-free transaction with competent employees who can do the work accurately, and who treat the customer fairly and justly.

A second characteristic of quality of service is promptness. Slow service is a common complaint in many major service agencies, such as banking, insurance, hospitals, government, auto repair, and retail stores. This is a problem also in doctors' offices, restaurants, and supermarket check-outs. For the company, it wants to reduce wasted labor time, but the customer wants to reduce the excessive time required to obtain services. *Time is just as important to the customer as it is to the service agency.*

A third factor in quality is price. Customers complain that the price is too high for the service received. This can be a valid complaint. An affordable price is of major importance to most customers. Customers want a price commensurate with quality. They do not want to pay increased prices when quality is going down, as it is with some products today. Residents want reliable, tidy pick-ups and our product (recyclables) users want materials that are clean and can be used without causing damage to equipment.

Another factor in quality of services that needs to be emphasized is human error. Customers want error-free performance everywhere. In many of our products, the goal of zero error is imperative because safety is paramount. Customers do not want to be blamed or inconvenienced because of errors and mistakes the company makes. Yet this situation is far too common. The customer resents the company that makes an error but is very slow or reluctant to correct it. Two examples:

- It takes a mortgage company about three months to correct a documented error of $314. The customer has to write letters, make telephone calls, and take a day to drive over 100 miles, before the error is corrected.
- A bank enters a deposit of $1,842 as $18.42. The depositor, a business man, calls attention to it after he is penalized for overdrawing his account. He finally has to sue the bank in court for wasting his time. He wins.

The service company should examine complaints promptly and carefully, and correct them quickly and fairly. If it is going to maintain the confidence of the customer, and its own integrity and credibility, it will take steps not only to correct its errors but prevent them in the future. The last thing it will do is force the customer to go into court to get justice.

The following summarizes what quality means to the individual:

- The customer is treated decently, fairly, and with courtesy.
- Excessive waiting, delay, and service times are avoided at drop-off centers and other contact centers.
- Prices are commensurate with quality. No low quality at a high price.
- Customers get what they order, what they request, what they need, what they like, and what they pay for.
- Products are free of defects and trouble.
- Complaints are taken seriously and corrected immediately.
- Promises that the service agency makes are kept.
- The customer is not penalized or inconvenienced by the errors and mistakes the service company makes.

- Employees are competent, careful, and qualified to perform the service jobs they are in.

TWO KINDS OF QUALITY CHARACTERISTICS _____

The first of these are characteristics which permit measurement within a range of a defined standard. Thus, *quality* exists when the variation around an aimed-at value is controlled and any variation that occurs is due to chance. Typical characteristics are the following:

- Delivery times
- Service times
- Absenteeism
- Turnover of employees
- Time required to do a job
- Percent utilization of machinery and equipment
- Percent utilization of employees
- Percent of recyclable materials accepted by processors

The second kind of quality characteristic is entirely different. These characteristics are the nonquality or antiquality characteristics which we want to get rid of, eliminate, and prevent. These are the ones we want to drive to zero. In other words, we do not accept a range of controlled variation. Characteristics of this type are the following:

- Human errors and mistakes
- Defects in purchased products
- Failure to do a job, for example, to produce usable materials
- Failure of equipment to operate
- Excessive time to do a job, perform a service, make a delivery or shipment
- Waiting time to have a service performed, waiting for work
- Indifferent or rude employees; unacceptable attitudes and behavior; unkempt or messy handling of waste at pick-ups
- Incompetent employee
- Refusal to correct a mistake or error
- Excessive time to correct a mistake or error
- Service that is not as advertised or claimed
- Faulty handling of a complaint
- Dissatisfied customers
- Lost customers

- Excessive price considering the quality of service
- Collection and use of inadequate and faulty data
- Faulty analysis and use of acceptable quality data.

Shewhart, the founder of modern statistical quality control, recommended that 25 consecutive samples of four be made in order to detect and eliminate "assignable causes" for the preceding characteristics. They could then be stabilized and brought under control. In other words, after making 25 samples, we could eliminate random occurrences and pin down problems caused by poor service—by people not doing their jobs right.

QUALITY OF PURCHASED PRODUCTS

Community recyclers are also buyers of products, which they need to render the services they perform. This means their ability to maintain quality of services depends upon the quality of the products they buy. As buyers, we can take several steps to insure that the products we buy are satisfactory. We can, for example:

- Prepare detailed specifications for each product for vendors to follow.
- Select vendors carefully.
- Work closely with vendors, including helping them with a quality improvement program.
- Have vendors submit evidence that specifications are met for each product in each shipment.
- Do business only with reliable and trustworthy vendors.

Basic Conflicts about Quality

Quality has been defined since Shewhart as meeting the needs of customers, of satisfying buyers, and of meeting human wants. This is easy to state but difficult to attain because the seller has different ideas of the nature of these needs than does the customer. Customers form heterogeneous groups whose needs vary greatly due to the following different characteristics:

• age	• income	• physical makeup
• sex	• occupation	• interests
• race	• education	• habits
• religion	• ethnic background	• life styles
• living standards	• residence	

There is no guarantee that the market, based primarily on profit, will find all of these needs a profitable undertaking to meet. The reasons are obvious:

- The individual does not buy according to his or her specifications based on needs to be met.
- It is not profitable for the seller to meet many of these needs.
- It is not convenient for the seller to meet the need.

In addition to the preceding reasons, customers sometimes fall outside the normal markets. Hence, they become victims of the tyranny of the marketplace. Their "needs are met," but only with available and often unacceptable goods or services.

Problems and Data Collection

Data collection is the key to problem detection, definition, and diagnosis. It is the first step to show what the present situation is; where operations now stand; what managers, supervisors, and employees are now doing. It is the first step to reveal what is in need of improvement. The following examples show how data collection can be used:

1. *To discover an unknown problem.* In a data processing division with 350 employees, a random time sample (RTS) (work sampling study) was made of the work of every employee for each of five consecutive days. The purpose was to estimate the time and cost of various functions, jobs, and projects. However, the study revealed something very unexpected. Several units reported idle time in the form of "waiting for work." This revealed a situation the director was not aware of so he took steps to have it corrected immediately.

   In another situation, a large public utility, working with a quality improvement team, discovered that the billing department was making 60,000 errors annually or about 250 daily on the average. Collecting a sample daily on errors in the billing department would have revealed the magnitude of the problem very quickly and what had to be done to eliminate it.

2. *To define problems.* Data can be used to define the magnitude and extent of a problem whose dimensions hitherto have been unknown. An example is noncompliance on federal income tax returns. This is done by taking a nationwide sample. (The data are published by the U.S. Treasury Department.) When this was done, for the first time, top-level officials and planners were able to establish the magnitude and the type of noncompliance. It now had a rational basis for the allocation of auditors (using Pareto's law) by going after the large offenders.

   Other examples are the monthly nationwide sample of households to estimate the number of unemployed in the United States, and the nationwide sample of shippers to estimate the shortage of freight cars.

3. *To resolve problems and correct management by hunch.* It is very easy for managers at all levels to jump to conclusions about the cause of a certain

situation. When management is by hunch, no data are needed but the dangers of being wrong are great. An example is a business whose sales had been dropping for some months. The president called in the sales force and rebuked them for falling down on the job. The surprised salespeople countered that they had been doing their job. They finally convinced the president to survey the lost customers. This showed that loss of customers was due to poor quality. It turns out that their quality went down when they changed vendors in order to save money. When they shifted back to the original vendor, quality improved and so did sales.

4. *To lead to immediate improvement.* Experience in the field of errors shows that *so long as the number and rate of errors are unknown, then whatever exists is accepted, and can be accepted indefinitely.* The mere act of collecting data on errors on a daily basis can bring about drastic changes. Once people know the error rate, they become motivated, under good supervision, to reduce it. We have numerous examples of this. Two examples are an insurance claim and a mail-order form in which the rates dropped below 1 percent in a matter of weeks. The work at Denver Airport mentioned at the beginning of this chapter is another.

5. *To show "problem" does not exist.* This is a different type of data problem. In this case the collection of biased or otherwise poor-quality data led to the creation of a "problem" situation that did not exist. In this case, the manager of a textile mill ran a test on one operator to find out how much yarn was being used per unit of output. From this figure he concluded that the employees were stealing $1 million of merchandise annually! He called in detectives who found nothing. He called in psychologists who also found nothing until one asked how the dollar figure was arrived at. This brought out the fact that the estimate was based on the performance of one of the best operators who used much less yarn per unit than the average of the group. There was no problem! The goods had not been stolen; they had never been made! The problem was not the employees. It was management.

In another case, the data from a faulty test created a public furor. The purpose was to test the difference in plutonium between Rocky Flats, near Denver, and a test site in Nevada. A herd of ten cattle was used at each site. Plutonium in lung tissue at Rocky Flats was 5.1 picocuries per kilogram; in Nevada the reading was 1.34 pc per kg. The press headline was that the level of plutonium was four times as great in the Rocky Flats area as in Nevada. A U.S. Senator got upset and called on the EPA to make a $100,000 study.

Examination of the data showed that the variation among animals within herds at each site was very high, indicating unstable averages—which in another test could be reversed. This is, in fact, what happened. A second test in Nevada yielded 12 pc per kg (a variation of almost 800 percent!). What appeared to be a striking difference was no difference at all. The test was not properly designed, nor were the data properly analyzed and reported. Apple arithmetic—four apples are four times one apple—did not apply. These were measurements, not counts.

Data Collection

Data collection is most vital in any quality improvement program because the quality of the inferences, estimates, decisions, and actions are no better than the quality of the data on which they are based.

Data are a means, not an end. It is a means as stated earlier to discover, define, and resolve problems, clarify situations, and defuse conflict. Data are collected with a specific purpose in mind. Collecting large masses of data to play around with is a waste of time and talent. Data should result from analysis of problems or problem situations relating to management and operations. In this way no more data are collected than are needed.

Good-quality data collection requires special knowledge not only of statistics but how to apply it. This means not only an ability to design probability samples but how to design questionnaires, data sheets, calculation layouts, observation forms, sample controls, and much more. A good-quality job requires careful planning, design, and execution. Data collection and analysis require the services of at least one good practitioner in statistics who knows how to apply that science to problems of management.

Those who do not believe this capability is necessary should see quality or quality assurance departments who have a large volume of data to process, analyze, and present, including sample data, *without having the slightest technical capability* to do so. These situations, which can be documented, *exist!* These businesses have a quality program that is running on one cylinder.

The simple methods used by Quality Circles are only the beginning. They can be effective in services, but they hardly scratch the surface. Many powerful techniques which are needed in service operations, such as random time sampling (work sampling), are completely ignored. The techniques needed are those which correct faults in the system and make breakthroughs that bring about substantial improvements.

All sample studies should be predesigned for a specific purpose using the principles of probability sampling, except for situations where an exploratory sample may be fitting. These designed samples have a number of advantages: They determine how the sample is to be selected, the method of estimation, and they may call for specified methods of analysis. They eliminate a lot of guesswork.[2]

---

[2] (For a detailed discussion of sampling techniques see W. Edwards Deming, *Sample Design for Business Research* (New York: John Wiley, 1960); A.C. Rosander, *Case Studies in Sample Design* (New York: Marcel Dekker, 1977); and A.C. Rosander, *Applications of Quality Control in the Service Industries* (New York: Marcel Dekker and Milwaukee: Quality Press, 1985).

Data Analysis and Interpretation

Just as important as collecting data is the interpretation of the data. One of the great advantages of the designed probability sample and the designed test or experiment is that the method of interpretation is an integral part of the design. In this way the maximum amount of information is obtained from the data at the same time that unsound interpretations are avoided.

Several methods are available, ranging from the simple to the complex. A wide variety of applications is described in my book mentioned earlier. Here are also some very useful techniques:

1. *Exploratory time chart.* This is a simple trend chart with numerical values such as counts, percents, aggregates, rates, averages, and ratios plotted vertically, and time plotted horizontally such as hours, days, weeks, and years. This is an effective way to show error rates, number of errors, volume of production, number of failures, downtime, sick leave, service time, and transit time.

2. *Simple tally of frequency of measurements.* This shows extreme values, bunching, discontinuities, and range. It can be used to show distribution of error rates, daily amount of production, downtime of each of the different kinds of equipment, sick leave and absenteeism by individuals, and the amount of time different people require to do the same job.

3. *Simple tally of frequency of counts of attributes.* This tally is made to study distribution of specific items under sources, causes, reasons, locations, and categories. Using this procedure to identify the most frequent causes of trouble is called Pareto analysis.

4. *Learning curve analysis.* The learning curve refers to a plot of some measure of learning as a function of time. This curve may take several forms: the error rate curve showing the reduction in errors as learning progresses, the volume of production curve showing the increase in production as errors are eliminated and learning eliminates wasted motion, and the unit time curve showing the reduction of time required to do an acceptable-quality job on each unit. This applies to a job that is entirely new to the employee, and a training course is necessary before the individual can do a satisfactory job.

Waste in Data Collection and Analysis

A major source of savings is to get rid of waste caused by excessive data collection and analysis. This means predesigned studies so that no more data are collected than the problem requires. It also means foregoing a sophisticated analysis of data when all that is needed is a simple analysis.

Organizations tend to suffer from the persistence of useless data. Annual reports issued by governments and large companies can easily be storehouses of data with little or no value. Data should be appraised periodically to see if they are serving a useful purpose, and those not needed should be eliminated.

HUMAN ERROR

The nation is beset with human errors, mistakes, and blunders. The resultant waste in time, resources, and people is tremendous. It may also result in human tragedy.

For our purposes, it is convenient to divide human error into two broad categories: common errors and critical errors. *Common errors* are those which are made in connection with paper work, data collection and analysis, operations, judgments, and decisions at all levels. Examples are the following:

- Errors in billing
- Errors in filling orders of all kinds
- Errors on claims
- Errors on reports
- Errors in financial transactions
- Errors in crediting receipt of payment
- Errors in processing carload waybills and other freight bills
- Errors in decisions and actions at lower levels.

Critical errors are of two types: those made by top-level managers which are destructive of the operation and its effectiveness, and those which are made at any level which are destructive of human life. Examples of management errors are the following:

- Changing vendors to reduce cost but losing quality and customers
- Using biased data to make false inferences and decisions about employees
- Refusing to face and meet competition. Using government action to restrict competition
- Moving into a new product line without adequate market research
- Moving into a highly competitive market
- Relying too much on government or community support.

The Prevention of Human Errors

A major part, if not the most important part, of a quality improvement program in services is making provision for the prevention of human errors at all levels of the organization. This means constant and persistent effort on the part of both management and employees. To do this it is first necessary to *reject* the common justifications of errors and mistakes, such as: "Making mistakes is human," "Everyone makes mistakes," or "To err is human." This attitude not only condones errors and mistakes, it fosters them.

Errors cannot be prevented until causes are identified and steps taken to eliminate them, or better yet prevent them from occurring in the first place. Space limitations do not allow an explanation to be made of the various types of errors and the various methods which can be used to prevent them; the following listings show that the types of error are numerous and that their prevention is not easy.

TYPES OF ERRORS

clerical	calculating	computer	sampling
observational	inspection	accounting	reporting
operational	procedural	transcribing	appraisal
statistical	recording	judgment	mathematical

METHODS OF PREVENTION

verification techniques

special training in knowledge and skills

audit methods

monthly error prevention meetings with supervisors, managers, and employees

screening at time of hiring and promotion

redundancy

self-checking

methods of review

effective use of technical knowledge

A program in prevention is justified when consideration is given to the waste that otherwise occurs because of corrections, rework, jobs that have to be done over, time spent on customer complaints, and other sources of loss.

The Prevention of Critical Errors

At the heart of critical errors is safety, the number one quality characteristic in pick-up operations, handling unsafe materials, working around machinery at transfer stations, and so on. The tragedy in most fatal accidents is that most of them are preventable.

The goal to stress is *safety first*. It is ABC (Always Be Careful). Of course it takes more than exhortations to bring about safety, but exhortations are a good way to let supervisors, managers, and employees know what the major goal is. To attain this goal requires a continuous error-prevention program at all levels.

Following are lists of causes of critical errors and possible remedies and preventive measures.

Some causes of critical errors are the following:

- Faulty judgment
- Refusal to follow operating rules
- Overriding of expert advice by management
- Lack of follow-up, lack of checking
- Absence of self-verification
- Lack of sound data
- Refusal to act
- Faulty storage
- Faulty labeling
- Faulty communication arrangements, breakdown of communication between those with know-how and the final decision makers.

Some remedies and preventive measures of critical errors are the following:

- Care in hiring (relative to knowledge and attitudes)
- Care in promotions (relative to knowledge and attitudes)
- Training in how to avoid error-prone situations
- Monthly safety seminars
- Error-prevention meetings and seminars
- Risk taking and how to avoid dangerous risks
- Monitoring and double-checking all operations of a critical nature
- Limited access to critical switches, valves, equipment, and so on
- Better and bigger labeling of all critical chemicals, explosives, gases, and so on
- Separate storage of all critical chemicals, explosives, gases, and so on.

THE COST OF QUALITY

The cost of quality is not defined the same way as the cost of a product or service. Crosby states that the cost of quality is the expense of doing things wrong.[3] The inference is clear: If things are done right, all of this expense is eliminated. Stated another way, the cost of quality is the cost of producing poor-quality products and rendering poor-quality services. It is now widely accepted that quality costs consist of four components:[4]

---

[3] Philip B. Crosby, *Quality is Free* (New York: McGraw-Hill, 1979), p. 11.

[4] *Quality Costs—What and How,* 2nd ed., American Society for Quality Control, Milwaukee, 1967. The *cost of quality* as currently defined is a misnomer. Really it is the cost of producing

1. *Prevention.* These are all of the personnel costs associated with the quality system: planning, designing, implementing, and maintaining a quality program.
2. *Appraisal.* These are the costs incurred in determining the degree of conformance to quality requirements: inspection, testing, audit, and evaluations.
3. *Internal failure.* Costs arising internally when products fail to meet quality requirements: scrap, rework, and repair.
4. *External failure.* Costs arising when products fail to meet quality requirements after transfer to the customer: complaints, returns, and replacing failures.

Internal and external failure are aspects of nonquality that need to be reduced if not eliminated. The first two components are aimed at reducing if not preventing the other two components. The success and effectiveness of a quality improvement program can be measured by the extent to which the first two components reduce the last two components. This is accomplished in a progressive manner by reducing the effects of the following aspects. In the source cited only the elimination of defects in products and the reduction of customer complaints are mentioned.

DEVELOPING A QUALITY PROGRAM

The basic elements of a quality program have been described: services, quality of services, quality characteristics, data collection and analysis, the critical role of human error, and the cost of quality. The next step is to describe how all of these parts are put together to form an effective quality improvement program. Two stages are necessary to accomplish this: a preparatory stage and an operational stage.

The Preparatory Stage

The purpose of this stage is to get managers, supervisors, and employees not only to understand quality concepts but to accept them to the extent that they are ready to apply them. This means teamwork. It means that the program cannot really start until all managers and supervisors are convinced of its value to them as well as to the operation.

Regardless of how a program is started, it will be necessary to educate everyone in quality goals, quality techniques, and the role of every individual in making the quality program a success. This can be done with the help of outside seminars and consultants, by courses in quality given in house, and by training on the job.

---

nonquality characteristics. The real cost of quality is the cost of producing goods and services without these characteristics.

How to start

There are two major ways that quality programs have been started:

1. Quality techniques are applied to a problem or problem area by a professional familiar with quality and quality control, as well as with important problems facing management.
2. Quality concepts are applied across the entire organization, with someone in charge of quality. This person takes the necessary steps to set up an organization for quality, such as a quality council, quality teams, quality policy, and quality plans. This person leads the organization through the preparatory stage into the operational stage.

There are several advantages to this approach:

- Can be a successful demonstration
- Can lead into the second approach
- Can be started with one professional with clerical assistance
- Can be used to convince doubting Thomases
- Can show benefits of quality
- Can show quality works as claimed
- Can convince managers opposed to the idea of quality.

It was the pioneering efforts of applying quality techniques to problem areas that proved beyond a shadow of doubt that Shewhart's theories of quality control would work successfully not only for products but for services as well.[5]

It had one serious weakness. There was no provision for continuity of the application. When the originator and promoter left, the quality project disappeared. No doubt this is why both Deming and Juran emphasize taking specific steps to insure continuity of the quality program.

This original approach was sound because it was based on applying quality control to important problems facing management. Some actual examples are: coding errors in data processing, errors on airline reservations, errors in filling mail orders, errors in processing insurance claims, and keypunching of federal census documents. The project-by-project quality improvement approach recommended by Juran today is similar.[6]

This suggests that the first approach stressing problems that may be very important but which are limited to a department or division, such as errors in billing, needs to be combined with the second approach to insure continuity.

---

[5] For examples, see issues of *Industrial Quality Control,* published by ASQC from 1946–1968; also transactions of various ASQC conferences 1950–1970.

[6] J.M. Juran, "Catching Up: How is the West Doing?" *Quality Progress* (November 1985), p. 19.

Starting at the top

The usual way to start is to appoint a senior official, such as the operations manager, to head the quality project. The first job of this official is to learn about quality, quality techniques, and quality improvement and what such a program requires within the community. It is assumed that this official is *not* already familiar with the management of quality.

Before this person can proceed, a *quality attitude survey* of managers and supervisors is necessary. Such a survey seeks answers to questions such as:

- What are you doing about quality?
- What does quality mean to you?
- Do you have any quality aims or objectives?
- How is quality measured?
- Can the quality of the work be improved?
- Should we have a quality program?

The quality attitude survey is critical. Unless it shows that all officials, managers, and supervisors are ready and willing to cooperate and undertake a quality program, it will be necessary to stop and back up. The program cannot proceed even if only a few are opposed or not convinced. There must be cooperation and teamwork if the program is to succeed.

If opposition exists, the first approach is recommended. This would consist of a pilot application on an important problem in an area where everyone is cooperating to make the application a success. It would be a demonstration that all could see planned and implemented.

If opposition exists, another step that is recommended is to make a cost-of-quality study. While this may be pushing ahead rather fast, it may be the most convincing approach of all. The purpose is to obtain from every department an initial set of estimates of what internal and external failures are costing the company. Indeed, determining the magnitude of this loss may convince the doubters that something needs to be done about quality immediately.

The quality council

When officials, managers, and supervisors have accepted the idea of a quality improvement program, then a Quality Council consisting of senior officials is formed to direct a community-wide program. Its functions include the following:

1. Develop and proclaim a quality policy for the company.
2. Develop a quality improvement plan.
3. Develop a quality training and orientation program.
4. Get quality programs started in every department.
5. Push the implementation of a quality program in every department.

6. Plan quality audits to insure that quality plans and policies are being carried out.
7. Plan an annual quality improvement budget so that continuity of the program is guaranteed.

The Quality Council sponsors *quality problem surveys* in every department. This means that every department surveys its operations and identifies problems and situations needing attention. Examples are errors, error rates, waiting time, lost time, downtime, idle time, service time, customer complaints, lost customers, lack of data, and inadequate data.

Once a quality problem survey has been made, it is necessary to analyze each problem and situation in detail to determine priorities. Problems selected for prompt attention are those that are considered most serious, involve the greatest amount of money losses, are most clearly defined, and for which remedies and solutions are readily available. If a new problem survey is made periodically, then a new list of priorities is required to adjust to the new situations.

The Quality Council can recommend one of three different ways of organizing for quality operations. First, it can recommend quality teams be established at each of the various levels of organization. These may be special groups set up at two or three different levels of organization of the company. These groups will concentrate on identifying quality problems and solving them. These separate groups will create problems in coordination and communication and jurisdiction which will have to be overcome.

Second, the Quality Council can recommend that every organizational group in the company be identified as a Quality Improvement Unit. This leaves the organization intact. It makes the supervisors and their employees a Quality Improvement Unit. Quality then is everybody's business, not that of a special group. This seems a natural way to handle organization since the basic premise of the quality improvement program is that every employee, supervisor, and manager is going to be involved as a participant, teamworker, and quality producer.

Third, the Council can suggest the formation of quality circles. The weakness of quality circles is that they are limited in their scope. They cannot solve problems that are the fault of the system, or other problems involving quality which are the responsibility of higher-level management. Their technical capability also is very limited.

The Operational Stage

It will take several years to progress through the preparatory stage to the point where the quality improvement program is really in full operation. Evidence that the operational stage has been reached is indicated by the following:

- A training, orientation, and education program is established and is beginning to pay off.

- All departments have quality plans fully operative with one or more successful applications.
- Losses due to poor quality are being reduced in every department.
- Quality Improvement Units are identifying faults which they must correct as well as faults only higher-level officials can correct.
- The necessary technical capability is on board and is contributing to quality improvements. This includes the necessary statistical capability to collect and analyze data, prepare reports, and resolve faults of the system connected with such aspects as errors and mistakes, wasted time, customer surveys, and inadequate data.
- A quality improvement plan is prepared as an integral part of the annual budget. This budget describes problems to be tackled and projects to be undertaken. Management recognizes that the quality budget is as necessary as the financial budget.

Management by quality

The final result is that management is motivated by and for quality, and combines into a unified creed three current management slogans:

- Management by exception (MBE)
- Management by objectives (MBO)
- Management by wandering around (MBWA)

This latter was not discussed earlier. It suggests the importance for managers to visit their operations and see regularly how the work is being done, including talking to workers.

References

1. Aubrey, Charles A. II, *Quality Management in Financial Services,* Wheaton, IL: Hitchcock Publishing Co., 1985
2. *Consumer Perceptions concerning the Quality of Products and Services,* Princeton, NJ: The Gallop Organization, Sept. 1985. Report of a survey for the American Society for Quality Control
3. Crosby, Philip B., *Quality is Free,* New York: McGraw-Hill, 1979
4. Deming, W. Edwards, *Sample Design in Business Research,* New York: John Wiley, 1960
5. Deming, W. Edwards, *Quality, Productivity, and Competitive Position,* Cambridge: MIT, 1982
6. Deming, W. Edwards, *Out of the Crisis,* Cambridge: MIT, 1986
7. Juran, J.M., "Japanese and Western Quality—a Contrast," *Quality,* Jan. and Feb. 1979
8. Juran, J.M., "Catching Up: How is the West Doing?", *Quality Progress,* Nov. 1985, 18–22
9. Juran, J.M., "The Quality Trilogy," *Quality Progress,* Aug. 1986, 19–24

10. Latzko, William J., *Quality and Productivity for Bankers and Financial Managers*, New York: Marcel Dekker and Milwaukee: ASQC Quality Press, 1986

11. Rosander, A.C., *Case Studies in Sample Design*, New York: Marcel Dekker, 1977

12. Rosander, A.C., *Washington Story*, Greeley, CO: National Directions, 1985 (Applying probability sampling and quality control to federal government operations)

13. Rosander, A.C., *The Early History of the Administrative Applications Division*, Milwaukee: American Society for Quality Control, 1985. Especially the last 17 pages

14. Rosander, A.C., *Applications of Quality Control in the Service Industries*, New York: Marcel Dekker, and Milwaukee: ASQC Quality Press, 1985

15. Towsend, Patrick L. and Gebhardt, Joan E., *Commit to Quality*, New York: John Wiley, 1986

Conclusion

When we began, we observed that enormous opportunities lie ahead for those who get into recycling. Our present knowledge and approaches have just thrown the first pitch.

More than a mere recitation of the systems and mechanical features of recycling, we have emphasized the general principles and methods for getting results through management techniques. In the long run, it is how well you run the business that counts. It is how well you achieve the goals of recycling and how efficiently this is done that is important.

Like all new businesses, with a completely undefined plan of action, recycling sits on the edge of a great deal of uncertainty and confusion. It offers challenges to the technical and creative abilities of society. There are no problems that do not offer potential solutions, and the challenge is to treat these difficulties and frustrations in a logical, clear manner. The sheer magnitude of the problem, with its endless generation of new piles of waste, are enough to dismay the mind. But life teaches us that you can overcome most obstacles, no matter how large, if you have the patience to tackle them one step at a time. A journey of great distance begins with a single step.

Recycling, to be fully effective, is really a comprehensive problem that requires the technical skills of all segments of society, from product design to reuse, from handling to processing.

I think that the middle of the next century will have seen so many changes and improvements in product design, new methods of packaging and handling, new markets for recyclables, perhaps the virtual elimination of some items such as newspapers, and major breakthroughs in the reuse of commodities and the handling of waste that the recycling stream will no longer be considered a liability. It will be sought after, like a gold mine of opportunity. We will be digging up the past to glean the lode of ores we once buried and discarded. We will be strip-mining the past and injecting it into the future.

No problem has ever been too big for the human mind. The key is to recognize that a problem exists. This we have done, thanks to a few young minds that began to warn us a decade ago. Once the problem is recognized, the solution cannot be far behind.

What makes recycling particularly exciting is that the challenge is occurring in 64,000 communities at once, offering thousands of local leaders a chance to apply their creative and administrative talents. The real job ahead of us belongs to the visionaries of the twenty-first century, geniuses with vision and leadership to show us what can be done and where we are going.

That's what we mean by progress. That's our future.

See the following panel for a summary of the steps to be followed in setting up a recycling program.

YEAR 2050 -
PEOPLE DID CARE!

SUMMARY

MAIN THINGS TO DO

1. PLAN FIRST!

2. KNOW YOUR VOLUMES

3. ESTIMATE YOUR COSTS

4. CHECK YOUR MARKETS

5. SET UP CASH FLOW

6. LOOK FOR SOURCES OF FUNDS:
    GRANTS (FREQUENCY?)
    COMMUNITY CHARGES
    SALES OF MATERIALS

7. INVESTIGATE EQUIPMENT NEEDS AND COSTS
    BUY? RENT? LEASE?

8. SHOULD YOU CONTRACT OUT?

9. COST TO SET UP TRANSFER STATIONS

10. SET UP MARKETING PLAN -
    CONTACT RECYCLER/MANUFACTURERS
    SHIP TO THEM
    BRING THEM TO YOUR TOWN

11. JOIN CO-OPS TO BUILD MARKETS, REDUCE COSTS

12. DEVELOP AND EMPLOY SOUND MANAGEMENT PRACTICES
    EFFICIENCY
    HUMAN QUALITY

13. BUILD AND *MAINTAIN* PUBLIC SUPPORT.

From "Community Recycling Seminars," by Institute for Global Action. Used by permission.

Appendix

Resources for Help and Information

MAGAZINES

BioCycle. The Journal of Waste Recycling. Monthly with combined issues in May–June and November–December.
Box 351, 18 South Seventh Street
Emmaus, PA 18049
215-967-4135

The Community Resource Report. Periodically. Emphasis is on creative approaches to recycling, marketing, management principles, financial and cash-flow planning. Written for Community Executives and operating officials.
P.O. Box 677
Bath, OH 44210
216-666-2815

Recycling Today. Monthly. Available in two issues: Scrap Metal Edition and Municipal Market Edition.
4012 Bridge Ave.
Cleveland, OH 44113
216-961-4130

Resource Recycling—North America's Recycling Journal. Monthly.
Resource Conservation Consultants
1206 N.W. 21st St.
P.O. Box 10540
Portland, OR 97210
503-227-1319

Waste Alternatives: The Magazine of Disposal Options. Quarterly.
National Solid Waste Management Association
Suite 1000, 1730 Rhode Island Ave., N.W.
Washington, DC 20036
202-861-0708

ORGANIZATIONS

Glass Packaging Institute
1801 K Street, N.W.
Suite 1105-L
Washington, DC 20006
202-887-4850

Aluminum Association
818 Connecticut Ave., N.W.
Washington, DC 20006

American Paper Institute
Paper Recycling Committee
260 Madison Ave.
New York, NY 10016

Can Manufacturers Institute
1625 Massachusetts Ave., N.W.
Washington, DC 20036
202-232-4677

Steel Can Recycling Institute
680 Andersen Drive
Foster Plaza X
Pittsburgh, PA 15220
800-876-SCRI
412-922-2772

Institute of Scrap Recycling Industries, Inc.
1627 K Street, N.W.
Washington, DC 20006
202-4466-4050

Society of the Plastics Industry, Inc.
Plastic Bottle Information Bureau
1275 K Street, N.W. Suite 400
Washington, DC 20005

National Recycling Coalition
1101 30th Street, N.W.
Suite 304
Washington, DC 20007
202-625-6406

National Soft Drink Association
1101 16th Street, N.W.
Washington, DC 20036
202-463-6700

Council for Solid Waste Solutions
1275 K Street, NW #500
Washington, DC 20005
202-371-5319

STATE RECYCLING OFFICES

For more information about recycling and for copies of *Recycling Works!,* call the EPA Solid Waste Hotline at 1-800-424-9346. In Washington, DC, call 382-3000.

ALABAMA
Department of Environmental
   Management
Solid Waste Division
1715 Congressman Wm. Dickinson
   Drive
Montgomery, AL 36130
(205) 271-7700

ALASKA
Department of Environmental
   Conservation
Solid Waste Program
P.O. Box O
Juneau, AK 99811-1800
(907) 465-2671

ARIZONA
Department of Environmental
   Quality - O.W.P.
Waste Planning Section, 4th Floor
Phoenix, AZ 85004
(602) 257-2317

ARKANSAS
Department of Pollution Control
   and Ecology
Solid Waste Division
8001 National Drive
Little Rock, AK 72219
(501) 562-7444

CALIFORNIA
Recycling Division
Department of Conservation
819 19th Street
Sacramento, CA 95814
(916) 323-3743

COLORADO
Department of Health
4210 E. 11th Avenue
Denver, CO 80220
(303) 320-4830

CONNECTICUT
Recycling Program
Department of Environmental Protection
Hartford, CT 06106
(203) 566-8722

DELAWARE
Department of Natural Resources
   and Environmental Control
89 Kings Highway
P.O. Box 1401
Dover, DE 19903
(302) 736-4794

DISTRICT OF COLUMBIA
Public Space and Maintenance
   Administration
4701 Shepard Parkway, S.W.
Washington, DC 20032
(202) 767-8512

FLORIDA
Department of Environmental Regulation
2600 Blairstone Road
Tallahassee, FL 32201
(904) 488-0300

GEORGIA
Department of Community Affairs
40 Marietta St., N.W., 8th Floor
Atlanta, GA 30303
(404) 656-3898

HAWAII
Litter Control Office
Department of Health
205 Koula Street
Honolulu, HI 96813
(808) 548-3400

IDAHO
Department of Environmental Quality
Hazardous Materials Bureau
450 W. State Street
Boise, ID 83720
(208) 334-5879

ILLINOIS
Illinois EPA
Land Pollution Control Division
2200 Churchill Road
P.O. Box 19276
Springfield, IL 62706
(217) 782-6761

INDIANA
Office of Solid and Hazardous Waste
   Management
Department of Environmental
   Management
105 S. Meridian Street
Indianapolis, IN 46225
(317) 232-8883

IOWA
Department of Natural Resources
Waste Management Division
Wallace State Office Building
Des Moines, IA 50319
(515) 281-8176

KANSAS
Bureau of Waste Management
Department of Health
   and Environment
Topeka, KS 66620
(913) 296-1594

KENTUCKY
Resources Management Branch
Division of Waste Management
18 Reilly Road
Frankfort, KY 40601
(502) 564-6716

LOUISIANA
Department of Environmental Quality
P.O. Box 44307
Baton Rouge, LA 70804
(504) 342-1216

MAINE
Office of Waste Reduction
   and Recycling
Department of Economic
   and Community Development
State House Station #130
Augusta, ME 04333
(207) 289-2111

MARYLAND
Department of Environment
Hazardous and Solid Waste
   Administration
2500 Broening Highway
Building 40
Baltimore, MD 21224
(301) 631-3343

MASSACHUSETTS
Division of Solid Waste Management
D.E.Q.E.
1 Winter Street, 4th Floor
Boston, MA 02108
(617) 292-5962

MICHIGAN
Waste Management Division
Department of Natural Resources
P.O. Box 30028
Lansing, MI 48909
(517) 373-0540

MINNESOTA
Pollution Control Agency
520 Lafayette Road
St. Paul, MN 55155
(612) 296-6300

MISSISSIPPI
Non-Hazardous Waste Section
Bureau of Pollution Control
Department of Natural Resources
P.O. Box 10385
Jackson, MS 39209
(601) 961-5047

MISSOURI
Department of Natural Resources
P.O. Box 176
Jefferson City, MO 65102
(314) 751-3176

MONTANA
Solid Waste Program
Department of Health
  and Environmental Science
Cogswell Building, Room B201
Helena, MT 59620
(406) 444-2821

NEBRASKA
Litter Reduction and Recycling
  Programs
Department of Environmental
  Control
P.O. Box 98922
Lincoln, NE 68509
(402) 471-4210

NEVADA
Energy Extension Service
Office of Community Service
1100 S. Williams Street
Carson City, NV 89710
(702) 885-4420

NEW HAMPSHIRE
Waste Management Division
Department of Environmental Services
6 Hazen Drive
Concord, NH 03301
(603) 271-2900

NEW JERSEY
Office of Recycling
Department of Environmental
  Protection
CN 414
401 E. State Street
Trenton, NJ 08625
(609) 292-0331

NEW MEXICO
Solid Waste Section
Environmental Improvement Division
1190 St. Francis Drive
Santa Fe, NM 87503
(505) 457-2780

NEW YORK
Bureau of Waste Reduction and
  Recycling
Department of Environmental
  Conservation
50 Wolf Road, Room 208
Albany, NY 12233
(518) 457-7337

NORTH CAROLINA
Solid Waste Management Branch
Department of Human Resources
P.O. Box 2091
Raleigh, NC 27602
(919) 733-0692

NORTH DAKOTA
Division of Waste Management
Department of Health
1200 Missouri Avenue, Room 302
Box 5520
Bismark, ND 58502-5520
(701) 224-2366

OHIO
Division of Litter Prevention
    and Recycling
Ohio Department
Fountain Square Building, E-1
Columbus, OH 43224
(614) 265-7061

OKLAHOMA
Solid Waste Division
Department of Health
1000 N.E. 10th Street
Oklahoma City, OK 73152
(405) 271-7159

OREGON
Department of Environmental Quality
811 S.W. Sixth
Portland, OR 97204
(503) 229-5913

PENNSYLVANIA
Waste Reduction and Recycling Section
Division of Waste Minimization
    and Planning
Department of Environmental
    Resources
P.O. Box 2063
Harrisburg, PA 17120
(717) 787-7382

RHODE ISLAND
Office of Environmental Coordination
Department of Environmental
    Management
83 Park Street
Providence, RI 02903
(401) 277-3434

SOUTH CAROLINA
Department of Health
    and Environmental Control
2600 Bull Street
Columbia, SC 29201
(803) 734-5200

SOUTH DAKOTA
Energy Office
217-1/2 West Missouri
Pierre, SD 57501
(605) 773-3603

TENNESSEE
Department of Public Health
Division of Solid Waste Management
Customs House, 4th Floor
701 Broadway
Nashville, TN 37219-5403
(615) 741-3424

TEXAS
Division of Solid Waste Management
Department of Health
1100 W. 49th Street
Austin, TX 78756
(512) 458-7271

UTAH
Bureau of Solid and Hazardous Waste
Department of Environmental Health
P.O. Box 16690
Salt Lake City, UT 84116-0690
(801) 538-6170

VERMONT
Agency of National Resources
103 S. Main Street, West Building
Waterbury, VT 05676
(802) 244-8702

VIRGINIA
Department of Waste Management
Division of Litter Control
    and Recycling
11th Floor, Monroe Building
101 N. 14th Street
Richmond, VA 23219
1-800-KeepIt

WEST VIRGINIA
Department of Natural Resources
Conservation, Education, and Litter
  Control
1800 Washington Street E.
Charleston, WV 25305
(304) 348-3370

WASHINGTON
Department of Ecology
Mail Stop PV-11
Olympia, WA 95804
1-800-Recycle

WISCONSIN
Department of Natural Resources
P.O. Box 7921
Madison, WI 53707
(608) 266-5741

WYOMING
Solid Waste Management Program
Department of Environmental Quality
Herschler Building
122 W. 25th Street
Cheyenne, WY 82002
(307) 777-7752

INDEX